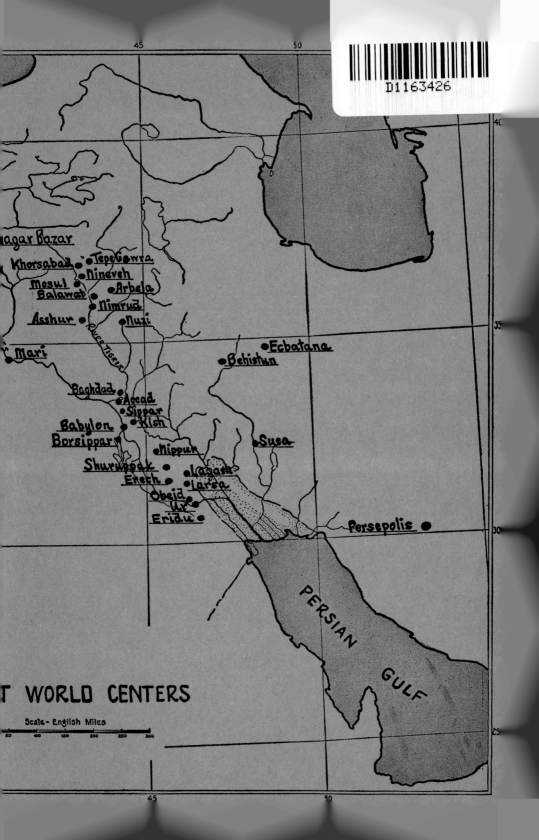

45

50

40

35

Nagar Bazar

Khorsabad • Tepe Gawra
        • Nineveh
Mosul • • Arbela
Balawat
        • Nimrud
Asshur • • Nuzi

• Mari

        • Ecbatana
    • Behistun

Baghdad • • Agead
        • Sippar
Babylon • • Kish
Borsippar •
        • Nippur   • Susa
Shuruppak •
Erech • • Lagash
        • Larsa
    Obeid •
    Ur
    Eridu •

Persepolis •

30

PERSIAN

GULF

T WORLD CENTERS

Scale- English Miles
50 100 150 200 250 300

45

25

50

Joseph W Morrell

ANCIENT RECORDS
AND THE BIBLE

THE MAGNIFICENT STATUE OF THUTMOSIS III, EGYPT'S OUTSTANDING WARRIOR AND CONQUEROR. IT NOW SEEMS PRACTICALLY CERTAIN THAT THUTMOSIS MUST BE CONSIDERED AS THE OPPRESSOR OF ISRAEL IN THE HOUSE OF BONDAGE.

ANCIENT RECORDS AND THE BIBLE

A SURVEY OF ARCHAEOLOGICAL EVIDENCES
IN THEIR BEARING ON THE INTEGRITY
OF THE HISTORICAL NARRATIVES
OF THE OLD TESTAMENT

J. McKEE ADAMS, Ph.D.

PROFESSOR OF BIBLICAL ARCHAEOLOGY
THE SOUTHERN BAPTIST THEOLOGICAL SEMINARY
LOUISVILLE, KENTUCKY

Author of
A Syllabus for Biblical Introduction Studies,
Biblical Backgrounds, Our Bible, The
Heart of the Levant, etc.

BROADMAN PRESS
NASHVILLE, TENNESSEE

PRINTED AND BOUND IN THE U. S. A. BY
KINGSPORT PRESS, INC., KINGSPORT, TENN.

This volume is gratefully dedicated to the
cherished memory of

President Edgar Young Mullins, D.D., LL.D.

THE SOUTHERN BAPTIST THEOLOGICAL SEMINARY 1899-1928

SOUTHERN BAPTIST CONVENTION 1921-1924

BAPTIST WORLD ALLIANCE 1923-1928

Equally poised in mind and heart

PREFACE

The gracious reception accorded my recent volume on *Biblical Backgrounds* in various quarters has greatly encouraged me in the preparation of this the second volume of a planned series of works dealing with matters of biblical interest in countries of the Near and Middle East. In the first book an attempt was made to give a geographical survey of Bible lands in the light of the Scriptures and recent research as those lands progressively appear in the framework of the redemptive movement. In the present work on *ANCIENT RECORDS AND THE BIBLE,* we seek to survey the recovered evidences growing out of scientific excavation and exploration, and to set forth their bearing on the integrity of the Scriptures in matters of historical detail. While many volumes on this and related subjects have appeared during recent years, none would probably claim to be definitive though recognized as of surpassing value in this particular field of scientific and biblical interest. The reason is obvious. Each year witnesses steady progress not only in the number of sites excavated and localities explored, but a marked increase also in the quantity of recovered evidences that bear primarily on the accuracy and trustworthiness of the Bible. These evidences must be continually sifted and evaluated in order to arrive at a clearer understanding of the historical foundations of the Bible and the numerous points at which it touched neighboring peoples in the ordinary affairs of life.

The astounding recoveries of the past few years which have thrown such a steady flood of light on the geographical and historical setting of the Scriptures, have likewise tended to elevate in critical opinion the historical narratives both of the Old Testament and the New. Furthermore, these same recoveries have made it increasingly evident that the Bible can no longer be neglected as the principal source book in any serious attempt to reconstruct the environments of ancient Israel and of early Christianity. Indeed, after a century now of diligent investigation in the countries of its origin and interests, scientific explorers and excavators of first rank agree that the conditions and events reflected in the Bible are in almost uncanny accord with results revealed by the excavations. Consequently, in undertaking this survey the author does not approach the writings of the Old and New Testaments under any obsession that they need to be *reconstructed* to conform to any of the advanced views which are now prevalent or to those which, like other of our little systems, have had their day. It is quite obvious that there is a revolt on the part of an ever-increasing body of teachers and students that many recent inquiries into biblical subjects have been comparatively obscured in a maze of theories *about* the Scriptures, and that there has been little disposition to receive at its face value the testimony which the Bible bears concerning itself. The upshot of the whole business has been an insistent demand that the Scriptures be allowed to speak from their own point of view and that their witness be received without prejudice. One can urge this proposition with utter frankness and still be conscious of the tremendous debt which he owes to those who have made distinctive contributions to the study of the Bible, or to those whose work has served to define biblical problems and issues more accurately and, in so doing, have provoked more earnest and intelligent effort to understand the sacred narratives. The main contention here is that criticism of

viii

the Bible may be *historical* and *scientific, accurate* and *discriminative, orderly* and *scholarly,* without being projected purely on a destructive basis. But the principle which operates in this connection will be founded on a reverent approach to the Bible, and this in turn will assure *constructive treatment.*

It is apparent that purely *subjective criticism* of the Bible has signally failed in providing adequate explanations for *biblical phenomena* and that its *disservice* to the cause of truth has been as conspicuous as its failure. In like manner, the insistent demand that all statements of the Bible shall be illustrated or corroborated by tangible evidence in support of their trustworthiness and accuracy, rests on a false assumption and is clearly unscientific. Now it is significant that biblical archaeology, the youngest of the sciences to be enlisted in the service of biblical criticism, has provided a stopgap for the extremes of subjectivism, on the one hand, and has definitely arrested or modified the contention that all statements of biblical import shall be rigidly subjected to the test tubes of proof as a condition of their credibility. It is now recognized that biblical statements of contemporary conditions and historical movements can be true even when unsupported by other contemporary records known to the scholarly world. Illustrations of this fact are presented in the following pages. The principal here emphasized and faithfully followed is that of an open approach and an open mind unfettered by prejudice. We seek all available evidences bearing on the veracity of the Scriptures, welcoming light from any quarter, and we seek to interpret these evidences in the light of their environment and antecedents. Where no special light is cast on disputed problems, we do not thereby assume the biblical record inaccurate or unreliable. Archaeology is continually unearthing for us substantial corroboration of biblical statements, and its contribution has been to enhance the historical value of the Scriptures on every hand. It is clear that what is needed in the present situation involving problems of the Bible is not more conjectures, but more light, and a corresponding mental humility produced by the recognition of the limitations of our present knowledge. Thus steering clear of the so-called avenue of "blind faith" or credulity, and of a presumptuous erudition, we will ultimately come to a wide space where truth may stand and prevail. And that, at least, is part of the approach adopted in this work. Without announcing dogmatically the solution of all problems and the elimination of all the tangled questions confronting the earnest Bible student, we have sought the truth, knowing fully that it alone has any secure footing either in *reason* or in *faith*.

For many years this work has been in the making. It has been placed in the forefront of all my travels and studies in the Near East and in extensive investigations in the principal museums of England and continental Europe, especially the British Museum, the Louvre, and the National Museums at Istanbul and Athens. Berlin and Rome have been most generous; Beirut, Damascus, Jerusalem, and Cairo have been incomparable for their wealth of antiquities in close association with native setting. In addition to these personal contacts with museums and fields of operation, there has been consulted a voluminous body of literature bearing on practically every phase of archaeological import, particularly the biblical, a partial summary of which will be found in the Bibliography. To one of my students, Rev. T. Lee Anderton, I am particularly indebted for the beautiful series of drawings appearing in this volume. To all of these authors, publishers, and works I am under profound obligation. I record here my sincere thanks. While appropriate acknowledgment is made in footnotes for all quoted sources, I wish to make more explicit my debt of gratitude to the Trustees of the British Museum, the Custodians and Directors of Antiquities at the Louvre, the National Museum in Cairo, and the Palestine Department of Antiquities in Jerusalem for permission to reproduce the magnificent photographs of many ancient monuments appearing in the text. These are now of priceless value in view of World War II conditions, which make impossible access to any original sources. The fine courtesies, together with practical helpfulness, shown by all, have touched me deeply.

Finally, to the Broadman Press I express abiding thanks for generous assistance in enabling me to share with an enlarged circle of teachers and students the fruits of travel and study whose prime interest has been a fuller understanding of the Bible and its claims.

J. McKee Adams

Louisville, Kentucky
April 10, 1945

FOREWORD

Dr. James McKee Adams, at the time of his death, was recognized throughout the Christian world as one of the greatest scholars in the field of Biblical Archaeology. Through prodigious work, research, and many personal visits to the Orient, he acquired a mass of knowledge, some of which has been put into book form.

Fortunately, he had completed the manuscript for a new book, *Ancient Records and the Bible,* before his death, but he never saw it published. The responsibility of putting the book into final shape for print fell upon two young men, his fellows in Biblical Introduction, William H. Morton and Marc H. Lovelace. Mrs. Adams is grateful to these young men for their fine service.

I recall distinctly the light of hope in Dr. Adams' face, just a little while before the book was finished, as he smilingly stated that he expected this book to be his greatest contribution in the field of Biblical Archaeology. It was obvious that he hoped that it would render even greater service than *Biblical Backgrounds,* which is used so extensively in colleges and seminaries.

ELLIS A. FULLER, *President*
Southern Baptist Theological Seminary

TABLE OF CONTENTS

MAPS

ILLUSTRATIONS

INTRODUCTION

ANCIENT RECORDS AND THE BIBLE

INTRODUCTION

IN introducing the present study, we may be allowed to state more definitely the scope of the investigation and the interests with which it is immediately concerned. The term "Bible" is employed to denote, first, the entire body of sacred writings which were produced through the Hebrew people during the early and middle periods of their national existence and which were gradually brought together to form what is now the accepted Canon of the Old Testament, and, secondly, the corresponding body of literature which came through the experiences of the first century Christians to constitute the present recognized Canon of the New Testament. Thus, whether regarded under the aspect of the Old Testament or the New Testament, or considered from the standpoint of combined Testaments which set forth a continuous and unified record of the redemptive movement, these are the narratives which are in view and which we propose to examine in the light of archaeological evidences provided by scientific excavations and explorations. It is our purpose to proceed on the specific proposition that the events and movements described in the historical narratives of the Old and New Testaments are accurate and authentic, and that the weight of modern critical investigation is definitely on the side of their credibility and trustworthiness.

Furthermore, while it is recognized that there is a tendency in certain quarters to approach the Scriptures with mental reservations, to assume that in the general structure of the Bible story there may be a *substratum* of fact or a *kernel* of truth which was later embellished with folklore, legend, and exaggerated tradition which finally lost all connection with reality, it may be stated plainly that such a tendency is no part of the present approach to the Scriptures, whether of the Old Testament or the New Testament. To assume the substantial correctness of the early portions of the Pentateuch, for example, and then by enlightened processes of scientific historical criticism to discredit, undermine, and demolish the remainder as accretions of later ages, is neither *scientific, historical, nor critical.* The predisposition to question every biblical statement, to put it into the test tube of a supersensitive critical experiment, is more reprehensible than the bald statement of Bible errancy and inexactitude, since the latter signifies open rejection which can be dealt with in the open and on the basis of reason and ascertained facts, while the former is largely the product of subjectivity and suspicion. To those who are thus disposed toward the Scriptures, the Bible can never speak with authority unless supported by extraneous evidences or contemporary records. But it may be pointed out incidentally that such an arbitrary demand on biblical accuracy has recoiled on the advanced critical position during recent years, and that some of its "assured results" have been rejected or radically modified.

In the second place, the phrase, "Ancient Records," while referring specifically to the significant number of epigraphic remains recovered through diligent research on the part of excavators and explorers, is not here used to exclude that larger body of material evidences whose testimony is equally decisive in questions of biblical accuracy and integrity. The principal result of scientific investigation in the Near and Middle East during the past century has been to provide the scholarly world with a body of archaeological information, written and unwritten, which has compelled con-

4

THE MIGHTY NILE FLOWING
OUT OF EQUATORIAL AFRICA
TAKES ITS COURSE TO THE
NORTH TO PROVIDE AND TO
SUSTAIN THE FERTILE SOIL
OF THE EGYPTIAN KINGDOM.
ALONG THE BANKS OF THIS
GREAT RIVER FLOURISHED
THE CITIES AND THE CIVIL-
IZATION OF THE ANCIENT
PHARAOHS THROUGH M A N Y
CENTURIES.

COMING FROM THE SECRET
SPRINGS OF THE ANTI-LEB-
ANONS, THE JORDAN RIVER
DASHES DOWNWARD TO THE
D E A D SEA IN SOUTHERN
PALESTINE. THE LIFE-STORY
OF THE JORDAN INCLUDES
ALL THE THRILLING CHAP-
TERS OF HEBREW AND CHRIS-
TIAN HISTORY IN THE BE-
GINNINGS.

THE BRITISH SCHOOL OF ARCHAEOLOGY, JERUSALEM, HAS LONG BEEN A
LEADER IN PALESTINE EXPLORATION AND EXCAVATION.

AMERICAN SCHOOL OF ORIENTAL RESEARCH. THE JERUSALEM BRANCH
HAS MADE SOME OUTSTANDING CONTRIBUTIONS TO THE FIELD OF
BIBLICAL ARCHAEOLOGY.

siderable modification of certain critical views on the one hand, and the definite correction of untenable and erroneous theories on the other, while further serving to present a more accurate and intelligible picture of actual conditions obtaining throughout the biblical period. It is now possible to use this new knowledge in describing the conditions and circumstances underlying the Scripture narratives, and to reconstruct the general framework of contemporary developments set forth so vividly in the Bible story. In so doing it will readily appear that the new representation is the correct one, that it reflects not only an inner connectedness which is in full keeping with actual conditions that obtained in the life of Israel at various periods, but is also in consonance with the general stream of historical conditions obtaining among surrounding peoples in their contacts with the people of God. It is held in this connection that the Scriptures afford us reliable and accurate accounts of the continuous movement of God in Israel for redemptive ends, and that the descriptions with which we are provided regarding the inner life of the Chosen People are true, whether viewed under the aspect of religion, politics, or any other phase of the social structure; and, further, that we have an accurate statement of Israel's contacts with its neighbors, including the overpowering kingdoms of Egypt, Babylonia, and Assyria on the one hand, and the lesser powers of nomad hordes such as the Midianites, Amalekites, and Ishmaelites on the other. In a word, the point at issue here is not that the Old Testament is an accurate historical narrative struck off at a late period of Hebrew development by competent writers who had access to necessary data and who were faithful to their sources, but that the ancient records now in hand tend to support the proposition that *beginning with the patriarchal period and continuing through the changing fortunes*

*of the Hebrew people to the final destruction of Jerusa-
lem, we have practically contemporary records, thoroughly reliable and authentic.*

It is through this amazing correspondence between
the biblical narratives and the materials provided by
archaeology that we can now reconstruct the physical
and historical framework of the world from the time
that Abram stepped forth from Ur of the Chaldees in
the East, up through the missionary campaigns that
touched the vital points of the Roman Empire in the
West. In the present survey our investigation will be
confined to the Old Testament in relation to ancient
records, the New Testament being reserved for separate
presentation.

CHAPTER ONE

THE OLD TESTAMENT WORLD

THE OLD TESTAMENT WORLD

THE historical narratives of the Old Testament are among the most fascinating records of ancient literature. They have their immediate setting in a geographical framework definitely related both to the developments therein described and to their significance. The modern emphasis on the study of geography for a fuller understanding of historical developments is a long stride in the right direction, though it comes as a rather belated recognition of the inseparable relations that always exist between persons and events on the one hand, and the places and circumstances referring to them on the other. History is rooted in the earth. To recapture the meaning of any movement or of any event, one must first of all see it in the light of its original setting. Historical orientation depends largely on historical geography. It is clear, therefore, that Old Testament archaeology, which is the reproduction of Old Testament life and thought in the light of scientific investigation, is deeply rooted in the geography of the Old Testament world; that both are complementary; and that in their combined contribution we obtain a faithful reproduction of conditions reflected in the Hebrew Scriptures.

Beginning with Genesis and continuing through the unfolding panorama of Hebrew history from Abraham to the Restoration from Babylon, there is presented an orderly and unbroken sequence of events. Here we find the dawn of creation, the spiritual biography of mankind, and the early history of the patriarchs issuing in the checkered experiences of their descendants, the Chosen People. As these people and events are described, they are immediately placed into a geographical framework which expands as the story unfolds. Vested thus with the dimensions of time and space, characters commence to breathe again, landscapes over which they journeyed take on life and movement, and cities of their habitation rise from the debris of the ages to throb once more with the bustle of life and its issues.

Properly conceived, the Old Testament world was centered at the heart of the great Tigris-Euphrates basin, in Mesopotamia, the land of beginnings, and from that definite region expands with lifting horizons. The geography of Genesis includes practically all the countries of the Old Testament narratives. Starting with the phenomenal career of Abraham (Gen. 12), we are introduced to the countries bordering the Persian Gulf. Advancing with him in his venture of faith to Canaan, the Land of Promise, we traverse the beautiful plains encompassed by the Euphrates and Tigris rivers; the upland country of Aram (the homeland of Rebekah, Laban, Leah, and Rachel); the territories of the powerful Hurrians and Amorites, who figure so prominently in all these narratives; the lands of the conquering Hittites, who came originally from the plateau of interior Western Asia; down through the marvelous valley of the Lebanon and Anti-Lebanon Mountains from whose secret springs come the twin rivers, the Orontes and the Leontes; through the Anti-Lebanons by the familiar route known to all travelers, ancient and modern, to Damascus, perhaps the world's oldest existing city and most beautiful oasis; passing through the borders of Syria and on to Canaan, west of the Jordan River; and to Egypt, the country of Father Nile. To these outstanding areas one could add other Genesis references which tell us of islands of the Sea of the Setting Sun (the Mediterranean) and of far-off hinterlands of neighboring countries. To all of this territory, stretching from the head of the Persian Gulf to the Nile Delta, Breasted applies the name of *Fertile Crescent*. "There is every reason to believe that somewhere along its attractive course was the beginning of human life and civilization. Though this was not all of Abraham's world, it was certainly the heart of it. Between these remote sections of the Tigris-Euphrates and the Nile River basin, following the highroads of the Fertile Crescent, was uninterrupted communication growing out of trade, travel, and war. Journeys were made with comparative safety from Ur by way of Haran, Aleppo, Damascus, and Jerusalem to the Delta of the Nile. The day of the pioneers had long since passed. We know now that Abraham himself was relatively a late traveler along this historic road as he pushed westward to Syria, Canaan, and Egypt."[1]* We also know that, subsequently, this was the territory that lay at the heart of the vast kingdoms created by the conquering Babylonians, Assyrians, Persians, and Medes. From these areas come the archaeological evidences discussed in this work. Let us turn for a brief consideration of the several parts.

MESOPOTAMIA

Ancient Mesopotamia, the land between the Tigris and Euphrates, was practically coextensive with the boundaries of the modern kingdom of Iraq. As shown on the map, it extends from the headwaters of the Persian Gulf to the foothills of the Taurus Mountains on the borders of modern Turkey. This stretch of territory, approximately 600 miles in length, had as its

---

*All footnote references will be found in back of book, beginning on page 363.

eastern boundary the Tigris River while on the west flowed the great Euphrates, whose name signifies the giver of fertility. Since the total rainfall in this area rarely ever exceeds ten inches a year, the rivers of Mesopotamia were regarded with deep reverence and their plentiful supply of water was utilized in a scheme of extensive canals, which was one of the greatest achievements of the ancient Babylonians and Assyrians.

In the middle section of this fertile country, probably in the immediate vicinity of ancient Babylon, stretch the plains of Shinar, and somewhere in this attractive region, which was so favorable for early man, we are inclined to locate the *Garden of Eden*. It is generally agreed that conditions of Eden described in Genesis find in lower Mesopotamia a fuller correspondence than in any other known section of the ancient world. In this same region was erected the *Tower of Babel,* perhaps not far from the great city of Babylon. But more important for our studies, it was in this region that many ancient cities flourished, cities which are mentioned in the Genesis accounts, whose later influence definitely affected the history of the Hebrew people. Among these cultural centers we mention *Eridu,* one of the oldest of the southern Mesopotamian cities, located very close to the Persian Gulf; *Ur of the Chaldees,* slightly north of Eridu, one of the outstanding political and religious centers, the original home of Abraham, Terah, Lot, and others whose departure for Canaan is described; north of Ur of the Chaldees we come to *Larsa* and *Kish,* historic towns, whose influence on early civilization was great; *Babylon,* located in the central area and outstanding even before the days of Abraham, was the center of Mesopotamian life and culture, the capital city of Hammurabi, the great lawgiver, and of Nebuchadnezzar, conqueror of Jerusalem, and later of Alexander the Great, whose death occurred

THE EGYPTIAN MUSEUM OF ANTIQUITIES, CAIRO. IN THIS CROWDED
BUILDING ARE BROUGHT TOGETHER THE PRICELESS MONUMENTS OF
EGYPTIAN LIFE AND THOUGHT THROUGH MANY CENTURIES OF CULTURAL
DEVELOPMENT.

THIS BEAUTIFUL MEMORIAL TO MARIETTE PACHA, THE FATHER OF
EGYPTOLOGY, STANDS IN THE CAIRO MUSEUM GROUNDS.

AN OSSUARY IN THE FORM OF
A DWELLING. FOUND IN
PALESTINE AND ASSIGNED TO
THE CHALCHOLITHIC PERIOD
ABOUT 4000 B.C. SUCH HOUSES
WERE BUILT OF REEDS PLAS-
TERED WITH MUD, STANDING
ON FIRM SUPPORTS.

IN THE HEART OF THE JORDAN VALLEY A DWELLER MAKES PROVISION
FOR THE ANNUAL FLOOD BY ELEVATING HIS HOUSE ABOVE THE USUAL
WATERLINE. EARLY PEOPLE IN THE MARSH AREAS FOLLOWED THE
SAME PRACTICE.

here in 323 B.C. Situated on the middle Euphrates, Babylon became the focal point of all world movements. Immediately east was the important city of *Agade,* located on the Tigris not far from the present town of Bagdad, capital of modern Iraq. Proceeding north on the Tigris we come to *Nineveh,* center of the ferocious Assyrians whose armies overran the whole of the Middle East. To the Assyrians is attributed the destruction of the Northern Kingdom in 722 B.C. and the captivity of Israel. West of Nineveh, close to the Euphrates, stood *Haran,* the town to which Abraham and his people came in their journey from Ur of the Chaldees. In addition to these great centers, numerous other cities, some of high antiquity, flourished throughout the area, particularly the centers represented by the mounds at Mari, Halaf, Tepe Gawra, Nuzi, etc., whose ancient names have literally perished. Life was pitched on a relatively high plane, the greater portion of the people in the southern sections following the exacting business of agriculturists, while in the rolling country to the north the nomads or pastoral peoples were seen everywhere. In ancient times the country of Mesopotamia was inhabited by approximately fifteen or twenty million people; today, its population does not exceed three and one-half million, the greater proportion being shepherds or nomads.

Syria

This area lies west of the Euphrates River, south of Western Asia, and north of Palestine. The territory runs parallel with the Mediterranean and consists of several lateral zones running north and south. The first of these is the coastal region which extends from the vicinity of Tyre and Sidon up to the Taurus Mountains in Asia Minor. In the ancient world this area was inhabited by the Phoenicians, a maritime people who made several first-rate contributions to human culture. Immediately to the east of the coastal region, and dominating the country from north to south, are the beautiful hills of the Lebanons mentioned so frequently in Old Testament narratives. East of the Lebanons runs the wonderful valley of the Lebanons, whose total length is approximately 200 miles. This area witnessed the early settled communities of the Hittites and Amorites, and was the general location of many prominent city strongholds mentioned in relation to the Hebrew people. To the east of the valley runs the Anti-Lebanon range, heading up in the south with Mount Hermon. Parallel with the Anti-Lebanons and extending toward the valley of the Euphrates lies the great Syro-Arabian Desert, more forbidding to early travelers than seas or mountains. In these several zones flourished many cities of outstanding importance, some of which are indicated on the map. Carchemish, Aleppo, Tudmor, Hamath, Homs, Karkar, Kadesh, Tyre, Sidon, and Damascus are full of historic lore. To this summary of outstanding cultural centers modern investigation has added Gebal and Ugarit (Ras Shamra), whose significant records of the fifteenth century B.C. have astonished the scholarly world.

CANAAN

This little country of perennial interest to all Bible students was located in the center of the Old Testament world. To the east was the fertile valley of the Tigris-Euphrates, while to the southwest was the great Nile basin with its marvelous soil replenished every year by the floods. Through Canaan ran the connecting highways penetrating every part of the ancient world. Indeed, the little country was on the way to everywhere,

14

and this relation determined practically the whole of its history through many centuries. In one sense it was "the least of all lands," while in another it was the most important. In Canaan, the Promised Land, we come to that central area which was to witness the gradual unfolding and culmination of the divine purpose to bless all the families of the earth.

The geographical features of Canaan are varied and full of interest. Its coastal region, extending from the Leontes River to the River of Egypt, averaging only a few miles in width, is characterized by subtropical climate and fertile soil. Here are the plains of Philistia, Sharon, and Acre, the regions which played such an important part in the history of the Hebrew people. In the Philistia Plain were the great cities of Gaza, Gath, Ekron, Ashkelon, and Ashdod, together with numerous other towns of outstanding importance. Joppa stood by the sea overlooking Philistia and Sharon. Dor was a little south of Mt. Carmel, Acre slightly north, while just beyond Acre stood the twin cities of the Phoenicians, Tyre and Sidon. Running parallel with the coastal plains was the great Central Plateau with its three sections of Galilee, Samaria, and Judah. This central section extended from the hill country of Galilee to the foothills of Judah in the vicinity of Beersheba, its total length being about 160 miles. This was the heart of the country. Here were located the outstanding centers of the patriarchs— Dothan, Shechem, Bethel, Jerusalem, Bethlehem, Hebron, and Beersheba. In this area was the Plain of Moreh, at the base of Gerizim, where Joseph was looking for his brothers, and farther south the Plain of Mamre at Hebron, where Abraham talked with the angelic visitors, and Machpelah, where the beloved Sarah was buried. This whole region is literally filled with historic events connected with the Hebrews from

Abraham to Jesus. East of the Central Plateau, and parallel from north to south, there is the great Jordan River valley with its three inland lakes—the Waters of Merom, the Sea of Galilee, and the Dead Sea, which in the Genesis records is called the Salt Sea. This region is one of the most striking sections of Canaan and one of the phenomenal areas of the earth's surface. In Abraham's day the lower sections of the valley were probably fertile. Here were the cities of Jericho, Sodom, and Gomorrah. Beyond the Jordan Valley stood the highlands of the country toward the sunrising, the territory of Moab, Gilead, and Bashan, inhabited in early days by Moabites, Ammonites, and Amorites. This little territory beyond Jordan was not a part of Canaan proper, though it was subsequently conquered and inhabited by the tribes of Reuben, Gad, and East Manasseh.

In the northern part of Canaan the Western Plateau is broken abruptly by a plain extending in a northwesterly direction from the valley of the Jordan. It is triangular in shape, with an extreme length of approximately forty miles. In the narratives of the Old Testament it appears as the Plain of Esdraelon, or Megiddo, whose eastern extension was the Valley of Jezreel. The area thus defined is one of the most beautiful plains in the world: "In fertility it compares most favorably with the delta sections of the Tigris-Euphrates, the Nile, and the Mississippi. In strategic importance, Esdraelon lay across the path of all approaches to central and southern Canaan from the north. In consequence of its position, it became the great battlefield of the nations. Here the great Thutmosis of Egypt triumphed, carrying off fabulous spoils from Megiddo; here, by the waters of Megiddo, the stars in their courses fought against Sisera in the victory of Deborah and Barak; here Pharaoh-Necho slew the young king Josiah

16

THE UNIVERSITY OF PENNSYLVANIA EXPEDITION AND THE BRITISH MUSEUM HAVE UNDERTAKEN THE STUPENDOUS TASK OF A SCIENTIFIC EXCAVATION OF THE ANCIENT CITY OF BETHSHEAN. THE CITY WAS ONE OF THE GREAT STRONGHOLDS OF THE CANAANITES AND CONTINUED INTO THE NEW TESTAMENT PERIOD WHEN IT WAS REGARDED AS THE CAPITAL OF THE DECAPOLIS.

VARIOUS TYPES OF DWELLINGS ARE USED IN PALESTINE, RANGING FROM THE REED HOUSES BY THE WATERS OF MEROM IN THE NORTH TO THE STONE BUILDINGS OF TOWNS AND CITIES. THE HOUSE HERE SHOWN IS MADE OF MUD-CLAY, WITH GRASS ROOF. NOTE THE ABSENCE OF WINDOWS.

AMONG THE LOW HILLS OF SOUTHERN PALESTINE OVERLOOKING THE VALLEY OF ELAH STANDS THE MOUND OF AZEKAH, PROMINENTLY MENTIONED IN THE OLD TESTAMENT RECORDS AND IN THE RECENTLY RECOVERED LACHISH LETTERS.

SAMARIA, THE CAPITAL OF THE NORTHERN KINGDOM, WAS FOUNDED BY OMRI ABOUT 880 B.C. THE ORIGINAL SITE OF THE CITY WAS ONE OF THE MOST CONSPICUOUS IN PALESTINE. LOCATED PRACTICALLY IN THE CENTER OF THE COUNTRY BETWEEN THE JORDAN AND THE MEDITERRANEAN, IT WAS ON THE GREAT HIGHWAY RUNNING NORTH AND SOUTH. THE DESTRUCTION OF SAMARIA IN 722 B.C. MARKED THE END OF THE NORTHERN KINGDOM.

who sought to block his passage to Carchemish, and here opposing armies continued to meet in decisive battles through succeeding centuries."[2]

In the extreme southern section of Canaan the Central Plateau begins to sprawl out into the vast areas of the Negeb or South Country. This territory is practically a barren waste at present, though Huntington, on the basis of scientific investigation, claims that civilization flourished here at an early date.[3] We know that it was traversed continually by hordes of nomads and that one of the decisive battles of the Hebrews was fought in this area. In general, the territory might have been occupied as early as the Hebrew invasion, but we know little of the culture of the Negeb peoples.

Altogether Canaan was an attractive country which, in comparison with the desert adjoining, was a "goodly land overflowing with milk and honey." It was inhabited by many peoples, some of whom go back to earliest antiquity. Among these peoples were the Hittites, the Amorites, the Canaanites, the Hurrians, the Philistines, and others. In Abraham's day Amorites and Hittites were well established in Canaan, living in great cities where they were powerfully entrenched. Abraham moved among them as a nomad, a shepherd, together with Isaac and Jacob; but in later years the descendants of Abraham were to re-enter this country to conquer it and to effect their own tribal settlements throughout the territory.

EGYPT

The Land of Father Nile gave to the ancient world its great Delta area and its unfailing granaries. It was the storehouse of antiquity. Abraham descended into Egypt in search of grain. That was the first contact of the Hebrews with the country which in later years was to be recalled as their *House of Bondage*. As a consequence the Hebrews always looked toward Egypt with deep bitterness and humiliation. But not the Egyptians. To them Egypt was one of the most attractive countries of the ancient world, and the most wonderful thing in Egypt was the Nile. Indeed, according to Herodotus, the Greek historian, Egypt is the Nile, and that statement is correct in every detail. The mighty Nile, rising in equatorial Africa, sweeps northward throughout its course to the Mediterranean a distance of 4,000 miles. From the uplands and the lowlands of Ethiopia come the tributaries to swell the volume of the Nile and to bring the floods with their rich alluvial deposits to replenish the whole of the valley area. In relation to Egypt proper the Nile begins at Assuan, the first cataract, continuing on to the Mediterranean, a distance of about 675 miles. The valley is narrow in the extreme southern portion, but as it proceeds north the valley widens until in the vicinity of Cairo it attains a width of about fourteen miles. From Cairo the Nile begins to spread, forming several branches which produce the great Delta area, the richest territory in the ancient world. The Delta region is approximately 115 miles in width, and its length 125 miles. In this region flourished some of the oldest cities of the Egyptians, while at the northeast was the attractive Goshen area which became the sojourn home of the Hebrews for 430 years. Shut in by the Arabian Desert on the east, by the Libyan Desert on the west, the kingdom of Egypt was relatively free from invading hordes, and as a consequence enjoyed a rather continuous cultural advance through many centuries. Its principal capitals in the early part of its history were located at Memphis in the north, and at Thebes in the south. Thus there were really two kingdoms. This twofold kingdom is reflected in the name of the country, Mizraim, which means the two lands. Later these sections were united to form one kingdom, the ruler being styled the Pharaoh, or lord over the Great House. Several of these rulers are referred to in the Old Testament. Abraham came in contact with one of the Pharaohs when making his journey into the Nile country in search of grain. Under similar circumstances Jacob and his sons made their advent into the Delta, where they were to remain through a period of four centuries. From this area they proceeded through the Peninsula of Sinai to their promised land of Canaan.

While the foregoing are the principal countries of the Old Testament world, the areas from which come the vast majority of our records of the past, there were other important sectors whose contributions have been of great significance. Among these Asia Minor, the land of the Hatti, stands out as the original home of the Hittites whose imperial organization successfully opposed the empires of Babylonians and Egyptians. The powerful stronghold of the Hittite Empire was located at Hattusas (modern Boghaz-koi, about eighty miles east of Ankara), while numerous other cities, stretching from the Aegean to the eastern boundaries above Mesopotamia, acknowledged the Hittite culture and domination. But we are just beginning to recover these mysterious people who are mentioned so frequently in the historical records of the Old Testament.

Along the coasts of Asia Minor and Syria stands Cyprus, one of the important sections of the Old Testament world. The island of Cyprus is referred to in the Hebrew records as Kittim, the name being derived from the great copper deposits developed both by the natives and by the Phoenicians who were the merchants and manufacturers of the ancient world. Immediately to the west of Cyprus, the island of Crete comes into view. Crete, which is in all probability the Caphtor of the Old Testament, lay along the perimeter of the Hebrew

19

world, but, in spite of its remoteness, played an important role in Hebrew affairs, particularly in connection with the Philistines who migrated from this area to Canaan and established themselves in the great cities of the southern maritime plain. Finally, Rhodes, lying off the southwestern tip of Asia Minor, makes its appearance in the Old Testament, but its contribution up to this time has not been very important for Old Testament studies.

CHAPTER TWO

THE RECOVERY OF ANCIENT CIVILIZATIONS

Gebal

DogRiver

Berytus

Sidon

RIVER LEONTES

MOUNT HERMON

Tyre

Dan Banias
Caesarea-Philippi
Waters of Merom

Accho
Ptolemais
Hazor
Chorazin
Capernaum
Khan Minyeh
Bethsaida-Julias
SEA OF GALILEE
Hippos
YARMUK
Haifa
Tiberias
Jokneam
Sepphoris
Dor
Nazareth
RIVER
Gadara
Megiddo
Taanach
Caesarea
Ibleam
Bethshean
Dothan
Tirzah
Pella
Samaria
Shechem
RIVER JORDAN
RIVER JABBOK
Gerasa

Joppa
Shiloh

Bethel
Ai
Rabbath-Ammon
Gezer
Mizpah
Ekron
Gibeah
Jericho
Heshbon
Ashdod
Jerusalem
Teleilat el-Ghassul
Tell es-Safi
Timnah
Bethshemesh
Ashkelon
Azekah
Bethlehem
Medeba
Maresha
Lachish
Beth-zur
Gaza
Hebron
Tell el-Hesy
Tell el-Ajjul
Kirjath-Sepher
Dibon
Gerar
RIVER ARNON
Sharuhen
Masada
DEAD SEA
Beersheba
Kerak

Khalasa

Khirbet et-Tannur

Sbeita

RIVER OF EGYPT

PALESTINE
PROGRESS OF EXCAVATIONS
Scale · English Miles

Kadesh-Barnea

Underscore Indicates Excavation Site

CHAPTER TWO

THE RECOVERY OF ANCIENT CIVILIZATIONS

DESCRIBING the results of his recent excavations at Ur of the Chaldees, Sir Leonard Woolley, the distinguished excavator, represents archaeology as "The Mirror of the Ages."[1] The description is very appropriate since it sets forth accurately the province and function of this the youngest of the sciences. Archaeology is simply the looking glass in which are seen the reflected images of the world's yesterdays. Its *province* includes all recovered material evidences associated with the civilizations of ancient peoples—their inscriptions, relics, implements of war and peace, scattered monuments, tombs, architecture, arts, and all likely representations of social customs and religious beliefs. The evidences thus recovered constitute the sole witnesses of peoples whose active participation in the affairs of life terminated thousands of years ago. It is the *function* of archaeology, patiently and effectively, to cause these remains to live again, to clothe them so far as possible with their original garments, and to allow them to move across a stage appropriate to their own times, and circumstances. It is one of the marvels of scientific development that, in this extremely difficult and exacting role as a rebuilder of the past, archaeology has already achieved signal success, and has assumed a commanding position among principal agencies making for an increase in human knowledge. It is

23

obvious that its great success at this point has been due to a keen sense of historical perspective, or orientation, which is one of the chief requisites for accurate interpretation.

But the handling of these recovered evidences of human culture together with a true appraisal and interpretation of their abiding values, constitutes only one phase of its work. Archaeology must also provide the materials with which it labors; must take up the pick and spade and proceed to the rubbish heaps of the ages to recover their buried wealth. Thus our science is not only engaged in rebuilding and interpreting for us the civilizations of ancient peoples, but is under compulsion to return to the sites of these early cultural centers and through arduous toil to bring to the surface the scattered and shattered parts of that which was once an organized and highly developed social structure.

The sites of these ancient cultures may be found in all sections of the Near and Middle East where excavations have been made with gratifying results by societies and institutions and by individuals of highest technical training. While the advent of war has brought practically all of these projects to an abrupt halt, a few enterprises continue in widely separated areas where the *mounds* are yielding their startling disclosures.[2] These are the dust heaps of the ages, the surviving witnesses to forgotten peoples and civilizations. Here are the sacred repositories of the millennia which hold the priceless evidences of progress when human culture was in the making. In these great mounds, accordingly, archaeology comes into the treasure houses of antiquity. Their story, whether regarded from the standpoint of the mounds themselves or from that of the mound builders, has all the elements of fascination and romance.

24

Mounds Described

It is generally recognized that the migratory movement of early peoples cannot be traced with absolute certainty. The explanation is probably found in the fact that they were largely nomadic peoples, and that in their frequent removals from one place to another they left no permanent evidences regarding either the time or nature of their settlements. With the progress of investigation, however, we have been able to go far beyond the nomad eras to other types of culture which had their own distinctive settings and characteristics. Among these, for example, appear the extremely interesting groups, the *marsh peoples* and the *troglodytes*. In Palestine, a country roughly characterized by mountains and plateaus, the earliest inhabitants drifted to the lowlands east and west of the Central Plateau in the south, while in the north they were attracted by the plains of Acre and Esdraelon and the Valley of Jezreel. Along the Mediterranean seaboard south of Mount Carmel there were evidently communities of *marsh peoples* flourishing as early as the Chalcolithic period (4000 B.C.). As illustrated by the accompanying photograph, these marsh people lived in houses securely propped up to clear the water. It seems that the houses consisted of a single room, probably a window, and an elevated doorsill or threshold. In comparing this type of dwelling with a modern reed hut in the Jordan Valley one may see the principle still in operation.[3] On the other hand, the *troglodytes,* or cave dwellers, while availing themselves of coastal caves, as in the Wady Mugharah on the western skirts of Mount Carmel, were generally disposed to seek the more elevated sections for their habitations, burrowing into mother earth as at Gezer, Megiddo, Bethshean, Jericho, and Jerusalem. The *troglodytes,* whose civilization is now rather fully known, were the immediate forerunners of the *mound peoples,* who in turn displaced them and appropriated their sites for permanent settlements. Of course hundreds of other sites, never occupied by cave dwellers, were also selected and subsequently developed into important mound cities.

These great mounds, the silent sentinels of hoary ages, may be seen anywhere in the Near and Middle East, the most conspicuous being located in Palestine, Syria, and Mesopotamia. Practically denuded of vegetation and usually deserted by inhabitants, they appear as hillocks, great knolls, or *tumuli,* rising almost abruptly from surrounding territory. This is particularly true of those sections where the country is relatively flat or slightly undulated, as in the great river basin of the Tigris-Euphrates in Mesopotamia, the Lebanon area in Syria, and the Mediterranean coastlands in Palestine. In all these sections climatic conditions were very favorable to primitive life and, consequently, they were among the first to witness the highly developed settlements associated with the outstanding cities of the Old Testament world. Our first glimpse of such cities in Palestine is provided in the report of the Hebrew spies who speak of Canaanite strongholds as "walled up to heaven" and very great.[4] It need not be added that this report receives full corroboration in the light of our present knowledge. We also know that practically all these strongholds which were to be conquered by the invading Hebrews had been in existence centuries before the conquest of Canaan began. But in order to have a clearer picture of the mound cities there are a few general considerations bearing on their antiquity, the acreage covered, and the nature of their fortifications which should be presented at this point. To those matters we now turn for brief discussion.

The *antiquity* of these mounds can be determined with a high degree of accuracy. In a few cases the con-

26

tents of a tell indicate human occupation extending through several thousand years. Tell ej-Jezer (Gezer), first inhabited by cave dwellers prior to 3000 B.C., represents the accumulated debris of eight distinct strata, each stratification referring to a different settlement in the course of its history. On the basis of Pottery Chronology,[5] dates for these successive settlements or cities can be fixed with almost scientific precision. Tell el-Hesy was shown by Petrie and Bliss to have been the site of eleven cities, each superimposed on the rubbish of its predecessor, the earliest of which dated prior to 2000 B.C. and the latest about 450 B.C. Recent excavations by Speiser at Tepe Gawra, a great mound located fourteen miles north of modern Mosul on the Tigris River, reveal twenty-six stratifications, which represent successive stages in the progress of prehistoric and early historic man.[6] Scores of other mounds tell the same story. Though varying both as to their beginnings and periods of duration as cultural centers, practically all of these tells go back to hoary antiquity, thus presenting to us a rather continuous account of social development among these early communities.

From the standpoint of *acreage* available for settlements, some of these mounds are large, others very small. The largest city mound in Palestine to come under observation thus far is Tell el-Hesy (probably Eglon of the Old Testament), which embraces slightly more than forty acres.[7] Next in order is the site of Gezer with a total spread of twenty-seven acres.[8] The powerful stronghold of Megiddo, figuring throughout Palestinian history as one of its principal cities, could never boast more than twenty acres, while Jerusalem, in its earliest days, covered approximately eight acres. The great majority of these mound cities, therefore, were characterized by relatively small acreage. Mizpah,

27

the home of Samuel, the prophet-judge, and an administrative center of the Babylonians after the destruction of Jerusalem by Nebuchadnezzar, enclosed about eight acres. Jericho, the first walled city west of the Jordan to fall before the advancing Israelites, consisted then of not more than seven or eight acres.[9] In comparison, the great pyramid of Cheops in Egypt covered almost twice as much ground as Jericho. But, in spite of their smallness, these cities should not be regarded as unimportant nor their population as insignificant. We may be certain that all available space was utilized to accommodate the population. There were no wide or convenient streets; movements here and there were, as a rule, along lanes or narrow passages. Houses were close together, many of them probably having more than one story. In addition, as in the case of Rahab's house at Jericho, some dwellings were even on the wall. It is clear that these cities were largely of the nature of citadels or fortresses, that they had garrison forces in addition to the civil population. We may also assume that there were considerable suburban areas whose inhabitants would avail themselves of the cities' protection in time of siege.

Finally, the mound cities were all *fortified*, the principal element in their defense naturally being the enclosing wall. Though all of the details are not known, we are probably justified in attributing walled settlements or fortified cities in Palestine to the Amorites, who arrived from the Lebanon area prior to 2500 B.C. In later centuries, about 2000-1500 B.C., the Hyksos and Hittite hordes made their way into Canaan, conquered or displaced resident peoples in many sections, and established themselves securely in fortified centers. The distinctive type of mural defense (the glacis or sloping revetment) adopted by these newcomers may be seen at Jericho, Jerusalem, and elsewhere. But,

28

whether Amorites, Hyksos, Hittites, or lesser groups, all seem to have been quite expert in planning walls, and some of the results of their labor are perfectly astounding. Materials used in construction consisted of brick, stone, and earth. Mortar was also very common as a binder for the various courses of the walls. Ordinarily stone foundations were laid for these walls, though it was sometimes possible by excavating to reach bedrock or to build on natural escarpments. In some cases we have found outer and inner walls designed to insure greater security. The dimensions of these ramparts are not uniform, but offer wide range, depending on the nature of the hill to be fortified. In height they were usually about 20 or 30 feet, while in thickness they ranged anywhere from 4 or 5 feet to 10, 15, and even more. It is obvious that such walls as these were practically impregnable. Besieging armies, even when equipped with battering machines, were frequently repulsed for months and, occasionally, for years. Samaria, for example, was besieged for three years by the Assyrians, but Troy held out against the Greeks for ten years, the fall of the former being due to starvation, while the conquest of the latter was attributed to a successful ruse on the part of the Greeks when the wooden horse was brought through the gate. The conquest of one of these cities usually made at terrible cost on the part of besiegers, was the signal for wholesale looting, murder of citizens, and complete destruction of walls and houses. It was not uncommon for curses to be pronounced against any attempt to rebuild them; even the sites were sown with salt.[10]

Mounds of Many Cities

In the foregoing summary we have sought to give a general view of early settlements with special reference to sites selected, areas included, and the nature of defenses constructed for their protection. But no attempt has been made to explain the process by which mounds gradually rose to considerable elevation above surrounding territory so that now the earliest civilizations are found at stages ranging anywhere between 60 and 100 feet in depth. This is a matter of first-rate importance to the student of archaeology, since it involves the sequence of cultural history as reflected in the accumulated debris of these specific sites.

It should be pointed out that the phrase, *buried cities,* as generally used, applies to all sites or places where civilization once flourished and where, at present, there is nothing but ruins. It is now known that many cities were originally founded on comparatively level ground, as over against the higher elevations of hills or undulating territory; that some occupied locations at the foot of mountain ranges, and some in the great river basins of the ancient world. All of these settlements, through long periods of time, would have been affected both by acts of man's violence and by the uncontrolled forces of nature. The abandonment of any of these centers because of effects of war, or destruction following in the wake of earthquakes, windstorms, or floods would result through successive centuries in actual obliteration of the sites so that they would become completely lost to view or buried. Cities engulfed by the encroaching sands of the Libyan and Arabian deserts can be found throughout Upper and Lower Egypt, along the North African littoral in the regions of Tunisia and Cyrenaica where Roman cities once flourished, and in other sections of the Near and Middle East where ancient empires rose and fell. In Italy, Herculaneum was swallowed up by the lava from Mount Vesuvius, while Pompeii was completely buried by the ashes of the same eruption. It is now known that cities situated along the water courses, or at the foot of towering mountains, have been subjected to natural causes which in time resulted in their burial. Shechem in Palestine succumbed to the erosion of Ebal and Gerizim flanking it on the north and south, while the earliest settlement at Jericho suffered a similar fate because of the Judean highlands. Excavations at Ur of the Chaldees and at Kish, cities situated along the course of the mighty Euphrates in southern Mesopotamia, indicate that these cities originally were founded on sites considerably below the present water level and that they were buried by the alluvium brought down by the annual floods. An illustration of this phenomenal increase of soil is found in the Obelisk of On whose submerged base shows a total deposit of 27 feet of alluvium made by the Nile through a period of 4000 years.

It will be of interest to note the process by which mounds gradually rose to considerable elevation above the original sites. As previously stated, early inhabitants preferred high or elevated places on which to establish permanent settlements, since they afforded greater security against the constant menace of invasion. Prior to the advent of the city builders, however, many of these sites had been occupied for centuries by cave dwellers, or troglodytes, who have left evidences of their culture. Displaced by the more advanced and aggressive invaders, the cave dwellers gradually disappeared and the sites of their settlements were appropriated by the newcomers. Instead of continuing the underground establishments for dwelling purposes, the new people converted them into tombs, granaries, and cisterns, and erected their houses on the surface of the mound. Around their houses, thus grouped in a settlement, they proceeded to build walls, which usually followed the contour of the hill. While stone was freely used in construction of the walls, little was employed in the erection of dwellings. The lower portions of houses ordinarily consisted of mud or clay walls, the upper sections of wood. Dwellings were built adjoining one another, as a rule; the streets or lanes were narrow and winding and usually littered with refuse. No departments of health operated either for city planning or public hygiene. As a consequence, broken vessels of pottery, useless and worthless, remained where they were cast, and all discarded implements were undisturbed by pedestrians.

Life was lived on a comparatively orderly and modest scale, with the extremes of society, then as now, expressed in terms of the wealthy, the near wealthy, the average lot, and the poverty-stricken. This representative settlement continued its daily affairs through many years, probably a century or more, when hostile invaders drew up their war machines before the walls. After prolonged siege the city was captured, its walls torn down or breached in many places, its houses burned or demolished, its inhabitants subjugated or killed, and all the visible booty taken away by the conquerors. With the departure of the victorious army another group of people, probably some of the survivors of the original population, made their way to the old site whose elevated position still offered greater security. They made no effort to remove the debris of the former city but began to build at once upon its ruins. Using the foundations of original walls, they constructed larger and higher ramparts to withstand siege and attack. In process of time the second city became a compact group of adjoining houses, with narrow winding lanes, and with bustling throngs. The city fathers, always alert to the menace of invasion, spared no pains in making the walls impregnable. With an eye to the inevitable siege of months, they further provided for the food requirements of an invested city and, most of all, for an adequate supply of water.[11] Hostile forces made

THE RESOUNDING CRASH OF THE TOPPLED WALLS OF JERICHO HAS
ECHOED THROUGH THE CENTURIES. GENERAL VIEW OF THE SITE OF
JERICHO AT THE FOOTHILLS OF THE JUDEAN HIGHLANDS. AT THE TIME
OF JOSHUA'S CONQUEST THE CITY OCCUPIED ABOUT SEVEN ACRES.

AN OCCUPIED MOUND, TELL BIREH, LOCATED IN THE UPPER SECTION OF
THE VALLEY BETWEEN THE LEBANON AND ANTI-LEBANON MOUNTAINS.
THE NAME OF THE ANCIENT CITY HAS PERISHED. THE ILLUSTRATION
SHOWS HOW CITIES BUILT ON HILLS APPEAR.

TAANACH, ANCIENT CITY OF THE CANAANITES, STOOD ONLY FIVE MILES FROM MEGIDDO AND WAS ONE OF THE STRONG FORTRESS CITIES GUARD-ING THE NORTHERN APPROACHES INTO THE COUNTRY. FREQUENTLY MENTIONED IN ANCIENT RECORDS.

TOWERING MOUND OF RABBATH-AMMON, PRINCIPAL CITY OF THE AM-MONITES. IN THE SIEGE OF THE STRONGHOLD UNDER JOAB THE NOBLE URIAH WAS SACRIFICED BY DAVID.

a second attack on the city, leaving complete destruction in the wake of their onslaught. Then other people came to the same site, rebuilt on the ruins of former settlements now probably twelve or fifteen feet below the surface of debris. Repeating this process through a period of ten or twenty centuries, with a succession of new cities and walls, new peoples and cultures, the mound gradually increased in height until the last city was completely destroyed and the site abandoned. Meanwhile the retaining walls, encircling the old cities from the beginning, protected the ruins from erosion, while natural phenomena gently threw over the abandoned sites a mantle of topsoil for protection. Thus the treasures of these former centers of culture were securely housed in the mounds to await the day of scientific excavation.

Uncovering the Past

It seems clearly providential that these mounds with their buried wealth should have been subjected to the natural elements which, in the long run, locked securely within the bosoms of the tells the treasures of the past, and that subsequently the sites were practically forgotten until the world was better prepared to uncover and to understand their mysteries. Never was an age more adequately equipped than our own to peer into these hallowed heaps of debris, to bring to light the materials with which men wrought in the actual struggle for existence, about which they thought in the realm of morals, religion, and social conventions, and from such visible objects as these to interpret the checkered experiences of men, women, and children who played their role on the stage of life and passed on.

In approaching these mounds with pick and spade, the excavator is undertaking a very serious business. The investigator who sets before himself a definite program of predetermined "finds," based on preconceived theories into whose mold all discovered data must be thrown, thereby shows himself disqualified for the work even before he begins. Irreparable damage has already been done to the cause of genuine scientific investigation by wandering excavators whose picks and hoes have been consecrated to some pet scheme or predetermined "find." No expedition whose sole purpose is the recovery of some special object, apart from its probable relation to a thousand other objects which might come to light during the process of the work, should ever be undertaken. To set out to find Megiddo, or Lachish, or Gath, or any other place, regardless of its capital importance, is not the proper motive which should actuate the labor of a serious excavator. If a tell is known by the name of ej-Jezer—and, in all probability, is the same as the old town of Gezer which Pharaoh gave to Solomon as part of the marriage dowry of his daughter—dig into it, excavate it, not for the sake of its name, nor for the sake of Solomon or his wife, but for the sake of itself! It should be uncovered for the sake of its treasure-trove! Every mound in Palestine, or elsewhere, is sacred ground to the extent that it holds within its bosom the secrets of the ages, and it is only by reverent handling of its charred ashes and scattered debris that we can hope to learn something of the conditions under which its inhabitants lived. These are the materials from which we must reconstruct at least the framework or general pattern of their social, political, religious, and economic life.

There are two considerations which convert this proposition into an urgent necessity and obligation. In the first place, no mound, once excavated, can ever be rebuilt according to its original state or stratification; the deposits of the ages, once disturbed, can never be rearranged to conform to the condition in which they were found. And, secondly, regardless of the thoroughness of the excavator's work, no civilization can be fully recovered; there will always be missing links. Every bit of evidence of ancient culture revealed in a tell is of inestimable value and, when properly related to contemporaneous objects, is invested with its true and significant meaning.

With this principle duly recognized by individuals and institutions entering the field of excavation, and with drastic requirements laid down by governments in whose territories work is to be done, methods of excavation practiced only a few years ago have become practically obsolete and the modern technique has been continually improved. Among the older methods was that of *tunneling,* or the use of underground passages for the purpose of examining the lower stratifications of ancient cities. This costly, dangerous, and unsatisfactory method was adopted by Warren at Jerusalem in 1867-68, under the auspices of the Palestine Exploration Fund. Apart from considerable information regarding the size and depth of Jerusalem's ancient walls, these underground operations proved unsuccessful and have since been discarded. Thirty-six years later, 1903, Schumacher, inaugurating excavations at Megiddo under the auspices of the German Palestine Society, resorted to a series of trenches extending at angles across the mound with a view to securing at least a partial picture of its early civilizations as revealed in these cross-sections. We give here an illustration of one of these trenches as it still appears. In 1890 Sir Flinders Petrie began the first project in scientific excavation at Tell el-Hesy, where he succeeded in removing the debris of eleven distinct cities dating from approximately 2000 B.C. to 400 B.C., when the mound was deserted. This work was done in a thorough manner although it affected only one-third of the tell, the other

two-thirds being occupied by an Arab settlement and
cemetery. The present appearance of Tell el-Hesy is
shown in the accompanying drawing.

THE MOUND OF EL-HESY IN SOUTHWESTERN PALESTINE IN ALL PROB-
ABILITY REPRESENTS THE OLD TESTAMENT CITY OF EGLON. WHEN
PETRIE EXCAVATED TELL EL-HESY IN THE EARLY YEARS, HE WAS NOT
PERMITTED TO COMPLETE THE WORK BECAUSE OF THE PRESENCE OF A
CEMETERY ON TOP OF THE MOUND. THE DRAWING SHOWS HOW THE
MOUND APPEARS TODAY.

One of the most systematic projects was that
inaugurated by Clarence Fisher at Bethshean in 1922
in connection with the British Museum and the University of Pennsylvania. Preliminary soundings to a depth
of 36 feet failed to reach bedrock, the stratifications
penetrated by the shaft indicating cultural periods

extending from 2000 B.C. to 800 A.D. Careful study of the accompanying illustration will show the progress of the work up to this time and the manner in which it is being done. But the most outstanding example of scientific excavation is the work of the University of Chicago at Megiddo, a project that will require twenty years or more for its completion. The method here employed is more on the strip order, i.e., the complete removal of the debris of each stratum, with a painstaking description of its contents, with photographs of all objects, classification of materials, and a precise plotting of each stratum to show where every object was found and its relation to all other objects on that particular level. With this precise and laborious method adopted, the excavations have progressed from the latest settlement of the late Greek period, through the era of David and Solomon, roughly between 1000 B.C. and 900 B.C., and are now concerned with the period of Thutmosis III (1501-1447 B.C.) of Egypt. Many cities on this mound remain to be uncovered. The final settlement will probably be found built over the subterranean chambers of the cave dwellers. When the Megiddo excavations are completed it is felt that we will have before us the most accurate and complete picture of its cultural development possible to obtain.

But Bethshean and Megiddo, together with other tells, are simply representative of the significant movement to return to the scenes of yesterday for enlightenment and orientation. Every year new societies and institutions enter the field with the older foundations; new faces among the upstanding archaeologists, new territories explored, and new sites excavated. With the success of each enterprise, additional light falls on the contents of the Bible whereby its customs and ceremonies become better understood and its historical narratives illustrated.

CHAPTER THREE

RECORDS FROM EGYPT

RECORDS FROM EGYPT

THE whole of the Near and Middle East represents a vast archaeological museum in which nature has preserved through many centuries the records of vanished empires and peoples. To the spirit of modern scientific investigation, Egypt, Palestine, Syria, Asia Minor, and Mesopotamia have yielded their hidden treasures, with the result that, item by item, we are now able to reconstruct the general outlines of historic development through several thousand years. No country has failed to provide some information, though Egypt and Mesopotamia, being the localities associated with earliest settlements and great empires, have been most generous in their contributions. Even the islands of the Great Sea, especially Crete, have given up their records of the past to shed light not only on their own immediate affairs, but to set forth in clearer manner their relations with other peoples around the Mediterranean basin. The imperishable desire of man to perpetuate the annals of his race and era, to record something of achievement and aspiration, to preserve the traditions of remote events, is seen on every hand, and explains at least in part the presence of these chronicles of early days.

As stated, these records of human interest and events have been found in almost every conceivable place. The great city mounds, where life was organized on a relatively high scale, have supplied the overwhelming majority of written accounts, but other areas have figured conspicuously. Increased knowledge has come from forgotten graves and abandoned cemeteries, from mountain slopes, temple walls, pyramids, subterranean passages, deserted fields, river beds, rubbish heaps, fortresses, mines, royal palaces, libraries, and desert sands. The wide distribution of these recovered monuments, the variety of circumstances under which they were originally produced, make it evident that they represent not one aspect of the social order of ancient peoples, but give a cross-section of their manifold activities in the realms of home, church, and state. It is clear that, if these records had never been written, the world would never have derived similar information from any other source. They are the sole survivors of the stirring events which they recount and are of priceless value. From these scattered historical fragments we are now able to formulate a fairly accurate outline of early peoples from the standpoint of their local interests and contacts with their neighbors.

In presenting the following summary of ancient records we are not concerned with any detailed discussion of their special significance and values, but seek here primarily to set forth the facts of their discovery. In doing this, we are proceeding on the general principle already stressed that the matter of first importance is to ascertain the facts, to master the details. The next step is the application of this knowledge to specific problems. And, as we proceed, it will be seen that practically every discovery herein described has a vital relation to some problem of biblical interest. The order of enumeration is not altogether satisfactory, but, in view of the wide diversity of subject matter, one wonders how it could be improved. Classification is always difficult, especially when dealing with materials that have so little in common, whether from the standpoint of language, race, history, geography, religion, politics, or trade. Of course the bond of interest in this work is their archaeological bearing on the Scriptures, and this is constantly to the front. In the following summary we have adopted a geographical framework rather than a chronological, in which we have arranged the various records according to the countries in which they were found. It is believed that this scheme will have the advantage of simplifying matters and that it will enable the student to orientate himself to kindred subjects and periods.

EGYPT

It is eminently fitting that this survey of ancient records should begin with Egypt, for the Nile area stands not only near the headwaters of human culture but, in a way hardly anticipated, definitely witnessed the birth of modern archaeology at the close of the eighteenth century. The Egyptian Expedition of Napoleon in 1798 was primarily of military significance, but the presence of about one hundred scholars who were interested in letters and antiquities disclosed that Bonaparte also associated with the invasion of Egypt a serious purpose to learn as much as possible concerning the mysterious kingdom of the Pharaohs.[1] The land of Egypt, extending from the Delta to Assuan, was a vast archaeological museum whose treasures were matters over which men dreamed, of which travelers told thrilling stories, but whose age-long secrets were practically unknown. Egypt was regarded by some as the cradle of civilization, by others as of hoary antiquity—how old, nobody knew—but there was none who could understand the voice of the sphinx, or interpret a single sign of the bewildering language which graced the halls and columns of ancient temples of Karnak, Luxor, Assuan, and Edfu. Stately edifices and monuments, stelae and statues, royal tombs and underground sarcophagi, all were inscribed with those picturesque and enigmatic characters which baffled explanation. But with the discovery of a master key which threw open all doors to the mysteries of Egyptian records, the Nile country began to make startling contributions to the story of historic and prehistoric culture. It is now generally held that we know more of Egypt's past, more of its historical development, more of its internal and external affairs and for a longer period of time than of any other country of the ancient world. Thousands of its historic monuments, consisting of inscriptions from temples and stelae, obelisks and pyramids, mural decorations in royal cemeteries, and retaining walls in sacred precincts, have been preserved. Thousands of feet of beautifully written papyrus scrolls, Books of the Dead, have come to light, depicting for us views of ancient Egyptians regarding life and its issues. Literally tons of inscribed records are now in hand, our museums are bulging with them, and more are being discovered every year. Among these records of Egyptian origin, five are of capital importance for our present investigation, namely: *The Rosetta Stone, The Tell el-Amarna Letters, The Stela of Merneptah, The Elephantine Papyri,* and *The Serabit el-Khadim Inscriptions.* To each of these we turn for a brief description.

1. *The Rosetta Stone*

While preparing fortifications at Rosetta, a town located on the Rosetta Branch of the Nile thirty-five miles northeast of Alexandria, one of Napoleon's soldiers unearthed a piece of black basalt about the size of a sewing machine table. The stone, bearing a trilingual inscription in Hieroglyphic, Demotic, and Greek,[2] was immediately turned over to the scholars, who commenced the laborious task of its decipherment. The extreme importance of the stone was not at first recognized, though copies of the inscriptions were sent to scholars and learned societies in various parts of Europe. In Sweden, Akerblad succeeded in finding the true values of fourteen demotic characters; Young rightly interpreted six hieroglyphic characters, while others made special contributions to the increasing knowledge. But it remained for the Champollion brothers to formulate a demotic and hieroglyphical alphabet that has stood the test of time and which is now in use by all Egyptologists.

Proceeding on the assumption that the Hieroglyphic and Demotic writings were repetitions of the facts given in the Greek (which was read without difficulty), and using the modern Coptic as a connecting link with the Demotic, the translators verified the theory that the accounts were identical. Then by a most ingenious method which began with the mastery of signs appearing in the *cartouches,* or ovals, which invariably represent royal names, true values were assigned to the Hieroglyphs. Almost a quarter of a century was spent in this difficult undertaking, but with the mastery of the picture language, the ancient records of Egypt began to give up their secrets. With the decipherment of the Rosetta Stone the question of translating Egyptian annals was lifted out of the realm of guesswork and hypothesis and placed on an accurate scientific basis, where it remains. No one can estimate the value of this discovery for the unrolling of the scroll of Egypt's past.[3]

2. *The Tell el-Amarna Letters*

The modern ruins of Et-Tell, located about 190 miles south of Cairo on the east side of the Nile, mark the site of the ancient capital of the heretical Pharaoh Amenhotep IV who, having outlawed the worship of the ancestral god Ra (or Amon-Ra), and having introduced a new religion which found its inspiration in Aton ("The Sun's Disk"), shifted the political and religious center of Egypt from Thebes to the new site which he designated Akhet-aton—i.e., "The Brilliance of the Sun's Disk." The rejection of Amon-Ra is also reflected in the discarding by the Pharaoh of his own name, Amen-hotep, and the substitution of the new description Akhnaton—i.e., "Aton is satisfied." These revolutionary events took place in the early part of Akhnaton's reign, the date being fixed at 1370 B.C., and inaugurated a period of unsettled conditions in Egyptian affairs both locally and among the foreign dependencies.[4] The young ruler had succeeded to a vast empire which had been held intact by his illustrious father, Amenhotep III, under whom the Theban Empire attained probably its greatest dimensions and glory. But the new king possessed neither the ability nor the disposition to administer effectively his vast domains, which extended from the southern regions of Nubia through Upper and Lower Egypt, Palestine, Syria to Mesopotamia. Furthermore, hand in hand with the violent religious innovations which alienated the loyal support of native priests and people, the outskirts of his empire were subjected to a series of attacks which were ignored by the Pharaoh and which were unsuccessfully met by his dependent rulers particularly in Syria and in Palestine.

The circumstances, as we are now able to reconstruct them, indicate that hundreds of urgent letters were sent to the Pharaoh by native rulers in adjacent territory imploring help against an armed invasion by a people called the Habiru (Hebrews), and pointedly stating that unless Egypt sent aid the dependent territories would be lost. The king of Jerusalem sent at least seven letters urging the Pharaoh to assist him.

46

But no help was given, nor even promised. In addition, engrossed in his religious revolutions and afflicted with problems in his own household, Akhnaton for the most part did not answer the letters of his foreign dependents but ordered them to be filed in the Foreign Office for future reference. Fortunately he had an efficient Foreign Secretary, who faithfully inserted the correspondence in the royal archives, probably under the head of urgent business. There they remained pigeonholed and unmolested. With the death of Akhnaton and the short reign of his son-in-law, Tutankhamen, at Akhetaton, the new capital was abandoned, the palace deserted, and within a short period even the site of the city was lost to view and remained unknown for over 2,500 years.

The discovery of the major portion of the Tell el-Amarna Letters in 1887 is attributed to a struggling peasant woman who, while digging into the rich soil of the ancient city, accidentally struck a section of the buried archives of Pharaoh Akhnaton with a cache of the precious clay tablets numbering several hundred, of which about 350 were saved. Later discoveries have increased the number to more than 400. Not knowing the value of the recovered treasures, it is reported that the woman sold her rights in the discovery for ten Egyptian piastres (fifty cents). News of the astounding discovery quickly reached merchants and archaeologists, with the result that brisk bargaining set in for permanent possession of the letters. In this way the Amarna tablets became distributed over wide areas, 81 being in the British Museum, 160 in Berlin, 60 in Cairo, 20 in Oxford, and a few more in other museums or in private collections.

The importance of the Tell el-Amarna Letters may be summarized as follows: (1) Written to Egyptian Pharaohs in the Babylonian cuneiform, and coming from vassal and independent kings in various sections of the Near and Middle East, the Amarna Letters show that the cuneiform, and not the Egyptian hieroglyphs, was the accepted language of diplomatic relations around 1500-1350 B.C. (2) The Letters enable us to reconstruct the political history of one of the most difficult periods in the life of Israel. (3) They will probably solve for us the urgent problem of the Pharaohs of the Oppression and Exodus with the determination of the date of the life and work of Moses. (4) The progress of the Hebrew conquest of Canaan under Joshua will be more clearly delineated. Finally, the letters from Canaan will set forth in sharper relief the cultural conditions obtaining in that country at the beginning of the fifteenth century B.C.

3. *The Stela of Merneptah*

The romantic discovery of the Stela of Merneptah at Thebes in 1896 is vividly recounted by Sir Flinders Petrie in the following: "The great discovery was the large triumphal inscription of Merenptah naming the Israelites. The site of Merenptah's temple was disastrously dull; there were worn bits of soft sandstone, scraps looted from the temple of Amenhetep III, crumbling sandstone sphinxes, laid in pairs in holes to support columns. I was tempted to leave it as fruitless; then came the half-length figure of Merenptah, a fine portrait work, and in the last corner to be cleared there lay a black granite stela, over ten feet high and five wide—on it a long inscription of Amenhetep III, which had been mostly erased by Akhenaten, and then piously re-engraved by Sety I. On looking beneath it, there was the inscription of Merenptah. I had the ground cut away below, blocking up the stela on stones, so that one could crawl in and lie on one's back, reading

TELL EL-MUTASELLIM, SITE OF MEGIDDO, ONE OF THE OUTSTANDING CITIES OF OLD CANAAN. LOCATED ON THE SOUTHERN BORDER OF THE PLAIN OF ESDRAELON. HERE THE ORIENTAL INSTITUTE OF CHICAGO UNIVERSITY IS COMPLETING ONE OF THE MOST THOROUGH-GOING EXCAVATION PROJECTS EVER UNDERTAKEN.

IN THIS DRAWING WE HAVE THE ARTIST'S CONCEPTION OF AN ANCIENT CITY WITH ITS WALLS INTACT. THE IDEAS HERE PRESENTED ARE ALTOGETHER IN KEEPING WITH THE ACTUAL FACTS OF A CITY'S APPEARANCE AND DEFENSES.

STREETS IN OLD WORLD
CITIES WERE SELDOM OF THE
BOULEVARD TYPE. AS A
RULE THEY WERE VERY NAR-
ROW AND WINDING. THE VIEW
HERE SHOWN RELATES TO A
MODERN STREET OF STEPS IN
OLD JERUSALEM. ORDINARILY
THESE STREETS ARE CROWD-
ED WITH CUSTOMERS, MER-
CHANTS, AND PEDDLERS AMID
AN ORIENTAL SETTING OF A
BEDLAM OF NOISE AND CON-
FUSION.

IN CONSTRUCTING WALLS FOR
DEFENSE OF CITIES, IT WAS
FREQUENTLY POSSIBLE TO
USE NATURAL ESCARPMENTS
AS SHOWN IN THIS PHOTO-
GRAPH. THIS IS A PART OF
THE NORTH WALL OF JERU-
SALEM JUST ABOVE THE EN-
TRANCE TO SOLOMON'S
QUARRIES.

a few inches from one's nose. For inscriptions, Spiegelberg was at hand, looking over all new material. He lay there copying for an afternoon, and came out saying, 'There are names of various Syrian towns, and one which I do not know, Isirar.' 'Why, that is Israel,' said I. 'So it is, and won't the reverends be pleased,' was his reply. To the astonishment of the rest of our party I said at dinner that night, 'This stela will be better known in the world than anything else I have found.' "[5]

Sir Flinders' judgment regarding the relative value of this discovery as compared with a long series of outstanding archaeological achievements ascribed to him, has been eminently justified, but his modesty forbade a more comprehensive claim that the monument stands, for biblical importance, among the most significant discoveries ever made. Its outstanding importance will be discussed later in connection with the question of the exodus of Israel from Egypt, but at this point we may note the following results of the discovery:[6] (1) It has compelled a re-examination and restatement of the traditional view which associated Rameses II with the oppression of Israel in Egypt, and his son Merneptah with the events of the exodus from Egypt. (2) The Stela has directed more exact study of the trustworthy character of chronological statements in the early historical narratives of the Old Testament. (3) The inscription provides evidence of Egypt's continued political activities in Palestine almost up to the threshold of the Hebrew Monarchy.

4. *The Elephantine Papyri*

Assuan, the southernmost city of Egypt, is situated at the first cataract of the Nile, about 675 miles from the Mediterranean. Regarded from the standpoint of the political divisions of ancient Egypt, the city was located in Upper Egypt or Pathros.[7] It appears in the later books of the Old Testament under the name of Syene.[8] The position of the city was of such strategic importance that it was converted into a border fortress guarding Lower Egypt from hostile incursions of peoples in equatorial Africa. Inscriptions in the vicinity indicate its close association with Lower Egypt, while its granite ledges supplied abundance of material for the magnificent columns and monuments found throughout Egypt and adjacent countries. Here, of course, was the point from which the commercial sailboats slipped along the great Nile into the Mediterranean.

In the Nile River, immediately opposite Assuan, is located a large island which in the modern period bears the name of Elephantine, but in the ancient world was called Yeb. In all probability, sharing with Syene the defense of Upper Egypt, it was converted into a fortified area with a considerable garrison of soldiers. It now seems likely that a large number of Hebrews, following the disorders and privations produced by the Assyrian invasion of Palestine (c. 700 B.C.), fled into Egypt and settled both in the north and south. It is practically certain that a larger group of refugees, fleeing the disorders of the Babylonian advance into Palestine (c. 600 B.C.), also went down into Egypt, perhaps compelling the prophet Jeremiah to accompany them. Some of these emigrants settled at Elephantine, where they organized their own society, built their own temple, and continued to conduct their religious and social life after the customs of their fathers in the native land. Abandoning the language of the Hebrews, the Elephantine colony adopted the Aramaic, which at this period was the common language of the Near and Middle East.

The Elephantine Papyri, discovered in 1904 and 1907, constitute the surviving records of this far-off

Jewish outpost. They are written in the Aramaic language and describe for us a period in the history of these Hebrews from the fifteenth year of Xerxes (471 B.C.) to the seventeenth year of Darius II (407 B.C.). They represent a general view of life as lived by these expatriated people, and provide considerable information concerning their legal, religious, and social practices. From the accounts we infer that a temple had been erected by the Jews at Elephantine approximately one hundred years prior to the invasion of Egypt by Cambyses, which occurred in 525 B.C., and that the Persians respected the sacred precincts though they ruthlessly destroyed the monuments of the native Egyptians. Subsequently the Egyptians, probably in retaliation, destroyed the Jewish Temple, and it is in the interest of its reconstruction that a part of the correspondence is directed.

Great significance is attached to these letters. "Next to the finding of the Tel-el-Amarna tablets, and as weighty in its bearing on all the questions concerning the books of the Old Testament, is the discovery of the Aramaic papyri.'"[9] In addition to the new light thrown on the Persian invasion and domination of Egypt, the letters enable us to reconstruct an aspect of the Jewish dispersion in these early days hitherto little known or even suspected. Furthermore, they describe conditions in Palestine as bearing on the probable relations among Persians, Jews, and Samaritans, and thus supplement at various points the historical and prophetical narratives of the Old Testament.[10]

5. *The Sinai Inscriptions*

The Sinaitic inscriptions are here classified with the Egyptian epigraphic discoveries solely on the basis of the close relations existing between the Peninsula of

Sinai and the Empire of ancient Egypt. "During the flourishing years of some of the Egyptian dynasties, especially the XIIth, XVIIIth, and XIXth, the Peninsula was regarded as a vital part of the Empire, and its most valuable foreign possession. From the numerous references to the region, we know that the Egyptians engaged in extensive mining operations in various parts of the country with great success, and that from these mines they obtained an almost unlimited supply of turquoise, iron, and copper. From the highly developed quarries of the western area came the red granite and pink gneiss, used so extensively in Egyptian public buildings and sculptures."[11] While native labor was employed in these mining activities, it is highly probable that the great majority of the workers came from dependent or subjugated people who were forced to do this service under taskmasters. This was certainly the situation at the mines of Serabit el-Khadim, where work proceeded with Semitic laborers.

Due to the comparative isolation of the Peninsula of Sinai in the modern period, only a few scientific expeditions have been concerned with either its general topography or possible monuments. Among the earliest explorers to penetrate the heart of the country was Edward Robinson, whose travels are described in several volumes published exactly a century ago. In 1906, Sir Flinders Petrie issued his splendid work on *Researches in Sinai.* It was during his visit to Serabit el-Khadim that Sir Flinders first made the remarkable discovery of the Sinai inscriptions. "He found a number of rocks carved roughly to simulate eight Egyptian stelae, which were, nevertheless, carved with a script that was neither hieroglyphic nor hieratic Egyptian. A figure of the god Ptah was evident, but not a word of ordinary Egyptian. The marks were not mere scribbles, but showed some organized attempt at orthography, for they were found at mines a mile and a half distant from the Sphinx near the temple of Serabit, where similar markings are to be seen. The direction of the writing is from left to right, contrary to the later Semitic, and most Egyptian, script. Judging by the fragments of pottery found near, the date of the inscriptions must be ascribed to the XVIIIth Dynasty, and probably to the reign of Thothmes III. Petrie considered the writing to be one of the many alphabets in use in the Mediterranean lands long before the fixed alphabet selected by the Phoenicians.'"[12]

Twenty years after Petrie's original discovery, the members of a Harvard Expedition to Mount Sinai in 1927 were persuaded by Alan Gardiner, an English Egyptologist, to make a special visit to Serabit el-Khadim in the interest of more information concerning the inscriptions reported by Petrie. In this re-examination the Expedition found additional inscriptions and became fully convinced that there were more to be discovered if the whole area were searched. This was done three years later when the Serabit Expedition of 1930 made a systematic and thorough examination of the region with the result that twenty other inscriptions were found. All of these were photographed, many removed intact from the virgin rock, others left *in situ* because of the danger involved in cutting without proper machinery. The full report of this Expedition, together with reproduction of photographs and drawings, is now available.[13]

The surpassing importance of the Sinai inscriptions may be summed up in the following: In these writings we have in all probability the earliest form of alphabetic script, marking the transition from the parent hieroglyphs of the Egyptians, and providing a connecting link with the later Phoenician. If this is a correct assumption, the Sinai inscriptions stand at the headwaters of all subsequent Semitic epigraphy and will assist us in showing the general relations subsisting among the scripts of the Phoenicians, Hebrews, Moabites, Arabs, and other Semitic peoples of the ancient world. In a special way the Sinai inscriptions will serve to illustrate the possibility and probability of Hebrew writings far earlier than we have been willing hitherto to admit.[14]

CHAPTER FOUR

RECORDS FROM MESOPOTAMIA

AN ARTIST'S CONCEPTION OF THE GREAT MOUNTAIN ON THE FACE
OF WHICH ARE FOUND THE BEHISTUN INSCRIPTIONS. THE HILL IS
ABOUT 1700 FEET IN HEIGHT. THE INSCRIPTIONS ARE 300 FEET
ABOVE THE PLAIN. HERE RAWLINSON RISKED HIS LIFE TO COPY
THE ANCIENT RECORDS OF THE PERSIAN KING, DARIUS V.

RECORDS FROM MESOPOTAMIA

T HE territory embraced in this division of our
survey includes the whole of the area stretching
from the Armenian Taurus range in the north to the
Persian Gulf in the south, and from the Arabian Desert
on the west to the Zagros Mountains on the east. To
this geographical unit the ancients applied the name
Mesopotamia, or "Land between the Rivers," the
great waterways being the Euphrates and the Tigris.[1]
The progress of excavations throughout this territory
tends steadily to show that the area witnessed some of
the earliest phases in the evolution of human culture.
Our present knowledge of the region is based not only
on the marvelous discoveries associated with the
uncovering of the ancient mounds of Babylon and
Nineveh, but also on the more recent excavations at
Carchemish, Kish, Tepe Gawra, Ur of the Chaldees,
and a score of other outstanding centers of the ancient
world. Gradually the spirit of modern scientific investigation, particularly in the fields of anthropology and
geological history, is recapturing the environment and
conditions of millenniums of cultural development and
delineating the then contemporary life in a most
astounding manner. As a consequence, the whole of
this Mesopotamian sector looms larger nowadays with
reference to the relations which it might have sustained
to the beginning of human life and habitation. In comparison some phases of Egyptian antiquity appear less
ancient than the Mesopotamian and in all probability

57

may have been derived from the latter. On this particular point it is the judgment of some recent excavators and historians that Mesopotamia stands at the headwaters of cultural evolution and that future excavations will tend to set this conclusion in sharper relief. It may be added in passing that this judgment corroborates the general statements of the early biblical narratives, which obviously point to this area as the cradle of the human race.

But our present interest in Mesopotamia is not concerned primarily with the geological history of the region nor with the earliest inception of human culture. We seek here rather to review its outstanding contributions to the field of epigraphic materials as these may bear on the integrity of the Old Testament, and as they may shed light on its narratives as historical documents of highest importance. With this purpose in view we must necessarily pass by thousands of ancient records which are not particularly germane to our study and present those only which vitally touch the Scriptures. Even so, the list will be found to include quite a number, as follows: *The Cuneiform Inscriptions at Behistun, The Creation and the Deluge Tablets, The Code of Hammurabi, Excavations at Tepe Gawra, Erech, Ur of the Chaldees, The Mari Tablets, The Nuzi Tablets, Records of Shalmaneser III, Annals of Tiglathpileser III, Cylinder of Sargon II, Cylinder of Sennacherib, Archives of Ashurbanipal,* and *The Babylonian Chronicle.*

1. *The Cuneiform Inscriptions at Behistun*[2]

The middle of the nineteenth century witnessed a great triumph of perseverance and skill in revealing the secrets of the difficult system of writing known as the cuneiform. The origin of this language is now associated with the early Sumerians who inhabited the lower regions of the Mesopotamian area, though until recent years it was generally thought that the Babylonians and Assyrians were chiefly responsible for its invention and development.

Numerous examples of the wedge-shaped writings were reported by travelers in the Near and Middle East long before there was any serious attempt to decipher them. One of the earliest notices regarding the cuneiform comes from Oderic, who made a visit to Persepolis, ancient capital of the Persian kings, in 1320. Later travelers brought back copies of the strange inscriptions which were placed in the hands of various European scholars. But progress in deciphering the characters was very slow. In 1835 Henry Rawlinson, a young British officer in Persia, discovered and began to copy at the risk of his life the great trilingual inscription on the Behistun Rock in the Zagros area. Facing the highway between Babylon and the Persian Plateau stands this lone rock at an elevation of 1700 feet. About 300 feet above the plain there is a prepared surface measuring approximately 25 by 50 feet. Within this space appears a great relief representing Darius's reception to rival kings. The accompanying illustration shows the face of the rock ledge with the panel inscriptions which consist of three types of cuneiform characters: The Old Persian with its 39 letters, the Babylonian with its hundreds of signs, and the Susian. The three inscriptions tell the same story.

The work of copying the inscriptions for careful study was accomplished by Rawlinson at intervals during a period of four years. Additional years were spent in faithful effort to decipher the mysterious signs. In 1846 Rawlinson published a complete translation of the Persian text, which became the basis for deciphering the Susian and the Babylonian. Proceeding on the assumption that "the two inscriptions told the same story, scholars began an attempt to translate them. Soon the second tongue, the Median or Susian, began to yield its secrets. Then the third series of texts, the Babylonian, was forced to give up its hidden treasures. This Behistun group was then found to sustain a similar relation to the cuneiform languages of Babylonia that the Rosetta Stone sustained to the tongues of ancient Egypt. It was the key to its ancient writings, life, peoples, and governments."[3]

The thousands of tablets subsequently found in widely separated parts of the Near and Middle East were readily translated in the light of the new knowledge. As a consequence we now have a fairly complete picture of Mesopotamian life and thought from the time of the Sumerians through the latest phases of the Babylonian, Assyrian, and Persian developments. The full significance of this translation achievement is found in connection with the later discoveries of the Code of Hammurabi, the Tell el-Amarna Letters, the Creation and Flood Tablets, and the numerous obelisks and cylinders of Assyrian kings and officials together with official records of Babylonian rulers. All of these historical annals, written in the cuneiform, were immediately read and the increased knowledge applied to points of interest and special problems of the Hebrew Scriptures.

2. The Creation and Deluge Tablets[4]

The deciphering of the Behistun inscriptions by Rawlinson was immediately followed by increased activity on the part of individuals, societies, and governments to recover every possible aspect of the ancient civilizations of the Assyrians and Babylonians. "The twelve years during which Rawlinson held his appointment in Baghdad mark the first great period of Assyrian and Babylonian excavations. It is true that he undertook but little work in the trenches himself, but he influenced and supervised the excavations of others, and personally examined all of the important ruins of Assyria and Northern Babylonia. His advice and assistance were sought by nearly all those who with pick and spade were engaged in uncovering the buried monuments of two great empires. While continental explorers won their laurels on the mounds of Khorsabad and Nimrud, Rawlinson forced the inaccessible rock of Behistun to surrender the great trilingual inscription of Darius, which in the quietude of his study on the Tigris became the 'Rosetta Stone' of Assyriology, and in his master hand the key to the understanding of the Assyrian documents."[5]

Now discoveries came thick and fast, as ancient sites were excavated by Botta, Place, Layard, Rassam, Loftus, Fresnel, Oppert, Thomas, Taylor, and others. "A large amount of cuneiform material had gradually been stored in the halls of the Louvre and of the British Museum towards the middle of the last century. Before other funds were likely to be granted by governments and liberal-minded individuals for the continuation of the excavations in Assyrian and Babylonian mounds, it became necessary to satisfy the learned and to prove to the public at large that the numerous monuments and broken clay tablets unearthed could really be read, and that their intrinsic value or the contents of their inscriptions were well worth the capital and time spent in their rediscovery."[6] Fortunately, it was at this transition period that George Smith made his great discovery of the Babylonian account of the Deluge which was readily seen to agree in many details with the biblical narratives. Through his mastery of the cuneiform and his almost uncanny ability to reconstruct original tablets

61

from broken pieces, he concluded that the complete account consisted of probably twelve tablets setting forth the legends of the great Gilgamesh and that the Deluge story was the eleventh tablet of the series. In process of time he found among the thousands of tablets in the British Museum portions of two other copies. So great was the reaction of the public to the announcement of these discoveries that the London *Daily Telegraph* contributed more than $5,000 for the purpose of sending George Smith to the ruins of ancient Nineveh (where the original tablets had been found by Rassam), in an effort to recover the missing fragments. Smith undertook the mission and succeeded not only in recovering the missing portions of the great legends of the Flood but found also additional materials which have proved invaluable in the light cast on the historical background of these ancient empires and on the narratives of the Old Testament. Including the discoveries made by Smith, Rassam, and others, we now have in hand the following inscribed accounts bearing on Creation and the Flood:

(1) Semitic-Babylonian version of the *Epic of Creation* consisting of seven tablets. These were recovered from the Royal Library of Ashurbanipal at Nineveh. The tablets are copies of Babylonian originals first written about 2000 B.C. It is now believed that the Babylonian accounts were based on earlier Sumerian records.

(2) *The Sippar Tablet,* a bilingual version of the story of creation. Discovered by Rassam in 1882 at Sippar, thirty miles north of Babylon, the Tablet comes from the Royal Library of Nabonidus, the last king of Babylon. It is inscribed with the early Babylonian and Sumerian cuneiform.

(3) *The Gilgamesh Epic.* These are the Babylonian legends regarding the exploits of the great demi-

god and national hero, Gilgamesh. The Epic consists of twelve inscribed tablets discovered and deciphered by George Smith in 1872. The tablets come from the Royal Library of Ashurbanipal at Nineveh. Of greatest importance is the eleventh tablet, which sets forth the Babylonian account of the Deluge. There is close correspondence between this account and the Genesis narratives of the Flood. These tablets date probably from the seventh or eighth centuries and are copies of original tablets which go back to approximately 2000 B.C., as shown by other archaeological evidence. Thus the Deluge story was current in the period of Hammurabi and of Abraham.

(4) *The Nippur Tablet.* This account was discovered at Nippur during the Third Babylonian Expedition of the University of Pennsylvania, but not translated until 1912. The tablet measures 5 5/8 inches in breadth, length originally about 7 inches. Only one-third of its original inscribed surface is preserved. In subject matter the tablet contains a combination of the Creation and Deluge stories. This is an independent fragment written certainly about 2100 B.C. It is now believed that the tablet is a copy of another composition which is much earlier than 2100 B.C. This conclusion is reached on the basis of the cuneiform which is not Semitic Babylonian but the older Sumerian, the language of the earliest known inhabitants of Southern Babylonia. It may be dated accordingly at approximately 3000 B.C.

(5) In addition to the foregoing principal recoveries, there are several tablets found at Nineveh, Nippur, and Kish which bear on the stories of Creation and the Flood. Some of these relate to the late Babylonian accounts, while others are certainly based on primitive Sumerian stories.

The tremendous importance of all these recoveries will be readily recognized. Here we find not only the surviving traditions of the early Middle East peoples regarding the Creation and the Deluge, but can trace their connection with remoter peoples who occupied the southern regions of Mesopotamia. Furthermore, these tablets have special significance from a biblical standpoint. The relations existing between the tablets and the Bible narratives indicate ancestral connections, or points of contact, which cannot be brushed aside or explained away as of no consequence. As will be pointed out later, the presence of similarities, together with equally obvious dissimilarities, in these Creation and Flood narratives has given rise to various theories in an effort to explain these relations, the most important being the theory of *Dependence,* the theory of *Independence,* the theory of *Intermediate Transmission,* and the theory of *Cognateness.* We are not here concerned with a discussion of any of these views, but simply state the problem as growing out of the recovered materials.[7]

3. *The Code of Hammurabi*[8]

One of the most significant recoveries ever made was the unearthing of the Stela of Hammurabi by J. de Morgan and Scheil during the excavations of 1901-2 at Susa, ancient capital of the Elamites and site of one of the earliest known cultural centers. As indicated by its contents, the Stela refers to the period of Hammurabi, sixth king of the first Babylonian dynasty, and actual founder of the early Babylonian Empire. In the closing section of the Introduction, Hammurabi describes himself in relation to his kingship and to his divine mission to establish law and order throughout his vast domains, as follows: "The exalted one who makes supplication to the great gods; the descendant of Sumulael, the powerful heir of Sinmuballit, the

WITH THE PROGRESS OF SCIENTIFIC EXCAVATION CITIES OF GREAT
ANTIQUITY ARE UNCOVERED AND THE GENERAL OUTLINE OF THEIR
MUNICIPAL DEVELOPMENT MADE CLEAR. THE ENTRANCE TO THE OLD
CITADEL OF BETHSHEAN IS HERE PICTURED. THE VIEW LOOKS OUT
FROM THE GATEWAY TO THE WEST, TO MOUNT GILBOA AND THE HISTORIC
VALLEY OF JEZREEL. ON THE WALL OF THIS CITY THE PHILISTINES
HUNG THE BODY OF KING SAUL.

SOME OF THE WORLD'S OLDEST EXISTING CITIES ARE FOUND IN PALES-
TINE. HEBRON APPEARS AS A DEFINITE SETTLEMENT ABOUT 3000 B.C.
IT WAS THE GREAT PATRIARCHAL CENTER. IN THE HEART OF THIS CITY
IS FOUND THE CAVE OF MACHPELAH AND THE TRADITIONAL TOMBS OF
ABRAHAM, ISAAC, AND JACOB.

HEWERS OF WOOD, MAKERS OF BRICK, AND DRAWERS OF WATER—THESE
ARE LISTED AMONG THE MENIAL TASKS OF SUBJECT PEOPLES IN THE
ANCIENT WORLD. IN THE LIST OF INDUSTRIAL ARTS, BRICKMAKING WAS
MOST COMMON. HERE THE PEOPLE OF JERICHO MOLD THEIR BUILDING
BLOCKS FROM THE JORDAN VALLEY MUD AND LAY THEM OUT IN ORDERLY
ROWS TO BE SUN-DRIED.

EXCAVATING ANCIENT CITIES IS A SERIOUS BUSINESS. UNDER THE
PRESENT REGULATIONS OF THE DEPARTMENT OF ANTIQUITIES THE MOST
RIGID REQUIREMENTS MUST BE MET BEFORE WORK IS UNDERTAKEN. THE
PICTURE HERE SHOWN RELATES TO THE SUCCESSFUL EXCAVATION OF
OLD SHECHEM BY THE GERMAN PALESTINE SOCIETY. THE SITE IS
KNOWN AS BALATA AND IS LOCATED NEAR JACOB'S WELL ON THE HIGH-
WAY BETWEEN EBAL AND GERIZIM.

ancient seed of royalty, the powerful king, the sun of Babylon, who caused the light to go forth over the lands of Shumer and Akkad; the king who caused the four quarters of the world to render obedience; the favorite of Innanna am I. When Marduk sent me to rule the people and to bring help to the land, I established law and justice in the language of the land and promoted the welfare of the people.'"[9]

The accompanying illustration shows the upper portion of the Stela of Hammurabi as it now stands in the Louvre Museum, Paris, the scene representing the king receiving the laws from the sun-god Shamash. The monolith is a black diorite (an igneous rock composed of feldspar and hornblende), 7 1/2 feet in height and 6 feet in circumference. The inscription, which is in the beautiful characters of early Babylonian cuneiform, consists of an Introduction, 282 sections of laws, and a Conclusion, all arranged in parallel columns extending around the monument and read from top to bottom. About one-eighth of the inscription on the face of the Stela has been erased, presumably for the purpose of recording some historical facts connected with Shutruck-Nakhunte (king of Elam, c. 1200 B.C.), who transported the stone from Sippar to Susa. The addition was never made, however, leaving us still in doubt regarding the circumstances under which the Stela was captured and its introduction into a foreign capital. Apart from these missing sections, the remainder consists of 248 enactments which stand complete. They cover a great variety of subjects: "Laws relating to property, the duties and privileges of royal servants and other officials, the tenure, rent, and cultivation of land, trade and commerce, family law (including, for instance, the rights of wife and children, divorce, inheritance, adoption), criminal law (penalties for different kinds of assault), laws fixing the rates of payment for the hire of different articles, and the rates of wages in different employments, and laws relating to slavery. It will be seen at once what a variety of subjects the Code embraces, and what an advanced stage of civilization, with commerce, agriculture, and other branches of industry fully developed, it presupposes on the part of the people whose life it was designed to regulate.''[10] In this summary of laws by Hammurabi we have the most ancient Code ever recovered, its date being generally fixed at 2100 B.C., more than half a millennium before the Hebrew laws attributed to Moses. In a later discussion we shall set forth the relations between these two great systems of ancient laws.[11]

4. *Tepe Gawra*

Excavations begun in 1927 by Speiser, and continued during the seasons of 1931, 1936-37, and 1938, have issued in the dramatic unfolding of the Tepe Gawra civilization. The mound is located about twelve miles north of the ruins of Kuyunjik (Nineveh) on the east side of the Tigris. Speiser has succeeded in uncovering the mound from top to bottom with astonishing results.[12] According to the announcement of the excavator, the city was abandoned during the fourteenth century B.C., but its stratifications indicate continuous occupation since the fifth millennium. Here at Tepe Gawra we have for the first time a representation of the successive stages of cultural progress by prehistoric and early historic man. Though far removed from the Mediterranean littoral, evidences recovered at Tepe Gawra show that its people had commercial relations with Palestine, Syria, and Asia Minor on the west, to the north with Transcaucasia, and to the east with Persia and India. Its cultural advance during the Early Bronze Age was far beyond anything hitherto

66

suspected. Actually, it had been confidently asserted that the culture of Tell el-Obeid (located about four miles west of Ur) was the earliest clearly defined civilization of Babylonia, that it antedated the cultures of Ur, Erech, Lagash, and Eridu by a considerable period. But, now, in the judgment of Speiser, ''The Obeid culture is preceded by at least two still older civilizations known in the north (Tepe Gawra and Tell Arpachiya), where human occupation was possible much earlier than in the southern alluvium.''[13] These are significant discoveries and have a definite relation to the backgrounds of the Hebrew patriarchs.

5. *Erech*

In 1912-13 excavations were begun at Warka, site of ancient Erech, by Jordan and Preusser, and resumed in 1928 by Jordan and Andrae. The work, prosecuted with usual thoroughness as to method, was extended to reach virgin soil, thus making possible a relative chronology for the stratified periods revealed by pottery styles and changes. As a result, it is reported that a distinctive type of pottery was established intermediate between the El-Obeid and Jemdet-Nasr Periods.[14] ''Two strata of flood deposits were noted, the relation of which to the Deluge, which made so deep a mark in Sumerian tradition, is still obscure. Very remarkable remains of walls and wall decorations were found, going back to about 3200 B.C. . . . At about the same date writing makes its appearance in the form of pictographic signs (amounting to some fifteen hundred in number), which become intelligible as a cuneiform script about three hundred years later. The lowest strata at Warka must go back far into the fourth millennium.''[15] Among the clay tablets recovered were inventories and business documents. Other characteristics of this far-off culture are summed up by Albright as follows: "Ownership and business responsibility were impressed by fixing seal cylinders, with exquisitely carved designs, on moist clay sealings and dockets. The designs on these seals show that even in the third quarter of the fourth millennium B.C. art had already passed far beyond any stage previously attained. Native skill, empirically developed by generations of artists and craftsmen, had reached the point where it became standardized, where canons of proportions were established, and where the prevailing motifs were processions of human and animal figures, temple facades, and fabulous monsters with interlaced necks and tails. Standardization was thus accompanied by abstraction and symbolism. The archaic cuneiform inscriptions so far published are not entirely intelligible, but enough can be made out to indicate a complex economic life and active cultic organization. The language of the country was Sumerian, as it probably had been for the whole of the Chalcolithic Age."[16]

6. *Ur of the Chaldees*

"In the year 1854 Mr. J. E. Taylor, British Consul at Basra, was commissioned by the Trustees of the British Museum to investigate some of the ruined sites of southern Mesopotamia. Amongst the places he visited was one called by the Arabs al-Muqayyar, the Mound of Bitumen, lying about eleven miles west of the Euphrates, a tangled mass of low, sandy mounds dominated by one great pile where above the debris rose walls of red kiln-fired bricks set in the bitumen mortar which earned the place its name. The obvious importance of the building attracted Taylor, and he determined to excavate it."[17] In the course of his work, Taylor fortunately discovered, in a cache of cuneiform inscriptions, several cylinders deposited by Nabonidus (555-

538 B.C.), last native king of Babylon, who describes his repairs to the temple of the Moon-God of Ur, and prays for the blessings of Nannar, lord of the gods of heaven and earth, upon himself and his son Belshazzar. These records were immediately accepted as confirming the identification of al-Muqayyar with Ur, the native city of Abraham. Many years passed by before systematic work was resumed at Ur. In 1922, under the auspices of the British Museum and the University of Pennsylvania, Woolley began excavations which were to revolutionize conceptions hitherto held regarding Ur of the Chaldees, and to inaugurate a new era in the history of Mesopotamian archaeology.[18]

Roughly, the city walls enclosed an area about two and a half miles in circuit. In the northwestern part stood the great Ziggurat, an artificial mound composed of solid brick work measuring 210 feet in length at its base, 138 feet in breadth, and ascending in three stages, the lowest being about 35 feet high. "Millions of brick had gone to the making of that massive Ziggurat, which was already old in Abraham's time and survives today as the chief of the ruined monuments of Ur; labour and cost had counted for nothing, and the king who built it was proud to commemorate on a monument of carved stone the building in which he had played a labourer's part; but it was no mere desire for glory, no megalomania that had inspired him; in a vision of the night his god had bidden him to build him an house: its magnificence was the measure of the greatness of Ur and on its maintenance hung the fortunes of the city."[19]

In the city were also found typical residences. Kenyon refers to them in the following vivid description: "These were substantial dwellings, presenting blank walls (except for the doorway) to the street, and consisting inside of an open courtyard, surrounded by rooms on two storeys, the upper storey being reached

69

by stairs leading to a timber gallery overhanging the court, out of which the rooms opened. As the explorers remarked, both in ground plan and in elevation the house of a well-to-do citizen of Ur in the days of Abraham was almost the counterpart of the house of the well-to-do citizen of modern Baghdad.''[20] Of special interest to Bible students was the small room in every dwelling which the excavators regarded as the chapel, set aside for the worship of the ancestral or household gods.

Furthermore, the city contained well defined streets, not boulevards, probably divided into business quarters, as in Near East cities today, with commercial houses doing business with distant peoples by both land and sea; financial institutions, the equivalents of modern banking houses, and schools. Woolley describes the curricular activities as including instruction in elementary matters, writing, dictation, reading, arithmetic, geometry, grammar, etc. ''About 2000 tablets were found in the ruins of this school. In another school for more advanced scholars there was a far greater proportion of literary (religious) texts and tablets with copies of inscriptions on the buildings and monuments of Ur apparently intended to inculcate ideas of civic patriotism.''[21]

Probably the most astonishing results of the excavations came to light in the recovery of the royal tombs, some relating to the middle of the third millennium, others to the middle of the fourth millennium, which seems to have been the era in which the culture of Ur came to its highest point. The objects recovered from these graves consist of various metals (gold predominating) and semi-precious stones, such as lapis lazuli, obsidian, carnelian, etc. Arts and crafts had attained a marked degree of proficiency, the goldsmith being particularly expert in his astonishing creations now in

70

our possession. Finally, life as a whole was lived on a relatively high plane, more or less characterized by accepted conventionalities which had been customary for generations, and subject to laws which, as in the Hammurabi compilation, reflect a civil order of unusual attainment.

From this environment came Abraham, the founder of the Hebrew people. If our conception of him is greatly modified by these phenomenal discoveries, it will not be to minimize his heroic proportions, but to exalt him further as one of the most remarkable men in world history.

7. *The Mari Tablets*

"Another site which has yielded texts, not only commercial and official, but also religious and historical, is Mari, in the neighborhood of the middle Euphrates, where excavations have been proceeding under the direction of M. Andre Parrot since 1933. Here M. Parrot has found several hundreds of tablets, the decipherment of which has barely begun. From the brief reports hitherto published, however, it appears that, in addition to documents dealing with metal-working and other industrial matters, there are diplomatic, historical, and religious texts. Their date is about the beginning of the second millennium."[22] Since 1935 there have been discovered 20,000 other tablets at Mari, nearly all belonging to the beginning of the nineteenth century B.C. The discovery of this great city (Tell el-Hariri), located on the west bank of the Euphrates about 250 miles above ancient Babylon, stands out as one of the astonishing results of excavations. It is now believed that the population of Mari was basically Amorite with a culture combining Akkadian and Hurrian elements.[23] The emergence of Mari as a city state is to be dated prior to Sargon I (c. 2500 B.C.), who founded the Akkadian empire centering around the great city Agade on the middle Tigris. The culture of Mari, distinctively Semitic, reached its culmination about the twentieth century B.C., a period contemporary with the movement of Abraham to Canaan. Incidentally, among these Mari Tablets appear the Habiru (the Hebrews), who are represented as enemies menacing the city. While these references probably do not bear on the migration of Abraham, they yet throw light on the subsequent movement of the Habiru set forth in the Tell el-Amarna Tablets. On the other hand, the information now before us makes it impossible for us "to think of Abraham as a lonely figure moving across uninhabited wastes to an almost unoccupied land, and taking possession of it as an arctic explorer claims the wastes of the north for his nation. The picture of him in Genesis 14, taking part with three hundred and eighteen followers in a war between one group of kings and another, becomes more comprehensible and convincing."[24]

8. *The Nuzi Tablets*

The mound of Nuzi stands east of the River Tigris about twenty miles south of Kirkuk, the great oil center from which pipe lines extend to Tripoli and Haifa on the eastern Mediterranean littoral. It was apparently one of the cultural centers affected by the Hurrian people who were dominant in areas north of the Masius Mountains and east of the Tigris during the period extending from the twentieth to the fifteenth century B.C. Practically unknown forty years ago, the Hurri now appear as one of the principal peoples of Western Asia at this early date, probably the same ethnic group as the enigmatic Horites or Horim of the Old Testament narratives.[25] "Perhaps the most striking feature in connection with the Hurrians is the established fact of their expansion over a vast area, in what was assumed by many to have been predominantly Semitic territory. The scholarly world, which has watched these developments with an increasing sense of wonder, cannot but find the rise of the Hurrians an even more remarkable phenomenon than the reappearance of the Hittites. For the latter we were prepared to a certain extent by Egyptian, biblical, and Cuneiform sources. But the same records contain no warning that we should be obliged to make room for the Hurrians, by whatever name they might be known, outside and far beyond the limits of the middle Euphrates area. Near Eastern history is still young enough for such startling surprises."[26] There are still many problems concerning these mysterious people—problems regarding their ultimate racial origin, their possible connection with other contemporary groups such as the Hittites, Hyksos, and Mitanni—but here we are interested primarily in their epigraphic remains, which consist of more than a thousand tablets found by Chiera and Speiser in 1925 in co-operation with the American School of Oriental Research. Subsequent campaigns have added hundreds of documents to the Nuzi collection.[27] "The Nuzi tablets are written in the Akkadian language, which the Hurrians of that place, like many other people of the age in Western Asia, had evidently adopted for public transactions. The language shows at many points, however, the influence of the Hurrian tongue. Elsewhere, for example at Ras Shamrah, documents in the Hurrian language itself have been unearthed, including lists of Sumerian words and phrases with their Hurrian equivalents in syllabic characters. All these materials give us an invaluable insight into the daily life of Western Asia in the Middle Bronze Age. It was in this period, as we have seen, that Abraham must have lived. Our knowledge of the political, racial, and cultural situation in Western Asia thus provides the scenery, so to speak, for the drama of Abraham's life, and also peoples the stage with a motley throng of races and nations.''[28]

9. Records of Shalmaneser III

The imperishable desire of man to record the achievements of his race, particularly his own accomplishments if they have been unusual, has resulted in the preservation of a few outstanding monuments of surpassing historical value. Among the early rulers of Assyria, Shalmaneser III was unusually successful in his military operations, which included more than thirty distinct campaigns of conquest, and took pains to chronicle his triumphs in a series of public notices written on clay tablets, cylinders, and stone.[29] These records depict the career of a despot whose conquests extended to the westlands of Syria and Palestine, to the regions of Cilicia in Asia Minor, to the southern sections of Mesopotamia bordering the Persian Gulf, and to the hinterlands of the Medes on the east. His numerous victories resulted in an expansion of the Assyrian kingdom which embraced the ancient world. It was natural, therefore, that an effort should have been made to preserve the records of such an exceptional career. It is to our great advantage that they were not lost. Among these priceless narratives of Shalmaneser, three are of vital interest because of their bearing on developments reflected in the Old Testament, namely, the *Monolith of Shalmaneser,* the *Bronze Plates of the Palace at Balawat,* and the *Black Obelisk of Shalmaneser.* To these we turn for a brief description.

(1) *The Monolith of Shalmaneser*. This stela, or small column, now in the possession of the British Museum, sets forth the account of a great confederacy formed by twelve nations in the Westlands, particularly Syria and Palestine, against Shalmaneser in 854-3 B.C., and of the decisive battle fought at Karkar (near Hamath on the Orontes), in which Ahab and Benhadad II of Damascus were defeated.[30] The same engagement is referred to on the Bronze Plates of the palace of Balawat described in the following section. The Battle of Karkar took place probably after the engagement at Aphek mentioned in 1 Kings 20:26-42, when Ahab, though victorious over Benhadad, made a treaty with him, perhaps looking forward to a coalition against Shalmaneser then threatening the Westlands. The inscription is of first-rate importance in introducing the earliest cuneiform account which explicitly makes contact with Hebrew history. In addition, the almost certain determination of the date of the battle of Karkar provides the most important point in outlining Old Testament chronology both prior to and succeeding the Assyrian period.[31]

(2) *The Bronze Plates*. The second source of information made possible by the court historians and sculptors serving under Shalmaneser is found in the beautiful Bronze Plates unearthed by Rassam in 1878 at Balawat, site of Imgur-Bel, twenty miles east of modern Mosul. The site was originally chosen by Ashurnasirpal II for one of his palaces and later restored by his son and successor, Shalmaneser. These Bronze Plates, so unique as specimens of art in ancient metallurgy, consist of a series of metal strips from two to four inches thick which had originally covered the cedar gates of the Assyrian palace. "The plates represent a variety of subjects taken from the life and cam-

paigns of a king, who, according to the accompanying inscription, was no other than Shalmaneser II'' [III].[32]

The inscription has special importance in that it describes Shalmaneser's battle with a western alliance in which Ahab, king of Israel, was confederate with Benhadad of Damascus, the outcome of which was the defeat of the allies (it now appears as probably a drawn battle since Shalmaneser did not follow up his supposed triumph). This was the Battle of Karkar and is dated 853 B.C.[33] The battle is not mentioned in the Old Testament narratives, but it seems most probable that it was subsequent to the engagement described in 1 Kings 20, where Ahab is represented as having made a covenant with Benhadad of Syria, with whom he appears against Shalmaneser. Subsequently, Ahab is defeated at the Battle of Ramoth-Gilead by Syrian forces under Benhadad (852 B.C.).[34]

(3) *The Black Obelisk.* One of the most conspicuous objects in the British Museum is the Black Obelisk of Shalmaneser III, king of Assyria 859-824 B.C. The accompanying illustration gives full view of one side of the Obelisk, a monolith of black alabaster, whose height is exactly six feet and six inches. The Obelisk was erected by Shalmaneser at Nimrud (Calah), eighteen miles southeast of Nineveh, the Assyrian capital. Its discovery by Layard in 1846 and decipherment by Rawlinson in 1847 produced consternation among scholars everywhere. "Until the present day this black obelisk has remained one of the choicest historical monuments ever rescued from the mounds of Assyria. Layard was not slow in recognizing the exceptional value of this precious relic."[35]

The monument was erected as a stela of victory to commemorate the outstanding events of Shalmaneser's military campaigns, which numbered about thirty-one. "Sculptured on all four sides, it shows

76

twenty small bas-reliefs, and above, below, and between them 210 lines of cuneiform inscriptions."[36] Among these bas-reliefs (which are simply illustrations of the historical text set forth in the cuneiform) appear the four scenes representing Jehu, of the "House of Omri," prostrate before Shalmaneser, and accompanied by attendants bearing tribute of gold, silver, lead, bdellium, etc. "The tribute-bearers are bearded and have a strongly marked Jewish physiognomy. 'The House of Omri' is the standing name for the Northern Kingdom in the Assyrian inscriptions. The same inscription, as Hincks and Rawlinson shortly afterwards independently discovered, mentions also how Shalmaneser defeated Hazael, king of Damascus, the general who (2 Kings viii.15) smothered Benhadad to death, and seized the throne."[37] As is now well known, confirmation of these events is given on a pavement slab from Calah: "Hazael of Damascus—I fought with him and defeated him. . . . At that time I received the tribute of the Tyrians, the Sidonians, of Jehu, the son of Omri."[38]

It will be recognized at once that in this epigraphic discovery of unsurpassed importance, we have one of the few contemporary records which enable us to reconstruct the chronological framework in which Israel moved among its neighbors and in which its own great events occurred. This particular event, according to the Assyrian claim, occurred in eighteenth year of Shalmaneser's reign, or in 841-0 B.C., accepting the recognized date for the beginning of his rule in 859 B.C.[39]

10. *Annals of Tiglath-Pileser III*, 745-727 B.C.

The official documents of Tiglath-pileser provide us with considerable information concerning three of the kings of Israel—Menahem, Pekah, Hoshea—and one of the kings of Judah, Ahaz. His contacts with Palestine were numerous, and we are fairly able to reconstruct the general outline of his triumphs. In the book of Kings, Tiglath-pileser is referred to as Pul, king of Assyria.[40] Pinches, in 1884, demonstrated to the satisfaction of scholars that Pul is to be regarded as the boyhood name of Tiglath-pileser. His invasion of Palestine in 738 B.C. was attended by the introduction of state policies regarding subjugated areas which had dire effects on the Northern Kingdom at this time and later, particularly in 722 B.C. Reference is here made to the protective policies of deportation (the dispersion of native population among foreign people), and of importation (the introduction of foreign elements among the native population not only to administer the affairs of state, but also to weaken morale). Accounts of these policies are contained in his public records, though partly in mutilated fragments, together with invaluable data regarding Menahem of Israel, who became a vassal of Assyria. Menahem was succeeded by his son Pekahiah, who reigned for two years.[41] According to the Hebrew records, Pekahiah was slain in the king's palace at Samaria by his chief captain Pekah, who in turn is said to have reigned for twenty years.[42] Furthermore, the Hebrew narratives claim that Pekah was assassinated by Hoshea during a conspiracy, probably instituted by Tiglath-pileser, since the Assyrian annals claim Hoshea as a vassal king of the great Tiglath-pileser.[43] Thus the Assyrian claim that Tiglath-pileser slew Pekah need not be in conflict with the biblical story since Hoshea was probably carrying out the orders of his overlord.[44] In a later section we shall return to these records in their bearing on Old Testament chronology.[45]

11. *Cylinder of Sargon II*, 722-705 B.C.

This baked prism of Sargon, now in the British Museum, is inscribed with an account of Sargon's expeditions. The king here mentioned is the Sargon in Isaiah 20:1, whose historicity was so long doubted because of the absence of extraneous or non-biblical records. The discovery of his palace and archives now renders him one of the best known of the Assyrian monarchs. From this cylinder we get the information that he conquered the city of Samaria in the first year of his reign, taking 27,200 captives from the Northern Kingdom into Assyria. The record here inscribed fixes the exact date of the destruction of Samaria by Sargon and the close of the three-year siege inaugurated by Shalmaneser V.[46]

12. *Cylinder of Sennacherib*, 705-681 B.C.

In the Babylonian Room of the British Museum is displayed the marvelous Cylinder, or Taylor Prism, shown in our text. "This is one of the finest and most perfect objects of its class ever discovered, and its importance as an historical document can hardly be overrated. It contains 487 lines of closely written but legible cuneiform text, inscribed in the Eponymy of Beli-murrani, prefect of Carchemish, 686 B.C. The text records eight expeditions of Sennacherib, viz., the defeat of Merodach-baladan, king of Babylon, and sack of the city; the conquest of Ellipi and subjugation of the Medes; an invasion of Palestine and siege of Jerusalem; a second campaign against Merodach-baladan, who was deposed in favor of Sennacherib's son, Ashur-nadin-shum; a campaign in the countries of the northwest of Assyria; an expedition to the Persian Gulf and defeat of the Elamites; and a final expedition to Elam and the conquest of the allied Babylonians and Elamites.''[47] Of special importance is the passage that describes the siege of Jerusalem in the reign of Hezekiah, king of Judah, paralleling in some respects the historical narrative of 2 Kings 18. From the Assyrian records, based on the Eponym calculations, this siege occurred in the year 702-01 B.C., a date that is probably accurate and will be used with confidence in determining Old Testament points of chronology.

13. *Archives of Ashurbanipal,* 668-627 B.C.

It is fitting that we incorporate here a reference to the splendid contribution made by Ashurbanipal in his preservation of contemporary and ancient Assyrian and Babylonian records in the great library at Nineveh. These were recovered through the years as a result of the excavations at Nimrud (Nineveh, southwest palace and library of Ashurbanipal) by Layard in 1849-1851, and at Quyunjik (Nineveh, north palace and library) by Rassam in 1853.[48] The results of these recoveries were revolutionary, particularly their bearing on the literary capabilities of ancient peoples. From a biblical standpoint, they are also important. ''There are no explicit references to Biblical history in the extant records of Ashurbanipal (668-626 B.C.), save the bare mention of the name of 'Manasseh King of Judah' among his tributaries. Nor is Ashurbanipal named in the Bible, except for the brief note in Ezra 4:10, where 'the great and noble Osnappar' is said to have colonized Samaria. Yet we cannot refrain from pausing to commemorate one to whom Archaeologists owe such a debt of gratitude, and who (as Pinches observes) 'is worthy of a statue in every land where the languages of Assyria and Babylonia are studied.' Not only did the art of historical inscription reach its zenith through the encouragement of Ashurbanipal, but by a happy

Level I Arabic and Crusader 636-1850 A.D.
Level II Byzantine 350-636 A.D.
Level III Hellenistic 300 B.C.-300 A.D.
Level IV Philistine, Israelite 1225-300 B.C.
Level V Rameses II 1292-1225 B.C.
Level VI Seti I 1313-1292 B.C.
Level VII Amenhotep III following 1412-1313 B.C.
Level VIII Pre-Amenhotep III 1447-1412 B.C.
Level IX Thutmosis III 1501-1447 B.C.

?
?

to about 2500 B.C. —
Early Bronze Age

THE MOUND CITY APPEARING IN THIS ILLUSTRATION IS THE MIGHTY
STRONGHOLD OF BETHSHEAN. EFFORT IS HERE MADE TO SHOW THE
VARIOUS STRATIFICATIONS OF A CITY AS THEY ARE UNCOVERED IN THE
PROCESS OF EXCAVATIONS.

IN THE EARLY EXCAVATIONS BY SCHUMACHER AT MEGIDDO IN 1903-1905,
HE WAS COMPELLED TO RESORT TO THE TRENCH METHOD IN AN EFFORT
TO RECOVER THE PRICELESS TREASURES OF THE GREAT CITY. HERE
SHOWN IS ONE OF SCHUMACHER'S TRENCHES AS IT APPEARED WHEN
THE ORIENTAL INSTITUTE OF THE UNIVERSITY OF CHICAGO BEGAN ITS
EPOCHAL WORK.

THE ROSETTA STONE, NOW THE MOST CONSPICUOUS EGYPTIAN MONU-
MENT IN THE BRITISH MUSEUM. IT CONTAINS A TRILINGUAL INSCRIPTION
EXPRESSING GRATITUDE OF PRIESTS TO PTOLEMY V FOR REMISSION OF
TAXES. DATED 195 B.C. THE HIEROGLYPHICS APPEARING IN THE TOP
SECTION WERE DECIPHERED AFTER A PERIOD OF TWENTY-FIVE YEARS
OF CLOSE STUDY. THIS STONE PROVIDED THE MASTER KEY FOR EGYPT'S
RECORDED HISTORY AND INSTITUTIONS.

accident it was the discovery of his magnificent library at Nineveh which provided the master key to Mesopotamian literature."[49]

14. *Babylonian Chronicle*, No. 21,901

This priceless little tablet recently discovered by C. J. Gadd, assistant in the department of Egyptian and Assyrian Antiquities, British Museum, is a contemporary record of Babylonian history falling within the period of 616-609 B.C., and setting forth the military achievements of Nabopolassar (625-604 B.C.) during this period, particularly the conquest of Nineveh under a combined attack of Babylonians, Medes, and Scythians in 612 B.C. "About the date of the destruction of Nineveh, as about the whole subject, there has grown up a considerable literature, which had not, however, succeeded in giving any impression of certainty to the results attained. The evidence was, in fact, insufficient, and there was no prospect of satisfaction upon these matters so long as there was nothing to supplement it. It is certainly the greatest single contribution of this Chronicle to ancient history that the date of this all-important event is now securely placed in the month of Ab (i.e., July-August), of the year B.C. 612."[50] As will be seen later, the Chronicle provides us with other *data* concerning a period which was wholly obscure, and the information, purely historical, is of transcendent importance.

CHAPTER FIVE

RECORDS FROM ASIA MINOR

RECORDS FROM ASIA MINOR

FROM the standpoint of Old Testament geography, Asia Minor was on the extreme northern boundary of the biblical world. The southern portions of Western Asia, particularly the area stretching from the Amanus Mountains across the Orontes and Euphrates sections to the upper Tigris Valley, were well known, but the interior plateau centering around Cappadocia was remote and uncharted. The great trade routes connecting the Tigris-Euphrates and Nile basins followed mainly the Fertile Crescent rather than the northwest passage through the Cilician Gates into the highlands of Asia Minor. In later centuries, with the emergence of the great Hittite Empire, contacts became not only more frequent but determinative. The Old Testament narrative, faithfully reflecting contemporary conditions and movements, persisted in calling attention to some of these far-off movements, especially to the Hittite, which filtered into southern Syria and Canaan, but the scholarly world was so prejudiced against these records as historical documents that no credence was placed in them. The charitable view was to regard them as products of later centuries and purely fantastic. It was not regarded as a matter of great moment that more than forty biblical references bore testimony to the continuous existence of a people through a period of more than a thousand years—i.e., from Abraham to the middle phases of the Hebrew monarchy, nor was there any serious proposal to rethink the problem of the Hittites. Where there was no corroborative evidence to support the biblical claims, there could be no alternative procedure; the case was regarded as closed.

Today that whole situation has changed. The startling recoveries made by Hugo Winckler at Boghaz-koi in 1906-7 have completely revolutionized our conceptions of the Hittites. Subsequent investigations have been no less conspicuous, the net result being to present the biblical world with a marvelous vindication of Bible accuracy in matters of historical detail.[1] These recovered records have special significance for us in our studies in that they delineate the general outlines of a kingdom which disputed with Egypt and Babylonia the mastery of the Near and Middle East. "The earliest tradition of them is preserved in the Book of Genesis. In 10:15 we are told that Canaan begat Sidon his first-born and Heth, which is only a way of saying that in the records on which this chapter is based Hittites were described as settled in north Syria. They next appear at Hebron in south Palestine, when Abraham bought from them the cave of Machpelah as a burial-place for Sarah (Cap. 23). If the Amraphel of Gen. 14:1 was really the great Hammurapi, King of Babylon, whose date is approximately known, this transaction must have taken place somewhere about 2100 B.C."[2] It now appears that the tradition is thoroughly trustworthy and that the Hittites were so connected with Canaan as to be regarded as part owners.[3] While it is true that the biblical narratives do not provide us with information regarding the early home and kingdom of the Hittites, the results of excavations enable us to trace them originally to the Cappadocian and Phrygian areas, centering at Hattusas (Boghaz-koi), and subsequently to the southern strongholds of Hamath on the Orontes and Carchemish on the Euphrates. It is now known that Carchemish became the southern capital of an extensive area which included particularly the fertile valley between the Lebanons and Anti-Lebanons, and which embraced some of the most powerful cities of the region, namely, Aleppo, Homs, Kadesh, Restan, Hamath, and Qatni.[4] The fall of Carchemish in 717 B.C. marks the end of the Hittite Empire as such, though, after the central power was gone, the population in various Hittite centers must have remained much as it had been—only paying tribute to Assyria instead of allegiance to its own Great King.'"[5]

In addition to the facts enumerated in the foregoing, an interesting bit of information concerning Egyptian-Hittite relations comes to the surface with these recovered archives. From the temple inscriptions at Karnak and the Ramesseum in Egypt, we have two copies of a treaty which was drawn up between Rameses II of Egypt and Hattusil of the Hittites as a result of the Battle of Kadesh on the Orontes in 1288 B.C. In the excavations of Baghaz-koi in 1906-7 the Hittite version of this treaty was found among the royal records. This is the oldest treaty known. It sets forth a nonaggression pact between the Egyptians and Hittites, a defensive alliance with a recognition of all obligations incorporated in all former treaties signed by the two empires. In addition the agreement stipulates that Canaan—the country lying between the two kingdoms—should constitute a borderland, the northern boundary of Canaan marking the southern border of the Hittite Empire. Thus Canaan was recognized as a vital part of the Egyptian kingdom.

Among other items of interest recovered during the excavations at Baghaz-koi was a copy of the Hittite Code of laws. It is now generally held that these laws antedate the laws of Moses by at least two centuries. It is interesting to note that these laws contain several modifications of or amendments to earlier laws among the Hittites, thus evidencing progress in social evolution. Unlike the Hebrew laws which are solidly based on high conceptions of ethics and moral requirements, the Hittite Code is far less exacting in its standards. "The prevalence of thievery and robbery, the laxness of sexual relations, the practice of magic, and the slight emphasis upon religion are all in striking contrast with the attitudes of the Hebrews toward the same things."[6]

CHAPTER SIX

RECORDS FROM SYRIA

RECORDS FROM SYRIA

SYRIA proper lies between the southern borders
of Asia Minor and the northern boundaries of
Canaan, and from the eastern Mediterranean littoral
to the Euphrates River. The area first swings into
importance in connection with the Amorites who penetrated the Lebanon–Anti-Lebanon region at a very
early date and established themselves in centers which
subsequently assumed historic significance. The coastlands witnessed the later developments now associated
with the Phoenicians, while Damascus became the flourishing center of the splendid civilization of the Arameans. The area as a whole has not been as methodi-
cally investigated as some other sections of the Near
and Middle East, but a few of its ancient centers, particularly Carchemish, Ugarit, Gebal, Arpad, Aleppo,
Hamath, and Sidon have yielded rich returns of biblical
interest. Among these great recoveries we present the
following: The *Ras Shamra Tablets,* the *Gebal Inscriptions,* and the *Dog River Gallery.*

1. *The Ras Shamra Tablets*[1]

In this diversified assortment of cuneiform tablets
we have one of the most important collections of ancient
epigraphic materials yet recovered. Modern Ras
Shamra, situated on the Mediterranean coast about
forty miles southwest of Antioch on the Orontes, marks
the site of the ancient city of Ugarit, an Amorite-

Canaanite foundation, which appears in a letter of Hammurabi and in the public records of Babylonians, Hittites, and Egyptians. Ugarit also appears in the Tell el-Amarna Letters in company with Gebal, Tyre, and other Syrian strongholds in their relations with Amenhotep IV, Pharaoh of Egypt. Its position on the coastland made it a natural mart for the islands of Crete and Cyprus, the adjacent territory of southern Asia Minor and southern Syria; but its commercial influence reached to other portions of the westlands and extended even as far as Akkad and Sumer in the Mesopotamian area. Its commercial interests, however, marked only one aspect of this cosmopolitan city, for it seems to have been a religious center of great significance. These two phases of the city's activities make up the chief items reflected in the Ras Shamra Tablets, and of the two the religious interest is by far the more important, particularly in view of the fact that the religious texts relate to the period of Israel's exodus from Egypt and settlement in the land of Canaan. "The tablets which are of clay and vary in height from four to twenty-six centimetres (one-and-a-half to ten inches), represent several languages. This arises from the fact that the town, as already stated, was a polyglot one, possessing an extensive maritime trade, and situated at the meeting-point of the oldest civilizations of the Near East. The languages are: (1) What may be called North Canaanite, or Proto-Phoenician, or Proto-Hebrew, or some language allied to those, which was the language spoken locally; (2) Accadian (Assyro-Babylonian), for dealing with neighboring states; (3) Sumerian, which was the Latin of the epoch, restricted to priests and scholars; and (4) Some unknown language of an agglutinative type, which is believed to be Subarean or some other language, related to Hurrian. The texts in the so-called Proto-Phoenician, which are the only ones of importance bearing on the Old Testament, are not written, as the Accadian are, in a syllabic and ideographic script, but in a new cuneiform of an alphabetic nature, hitherto unknown.''[2]

Here, then, is epigraphic material of a neighboring people contemporary with Moses and Joshua. It is in this connection that their value is accentuated for every student of the Old Testament, for, according to Jack, ''they contradict one of the principal assumptions of the Reuss-Graf-Wellhausen school, namely, that the Israelites could not have had documents at their disposal written before the epoch of the Kings.''[3] Indeed, one of the startling revelations made by these Tablets is not only a kindredness in the use of religious terms by people of Ugarit and the Israelites, but they reveal also a series of similarities in ritual, sacrifice, feast, and other religious observances. The divine names El, Elohim, and probably Yaweh, appear, together with Baal, Dagon, Asherah, Asherim, etc., though not with the same significance or meaning reflected in the Old Testament. A study of these texts will set in sharp relief the deeper content of Old Testament practice and revelation.

2. *The Gebal Inscriptions*

About eighty miles south of Ras Shamra lies the ancient seaport of Gebal looking straight into the Mediterranean. In the Greek period the town was called Byblus, and was regarded as the chief center of the Adonis cult which spread over the whole of surrounding territory. Numerous references are made to the city during the Tell el-Amarna period (1412-1362 B.C.) when it was regarded as a part of the disintegrating empire of the Egyptian Amenhotep IV. In the Old Testament

Gebal is distinguished by its artisans who assisted Solomon in the building of the Temple at Jerusalem (1 Kings 5:18), and by its shipbuilders who added greatly to the glory of Tyre (Ezekiel 27:9). It is of interest to note also that Gebal was the scene of the principal actions described in the adventures of Wen-Amon, an Egyptian dispatched by Rameses XII (c. 1110 B.C.) to Syria on a semi-religious and semi-diplomatic mission which mainly concerned the purchase of cedars of Lebanon for the sacred barge of Amon-Ra, king of the gods.[4]

Here at Gebal two discoveries of first-rate importance have been made. During the progress of the French excavations conducted by P. Montet in 1922, there came to light a large royal sarcophagus with an inscription of five lines in the Phoenician language, which is now known to have been the immediate ancestor of the Hebrew. This monument is now housed in the museum at Beirut with other outstanding results of the Gebal excavations. We quote the following: Itobaal, son of Ahiram, king of Gebal, has made this sarcophagus for Ahiram his father as a resting place for eternity. "This inscription, which is dated as early as 1250 B.C., is the oldest known example of a Phoenician inscription, and indicates that already in the neighborhood of Palestine the older cuneiform had met with the rival which was ultimately to prove the 'Mother of Alphabets.' "[5]

Another important discovery bearing on the history of writing was made at Gebal. "In 1930 Professor Dussard discovered there an inscription on stone in a new form of hieroglyphic script. Subsequently he found a number of inscriptions on copper in the same writing. The total number of characters identified is over eighty. According to Dussard, the language is Semitic and the date not later than 2200 B.C."[6]

3. The Dog River Gallery

Looking down on the modern highway and railroad that skirt its base stands an ancient stone mountain whose face is adorned with figures of old world rulers whose military achievements are set forth in a series of panel inscriptions hewn some five or six inches in depth and averaging about seven feet in height and three feet in breadth. In this international Hall of Fame great conquerors of the ancient world meet in common to tell of exploits which resulted in the enslavement of millions and to boast of conquests which included practically all of the biblical world. Among the earliest of these inscriptions is that of the great Egyptian Pharaoh, Rameses II—until recently regarded in most quarters as the oppressor of Israel in Egypt—who is represented as offering sacrifice to the god Amon-Ra in commemoration of Syrian conquests (c. 1240 B.C.). Six hundred years later (670 B.C.) Esarhaddon returning from an invasion of Egypt records on a panel, next to that of Rameses II, his victory over Tirhakah, Ethiopian ruler of Egypt 693-667 B.C.[7]

Hall describes the event in the following: "The Assyrian then returned to Assyria, setting up stelae at Samalla and at the mouth of the Nahr el-Kelb in Phoenicia, on which we see him standing in majesty, while Baal of Tyre and Tirhakah of Egypt, whose negroid features are malignantly caricatured, kneel in chains to lick the hem of his robe. With supreme irony, the Assyrian monument is placed immediately by the side of the ancient stele of Rameses II."[8]

In addition to these inscriptions made by Rameses and Esarhaddon, other Oriental despots left here the records of their triumphs. Among these was Sennacherib, the conqueror of Lachish (2 Kings 18:13f), Tiglath-pileser III (Pul), whose reign (745-727 B.C.)

definitely affected the political fortunes of five kings in the Hebrew Northern and Southern kingdoms;[9] Shalmaneser III, the conqueror of Ahab at the Battle of Karkar (854-3 B.C.) and of Jehu (841 B.C.), describes his sixteenth crossing of the Euphrates, his arrival at Dog River, and the setting up of the royal portrait in that place. In later days Greeks and Romans, Arabs and Crusaders, and in the modern period French and English, all have recorded notices of their military exploits. While most of these memorials have been defaced either by forces of nature or by vandalism, some are still legible and provide useful information.

SCRIBISM AMONG THE AN-
CIENT EGYPTIANS ATTAINED
A STATUS OF PROMINENCE
AND PROFICIENCY. THE
SCRIBE HERE REPRESENTED
IS READY TO TAKE DICTATION.
THE QUILL AND PAPYRUS
ROLL ARE PLAINLY IN VIEW.
THE MONUMENT COMES FROM
THE PERIOD OF THE FIFTH
DYNASTY.

THE IMPOSING COLUMNS OF THE GREAT HYPOSTYLE HALLS OF KARNAK
DO NOT OBLITERATE THE MAGNIFICENT SHAFTS THAT RISE FROM ITS
RUINS. THESE ARE THE OBELISKS OF THUTMOSIS I AND HATSHEPSUT,
HIS DAUGHTER. THE OBELISK OF HATSHEPSUT WAS THICKLY COATED
WITH ELECTRUM, AN AMALGAM OF GOLD AND SILVER. HEIGHT 97½ FEET,
WEIGHT 700,000 POUNDS, RED GRANITE FROM THE QUARRIES OF ASSUAN.

ON THE DESERT PLATEAU OPPOSITE THE ROYAL TOMBS OF SAKKARA STANDS THE EARLIEST OF THE PYRAMIDS—THE STEPPE PYRAMID OF ZOSER OF THE FOURTH DYNASTY, THE FIRST BUILDING ON EGYPTIAN SOIL TO BE CONSTRUCTED ENTIRELY OF STONE.

THE RAMASSEUM LOCATED ON THE WEST SIDE OF THE GREAT NILE AT THEBES.

CHAPTER SEVEN

RECORDS FROM PALESTINE

RECORDS FROM PALESTINE

FROM the standpoint of the biblical narratives, Palestine, the land of Israel, lay at the heart of all old world relations, inseparably bound up with the fortunes of the early Babylonians, Egyptians, Hittites, Assyrians, and, subsequently, with the Persians, Greeks, and Romans. In our search for epigraphic materials relating to the earliest of these groups of peoples, naturally we have welcomed most heartily those records which throw light on Israel's relations with its neighbors and which enable us to evaluate the historical narratives of the Old Testament with a greater degree of fairness and fidelity. Our interest, accordingly, has been strictly biblical, and the survey which we have followed up to this point has been marked by that principle of selection which is our main concern. Egypt, Mesopotamia, Asia Minor, and Syria have made startling contributions to an increasing body of knowledge relating to biblical subjects, and with the steady advance of scientific investigation they will certainly add more extensive data on practically every aspect of biblical study. In this increase of knowledge, however, Israel's neighbors have not been the only contributors, probably not even its most important, though that is perhaps merely a relative matter, for Palestine itself has proved to be an almost inexhaustible storehouse of illustrative materials from which we may proceed to

99

delineate with fair accuracy the backgrounds of the Chosen People. But, unfortunately, this unsurpassed body of general information has not produced much written material which could be characterized as startling or phenomenal, though this is not meant as any disparagement of aught that we possess.

Probably, in the very nature of the case, we should not have expected any great papyrus discoveries, since the preservation of papyri depends on dryness of soil and climate; architectural genius was never a characteristic of the Hebrews, hence we look in vain for great public buildings adorned with decorations and inscriptions in true Oriental style; no perfection was ever attained in sculpture, hardly any attempt at representing living creatures in stone or bronze, seeing that the Second Commandment specifically prohibited. Scribes cherished and preserved with meticulous care the writings of the fathers, but when accurate copies of old scrolls were made the originals were invariably disposed of with solemn ceremonies. As a consequence, we possess no ancient manuscripts of the Hebrew Scriptures comparable to the codices of the Christian writings. Furthermore, many attempts were made among the Hebrews by outsiders to destroy literally every inscribed monument and every written record to the end that the religion of Israel and the laws of God should be obliterated. But this vandalism never completely succeeded, for we are now in possession of some great monuments from Palestine, some records of priceless value, to which we now turn for brief description. The list is not exhaustive, but rather selective in their bearing on the narratives of the Old Testament; namely, *The Lachish Letters, The Siloam Inscription, The Samaria Ostraka, The Moabite Stone, The Gezer Agricultural Tablet,* and *The Lachish Ewer.*

1. *The Lachish Letters*

The imposing mound of Tell ed-Duweir, located about seven miles southwest of Beit Jibrin on the main road from Gaza to Hebron, represents the site of the Old Testament city of Lachish. In the light of the excavations conducted here by the Wellcome-Marston Expedition during the period 1933-1938, it appears as one of the most strongly fortified cities in Southern Palestine. Lachish is mentioned in the early historical narratives of the Old Testament in connection with the conquests of Joshua and later in relation to the kings of Judah.[1] In the Tell el-Amarna Letters it is named as one of the important strongholds resisting the advance of the Habiru invaders. It is represented in the Assyrian records of Sennacherib, who claims to have captured it together with forty-five other cities of Judah.[2] This campaign is referred to in the Old Testament narratives in connection with the reign of Hezekiah, whose capital city, Jerusalem, was threatened but not captured (although Sennacherib states that Hezekiah forwarded to Nineveh thirty talents of gold, $900,000, and eight hundred talents of silver, $1,596,-000, in addition to numerous other items of tribute).[3] A century after the Assyrian conquest Lachish was again subjected to a disastrous siege, this time by Nebuchadnezzar, king of Babylon, who probably destroyed it.[4] As will be observed, its destruction synchronizes with the final fall of Jerusalem, 587-586 B.C., under the same monarch.

In the course of Starkey's work at Lachish, January, 1935, there came to light in the gate tower of the city a collection of eighteen written documents, ostraka, which are now referred to as the Lachish Letters.[5] They are regarded as among the most important recoveries in Palestine archaeology. "Until the Lachish Letters were found, there was little knowledge of the script in which the Old Testament would have been written in the time of Jeremiah, and no certainty that it was written in the Hebrew language."[6] In the light of these records, which are contemporary with Jeremiah, the prophet, and the last kings of Judah, we not only have copious evidences of archaic Hebrew (Phoenician), but actual examples also of personal correspondence which indicate that writing was very common and not exceptional. The translation of these documents has brought to the front some startling suggestions with reference to the military, political, and religious history of the people immediately preceding the fall of Jerusalem and the captivity of Judah in 587-586 B.C.[7]

2. *The Siloam Inscription*

The Hill Ophel, southern spur of Mt. Moriah, Jerusalem, represents one of the oldest cultural centers in Palestine. Here we have a continuous habitation from the period of the cave dwellers through the changing phases of political developments associated with Salem, Urusalim, Jebus, and Jerusalem. The entire Hill consists of not more than fifteen acres, a rugged, rocky spur in the shape of a wedge extending north and south. Its association with the city builders is to be attributed entirely to the circumstance that gushing from its side into the valley on the east was a spring, the only water supply in the vicinity. In the Old Testament this spring is called the Gihon, its modern equivalent the Virgin's Fountain, which stands at the head of an underground passage leading to the Pool of Siloam on the southwest of the Hill Ophel. This passage is the famous Siloam Tunnel. Its construction is probably to be attributed to Hezekiah during the emergency created by the Assyrian invasion of Judah fully described in the Old Testament

102

narratives.[8] The account in Chronicles definitely states that Hezekiah "stopped the upper spring of the waters of Gihon, and brought them straight down on the west side of the city of David."[9] In this citation we identify the Gihon with the present Virgin's Fountain, the Siloam Tunnel as the connecting subterranean passage by which the waters were brought down to the western side of the city of David (Hill Ophel) to the Pool of Siloam. The pool itself is located at the southern end of the tunnel and was subsequently enclosed within the wall of the city of Jerusalem. These details are all illustrated on the accompanying graph.

In the interior of the tunnel, about fifteen feet from the southern entrance, there was discovered in 1880 a mural inscription which turned out to be an eyewitness account of the digging operations by two groups of workmen starting at opposite ends of the tunnel and by dead reckoning meeting practically in the center. Further details set forth how the water flowed down when the passage was completed, and the approximate length of the tunnel itself.[10] It is of interest to note that the workman's estimate of the length of the passage—i.e., 1200 cubits, is approximately correct. If the excavation had followed a straight line, the actual distance would have been only 1050 feet, but following a serpentine course, based on dead reckoning, the actual measured distance is 1740 feet. The inscription, consisting of five lines on a surface of about 27 inches square, was cut from the wall of the tunnel and is now one of the priceless objects of the Museum of Antiquities, Istanbul. In this inscription we have one of the early examples of Semitic writing, particularly the proto-Hebrew or Phoenician, which will be used with confidence in establishing the genealogy of Hebrew epigraphy.

"The tunnel and Siloam inscription are not the only interesting things connected with the Gihon-Siloam aqueduct. A most remarkable discovery was made on October 24, 1867, during the explorations of Sir Chas. Warren. About 50 feet from the entrance of the tunnel from the pool in the cave at the Virgin's Fount, another passage coming from the north-west was discovered, and when cleared out, proved to be 17 feet long and ending in a cave. The bottom of this cave, 3 feet lower than the aqueduct, was also that of a great rock-hewn shaft or chimney rising 40 feet into the very heart of the hill and opening out into other rock-cut passages and a great chamber."[11] This is the approach to the Gihon from the interior of the city during time of siege when the mouth of the spring was concealed from the enemy. It was probably the discovery of this secret passage into the Jebusite stronghold which enabled Joab to conquer it as described in the Old Testament narrative.[12]

3. The Samaria Ostraka

When Omri, the father of Ahab, was chosen by the people of Israel to be their king, he proceeded to move the capital from Tirzah, a commanding point seven miles north of Shechem on the road to Bethshean, to the Hill of Shemer, eight miles north of Shechem on the highway to Dothan. "His wisdom was fully justified in selecting the hill of Shemer for the chief city of Israel, and in building on its summit a capital of considerable proportions and strength. Omri called the new city Samaria, after the name of its original owner. The term means 'watchtower,' and the idea suggested finds complete justification in the nature of the location. The elevation of the hill ranges from 300-400 feet above the surrounding plains. It is practically impregnable on all sides, except the northeast, where the mound is approached by a slow ascent. The hill was protected by an immense stone wall so elevated above the plains that no engines of war could be used to assault it.''[13] The highest point on the hill was in the southwest portion overlooking a massive gateway, the principal entrance into the city. Here Omri built his palace, the substructures of which were exposed during the Harvard excavations by Lyon and Reisner in 1908-10. In the course of the work the excavators also uncovered the foundations of Ahab's palace which was an enlargement of Omri's residence. During the season of 1931, excavations at Samaria were resumed under the direction of Crowfoot. ''Further examination of Ahab's palace revealed that even its furnishings were ivory inlay, and that they often show a strong Egyptian influence; for example, on many of them are figures of the hawk-headed Horus, of Isis with her lotus-flower, of Thoth with his Ibis beak, 'sacred Horus eyes,' etc.''[14] But more important than the ivory fragments are the potsherds which came to light in the operations of 1908-10. These consist of a total of about 75 Ostraka, 63 of which are written in fairly legible Hebrew, practically the same script used on the Siloam Inscription and in the Lachish Letters. As will be seen later, these Ostraka are also of the same family as the Moabite Stone and the Gezer Agricultural Tablet. From the data given on the Samaria Ostraka, Jack has been able to reconstruct the administrative, religious, and political developments at Samaria during the reign of Ahab 874-852 B.C.[15] Subsequent appraisal of these Ostraka puts the general date about a century later than Ahab, i.e., 776-774 B.C., during the reign of Jeroboam II (c. 780-746 B.C.),[16] but this does not materially affect either the general cultural background of the Northern Kingdom as reflected in the Ostraka, nor the value of

105

the writings as among the earliest examples of Hebrew epigraphy. As a matter of fact, the later date enhances their value in providing a more immediate step between the Siloam inscription and the Moabite Stone.

4. *The Moabite Stone*

In the classification of various tribal groups appearing at an early date in the west and east Jordan area, the Moabites occupy a position of great importance. The Old Testament represents them as a branch of the Semitic family specifically tracing their ancestry to Lot, the nephew of Abraham.[17] In this respect they share a common descent with the Ammonites who inhabited the open spaces immediately east of the Dead Sea. Although both tribes were practically semi-nomadic, they succeeded in establishing some centers of culture which exerted powerful influence on the Hebrews in the course of their checkered history. Among these centers Rabbath-Ammon belonged to the Ammonites, while Dibon, Medeba, Heshbon, etc., were strongholds founded by the Moabites.[18] One recalls particularly the hostile attitude of the Moabites against the Hebrews at the time of the invasion of Transjordan under Moses,[19] and subsequently the engagement with Israel when the king of Moab offered his sun as a burnt offering upon the wall.[20] On the other hand, the incomparable story of Ruth the Moabitess, so simply told in the book of Ruth, has a part of its setting in Moab.[21]

The Moabite Stone, discovered by Klein in 1868, is now one of the priceless treasures of the Louvre. It sets forth a narrative of considerable detail regarding the Moabites during the days of Mesha, their king, in relation to the people of Israel following the days of Omri. The stone was erected by Mesha at Dibon in honor of his god Chemosh, and probably as a memorial of the successful revolt against the Northern Kingdom as described in 2 Kings 3:4-27. If that is the event referred to, it is to be dated about 850 B.C., or a little earlier. The narrative complements the Old Testament account, while providing data which are not contained in the Hebrew parallel.[22] Its importance as a historical document is very great. From the literary point of view it is unsurpassed since it provides overwhelming proof that writing, particularly the archaic Hebrew represented by the Phoenician script, was in existence even among a semi-nomadic people such as the Moabites. The discovery of this monument has proved one of the greatest helps in tracing the development of the Hebrew language.

5. *The Gezer Agricultural Tablet*

In the historical records of Thutmosis III of Egypt, Gezer is mentioned as one of the cities of his conquest about 1475 B.C. The city is much older, however, as indicated not only by the Egyptian evidences uncovered during the excavations by Macalister in 1902-1908, but also by the emergence of cave dwellings associated with a non-Semitic people who occupied the site approximately 3000 B.C. Gezer appears as an important stronghold in the Tell el-Amarna period (1412-1362 B.C.) and later as a victim of Merneptah's invasion of Canaan (1220 B.C.). In the Old Testament narratives, from the time of Joshua and the Hebrew invasion, it is frequently mentioned as a great Canaanite fortified town which successfully resisted Hebrew occupation. It was finally brought under Israelite control when the Pharaoh of Egypt gave it to Solomon as a part of the marriage dowry of his daughter.[23]

"In 1907, while a new trench was being dug on the west hill, just west of the city gate, there was found, when the rock was reached, a large entrance to what at first appeared to be a pool, but upon the explorers penetrating further, it was found to be the entrance to a long and remarkable subterranean gallery or tunnel, descending by eighty steps, and leading ultimately to a large cave containing a spring of water. This tunnel was altogether 219 feet long and for the greater part of its length 23 feet high and 12 feet 10 inches across, but for the last third of the course, when the rock became harder, its dimensions contracted considerably. The water, which the tunnel ultimately reached, was 94 feet below the surface of the rock, and 130 feet below the present surface of the soil. The tunnel appears to have been excavated before 2000 B.C., and to have been abandoned between 1400 and 1200 B.C. It is a remarkable work for such an early date; and, as Pere Vincent has remarked, cannot but enhance our estimate of the engineering capabilities, and, indirectly, of the civilization generally, of the race who produced it.''[24]

The Gezer Agricultural Tablet recovered at this site is to be associated with these people whose accomplishments were so noteworthy. It is a small plaque 4¼x2¾ inches, inscribed with eight lines in archaic Hebrew characters, and setting forth the various months of the year according to their agricultural importance. ''The whole appearance of the script is very ancient. There are no traces of the characteristics of the later Hebrew writing, such as the lengthening and curving of the shafts of the letters, the supplementary additions, and the overlapping, intersection, and prolongation of the strokes. If the characters on it be compared with the Phoenician ones at Byblus in the tenth century and with those on the Samaria Ostraka, they will be found to be intermediate between these two.''[25] Its approximate date, accordingly, is to be placed at 900 B.C., not later. ''Seeing that some characters on the plaque exhibit slight changes from the Phoenician, it must have been at this time that the Hebrew writing showed a tendency to deviate from the latter. It was probably at this time also—or a little before it, certainly not later —that the Greeks borrowed their alphabet from Phoenicia."[26]

6. *The Lachish Ewer*

This splendid example of archaic Hebrew script came to light in the course of Starkey's excavations at Lachish in 1934. It was immediately recognized as an epigraphic monument of unsurpassed value, Langdon pronouncing it "the most important discovery of modern times in respect to Biblical criticism."[27] It is the finest example of archaic Hebrew script yet discovered, probably the connecting link between the Phoenician Akhiram inscriptions and the alphabetic writings of Serabit el-Khadim in the Peninsula of Sinai. It is not possible to determine its exact date, but the consensus of opinion is that it cannot be later than the middle of the thirteenth century and not earlier than the sixteenth century B.C. Professor Langdon, on the basis of orthography, puts it at 1500 B.C.

CHAPTER EIGHT

EARLY HEBREW RECORDS

1. HITTITE

2. AMORITE

3. SUMERIAN

4. HYKSOS

5. HEBREW

6. PHILISTINE

7. ASSYRIAN

8. EGYPTIAN

MANY PEOPLES APPEAR IN THE RECORDS OF THE OLD TESTAMENT AS CONTEMPORARIES OF THE HEBREWS. THOUGH NOT MENTIONED IN THE BIBLICAL NARRATIVES, THERE WERE OTHER GROUPS WHOSE CULTURAL CONTRIBUTION IS GRADUALLY BEING RECOGNIZED THROUGH THE EXCAVATIONS. THE DRAWING HERE PRESENTS THE MOST IMPORTANT AMONG THESE INTERESTING PEOPLES.

THE PYRAMID OF CHEOPS OR KHUFU AT GIZEH. THIS TOMB OF THE
PHARAOH IS REGARDED AS THE GREAT WONDER OF THE ANCIENT WORLD.
85,000,000 CUBIC FEET OF STONE. PERPENDICULAR HEIGHT 480 FEET.
DATES FROM THE FOURTH DYNASTY.

FOURTH DYNASTY PYRAMID OF CHEPHREN OR KHAFRE AT GIZEH. ORIGI-
NALLY COVERED WITH BEAUTIFUL ALABASTER. THE APEX IS STILL
FRINGED WITH ALABASTER. A GREAT DEAL OF THIS MATERIAL HAS
GONE INTO PUBLIC BUILDINGS OF CAIRO.

THE PICTURESQUE COLOSSI
OF MEMNON SEATED ON A
PLATFORM ELEVATED TO THE
CUSTOMARY NILE FLOOD LINE.
THEY ARE LOCATED AT THE
ENTRANCE TO THE EXTENSIVE
AREA OF THE GREAT THEBAN
NECROPOLIS ON THE WEST
SIDE OF THE NILE. THE
MONUMENTS ARE ATTRIBUTED
TO AMENHOTEP III AND HIS
WIFE, TIY.

THE INTERIOR OF THE VAL-
LEY OF THE KINGS WHERE
THE BODIES OF EGYPT'S
MIGHTY RULERS WERE EN-
TOMBED AND SEALED IN
MOTHER EARTH. EXACTLY IN
THE MIDDLE GROUND OF THE
PICTURE IS THE SITE OF
TUTANKHAMEN'S TOMB.

EARLY HEBREW RECORDS

T HE mere enumeration of the foregoing significant recoveries from the Old Testament world, together with others not specified but equally important, would justify the conviction that we are on the threshold of a new day in our approach to the Hebrew Scriptures. It is also clear that the field is bristling with problems new and old, that one must proceed with caution as well as with confidence as he undertakes to relate the recovered evidences to Scripture statements bearing on the history of Israel and surrounding peoples. We do not mean that the student should be apologetic or labor under the apprehension that he will claim too much where the evidence warrants unequivocal affirmation. On the contrary, he must be guided by discrimination and impartiality but ready to appropriate the benefits of every real discovery bearing on the accuracy and consequent authority of the Old Testament. An illustration of the position here adopted is found in the present discussion on the possibility and probability of written records among the Hebrew people from patriarchal times down to the periods of exiles and restoration.

It now appears that the science of writing was brought to perfection by the Egyptians in their hieroglyphical system two thousand years before Abraham, by the Sumerians and Babylonians in the cuneiform millennia before Moses, and by the Semites in the westlands around Canaan centuries before the Hebrew ever arrived from Egypt to occupy the Land of Promise. Consequently, the debate among scholars now revolves around the interesting question as to which of these vehicles of expression—the hieroglyphics, the cuneiform, or the alphabetic—was actually employed in chronicling these early events.[1] From cumulative evidence now in hand, reinforced by the Serabit el-Khadim Inscriptions, the Lachish Ewer, the Akhiram Sarcophagus, the Gezer Agricultural Tablet, the cuneiform-alphabetic script of Ras Shamra, and the Tell el-Amarna correspondence, it was entirely possible for an early Hebrew writer to select from these the medium with which he was most familiar. Naville, for example, contends vigorously for Mosaic authorship of the early chronicles of the Pentateuch and argues for the use of the Babylonian cuneiform as the vehicle of expression.[2]

Up until recent years conservative scholars have consistently contended for the possibility of written records among the early Israelites, though they had little material proof in hand to support their position. Today the situation is entirely different. In the light of overwhelming evidence of literary capabilities and actual achievements among other ancient peoples, long antedating the Hebrew patriarchs, there is no longer any justification for denying to the Hebrews the art of writing, particularly during the Mosaic age, nor to think it improbable that they used it in chronicling the earlier phases of their unparalleled history. Obviously, unless they were wholly uncultured, the Hebrews knew the art of writing, and actually composed records of their own traditions comparable in importance to the accounts produced by contemporary and neighboring peoples. It is no longer necessary to conjecture about the probability of such records, especially when we are confronted with the astonishing epigraphic materials

114

produced by highly cultured communities in Egypt, Mesopotamia, Asia Minor, Syria, and Palestine long before the Hebrew invasion and conquest of Canaan. Actually, we now know that the art was practiced even among some of the lesser ethnic groups, for example, the Moabites, a semi-nomadic tribe dwelling in the highlands of Transjordan, who have left for us an inscription of one of the critical periods of their national life.[3] It is admitted that the orthography of this particular inscription is of such character as to argue for a considerable period of development. But the Hebrews were not a semi-nomadic tribe; they were a sedentary people occupying the strong centers of a country dominated, since the period of the Judges and the Monarchy, by their power and culture. It is perfectly clear that recent adverse criticism has greatly erred in denying to this established people the elementary knowledge attributed to their neighbors and contemporaries. Particularly at fault has been the abrupt rejection of any suggestion that such a people could have produced in the early period the literature ascribed to them.

The position generally advanced regarding the early narratives of the Old Testament is summarized by Woolley in one of his latest volumes, as follows: "It was not until the nineteenth century that the old uncritical acceptance of the Biblical narratives was seriously challenged, and then the results of critical study seemed to be purely destructive. Scholars were able to prove that the five books of the Pentateuch, so far from being due to the inspired authorship of Moses himself (a claim never put forward in the Old Testament), were in their present forms late compilations, written by scribes after the Jewish exile in Babylon, that is, very many centuries after the events narrated in them were supposed to have occurred. And it was assumed that for these late writers no early written sources could have been available. Nomad sheikhs such as were the patriarchs, guerilla fighters like Joshua and Caleb, the down-trodden peasantry of Palestine under the Judges, all were too ignorant and too cut off from the centers of civilization in Egypt and Babylonia to have committed to writing anything of their tribal laws and annals. The scribes who composed the books were religious propagandists who tried to commend their views by attributing them to the remote past of the nation, but they really could not have had any knowledge of the doings of Abraham or the legislation of Moses. At best they depended on oral tradition, and a record passed from mouth to mouth during such long ages could not be taken as authentic; at every stage it was liable to embellishment and alteration, and there was nothing to show that originally it had even pretended to be a record of facts; rather, comparison with the legends of other countries brought to light parallels which tended to show that all alike sprang from man's imagination. Such were the arguments alleged, and there arose towards the close of the nineteenth century an extreme school of critics which was ready to deny the historical foundation of practically everything related in the earlier books of the Old Testament. Abraham became for them merely the eponymous hero of his race, a mixed creature of mythology, poetry, and folk-lore, given human shape and name with the idea of assuring the essential unity of a nation. *Today the whole position has been changed. While it is still true that Palestine has produced curiously little in the way of early inscriptions, archaeological discoveries made during the last half century have proved that there was no period in Hebrew history for which contemporary written authority of one kind or another could not possibly have existed.*"[4]

It will be observed at once that this sweeping statement makes room not only for the copious records of the days of the kings and kingdoms of Judah and Israel, but permits us to approach the Mosaic and Patriarchal eras with reasonable expectation that they also could have produced narratives of historical and religious value. That they did create a certain body of literature is now one of the assured results of biblical archaeology and criticism. The conclusion has not been reached in any arbitrary manner, nor is it based simply on a deduction that the Hebrews had attained a cultural stage comparable to that of their neighbors and were therefore recording their own history. It grows out of the clear recognition of certain internal evidences in the Hebrew narratives themselves which can be adequately explained only on the ground of such an assumption. Among these evidences deeply imbedded in the writings, perhaps the most important are the following: unusual correspondence of the narratives with *Original Setting;* accuracy with regard to *Geographical Details;* reliability in *Ethnographical References,* and, finally, a *Chronological Framework* for historical events and movements completely in agreement with the then contemporary life.

1. *Original Setting*

One of the most characteristic features of great sections of the early narrative in the Pentateuch is the reflection of local settings thoroughly in keeping with the events or situations described. It is obvious, for example, that the niceties of social conventions reflected in certain passages bearing on the experiences of Abraham, Joseph, and Moses, could never have been made by any writer far removed from the events, and that they could have emanated only from an eyewitness or

117

a participant. Fidelity to local coloring or environment is largely a matter of personal observation and not historical imagination. As suggested by Duncan: "When we turn to the narratives of Joseph and Moses, where the various scenes are set in Egypt, we find that the local colouring is historically accurate, and so true are they to their respective periods as reflected in Egyptian documents and inscriptions that we are irresistibly driven to the conclusion that the original narratives were written down at the time of the events recorded. In short it must have been Moses himself, or someone with the same education and facilities, who wrote the original narrative of the oppression and the Exodus. . . . The Exodus narrative leaves us in no doubt that Moses was an outstanding figure of the period, and was the actual author of much of the Pentateuch."[5] Again: "Professor Yahuda's work supports my contention made in 1908 that the original documents of the Old Testament were written as early as the period of serfdom in, or emancipation from, Egypt, and that Moses himself wrote these narratives. . . . Numbers 33:2 makes the simple, straightforward statement, 'And Moses wrote the goings of the people according to their journey.' I do not know why that statement has ever been disputed or the fact regarded as impossible. I believe the author of Numbers is speaking the truth, and all the evidence of archaeology goes to confirm it."[6] The point at issue here, however, is not the Mosaic authorship either of the book of Numbers or of any other section of the Pentateuch—rather, that the multiplicity of detail so perfectly in keeping with local setting of events described requires authorship based on firsthand information. The definite character of the information given makes it entirely unlikely that it could have been derived from accidence, imagination, or invention.

118

2. *Geographical Details*

The assumption of early composition of narratives, particularly those involving movements of the patriarchs from one definite point to another, is justified. It is claimed that these are writings of high antiquity; their genuineness is shown in the fidelity and accuracy reflected in referring to contemporary places. The ease with which a writer moves around in a world which he is describing, accurately referring to geographical details such as cities, districts, countries, waterways, and climate, is the result of experimental knowledge and not of hearsay or surmise. We would hardly expect that a writer, recording events centuries after their occurrence and with no written sources before him, could have been able to steer clear of grave mistakes in geographical and topographical details (provided he wanted to give full information, as these early records indicate). In a word, it is obvious that no author could have invented these accounts which are characterized by accuracy and consistency throughout. For example, take the much debated passage regarding the Battle of the Kings in Genesis 14, concerning which Professor Albright makes the following observation: "This account represents the invading host as marching down from Hauran through eastern Gilead and Moab to the southeastern part of Palestine. Formerly the writer considered this extraordinary line of march as being the best proof of the essentially legendary character of the narrative. In 1929, however, he discovered a line of Early and Middle Bronze Age mounds, some of great size, running down along the eastern edge of Gilead, between the desert and the forests of Gilead. Moreover, the cities of the Hauran (Bashan) with which the account of the campaign opens, Ashtaroth and Karnaim, were both occupied in this period, as shown by archaeological examination of their sites. The same is true of eastern Moab, where the writer discovered an Early Middle-Bronze city at Ader in 1924. This route, called 'the way of the King' in later Israelite tradition, does not appear to have ever been employed by invading armies in the Iron Age.'" This is corroborative evidence that the record in Genesis 14 is based on an extremely early source, since no scribe centuries later could possibly have invented the account or known of places long since forgotten.

The same explanation must be given for absolute exactness on the part of these records when referring to such ancient places as Shechem, Bethel, Ai, Salem, and Hebron, all of which were established centers of culture, as shown by archaeological investigations, and in existence even prior to the days of the patriarchs. It is interesting to observe in this connection that the journey of Abraham from Ur of the Chaldees to Egypt can be traced geographically and topographically without a slip. The author of these early narratives knew the route of the ancient highway from northern Canaan to the South Country, the order in which the cities were reached and their relation to each other. No error has been found in these details. On the other hand, the accuracy reflected in these ancient writings, and now generally recognized, commends the Old Testament to excavators as an indispensable guide in locating the probable sites of ancient cultural centers. If, for example, one should take the clear implications of the Genesis narratives in his search for the forgotten sites of Sodom and Gomorrah, he would probably see them across Jordan at the northeastern shore of the Dead Sea, in the same locality where in recent years the astounding discoveries at Teleilat el-Ghassul have occurred.[8] But, apart from conjecture, the accuracy in geographical notations appearing in these records is not to be attributed to coincidence; there were too many possible

120

pitfalls for an uninformed writer to miss them all. And this correspondence with the geographical backgrounds as now known argues not only for the integrity of the narratives but also for their high antiquity.

3. *Ethnographical References*

Again, the astonishing correspondence between these claimed early narratives and the findings of archaeology regarding primitive peoples in Canaan is also a matter of great importance. Ethnic groups known as Hittites, Horites, Jebusites, Amorites, and others make their appearance frequently in these early sources and, in the light of excavations, there is no proof of anachronism in any reference. For later scribes these peoples would have had no significance either with reference to their existence or to their specific relations with the early Hebrews.[9] But the writer in Genesis knew the full story of the Hittites and Hurrians many centuries before they completely disappeared, and continued to write with confidence about their affairs and their importance. The excavations by Winckler at Boghaz-koi provide an overwhelming vindication of biblical claims regarding the Hittites. In like manner recent investigations in the field of ethnic movements during these early centuries give support to biblical notations concerning another people hitherto considered not only mysterious but mythical to all intents and purposes—the Horites, or Hori, referred to in several passages.[10] "Perhaps the most striking feature in connection with the Hurrians is the established fact of their expansion over a vast area, in what was assumed by many to have been predominantly Semitic territory. The scholarly world, which has watched these developments with an increasing sense of wonder, cannot but find the rise of the Hurrians an even more remark-

121

able phenomenon than the reappearance of the Hittites. For the latter, we were prepared to a certain extent by Egyptian, biblical, and cuneiform sources. But the same records contained no warning that we should be obliged to make room for the Hurrians, by whatever name they might be known, outside and far beyond the limits of the middle Euphrates area.'"[11] It should be recalled, however, that the biblical notices gave us sufficient warning with reference to the Hurrians even as they did regarding the mysterious Hittites. Indeed, we have in the rediscovery of the Hittite and Hurrian peoples not only the signal triumphs of modern investigation but also a phenomenal vindication of Old Testament accuracy. Other triumphs may come in the future. But for the present we have no great difficulty in recognizing the many racial groups which move vividly across the stage of the Old Testament. All of these ethnographical details are so minute and so exact that they must be regarded as based on sources almost, if not actually, contemporary. Oral tradition, however persistent, could not possibly have preserved these details which have all the earmarks of written records of high antiquity.[12]

4. *Chronological Framework*

Characteristic of these early records of the Old Testament is their complete correspondence with the general chronological framework in which individuals, events, and nations are set. Events and eras, persons and periods, appear on the stage of action in closest harmony. Anachronisms disappear and orderliness is maintained throughout. The continuity of development here claimed, however, is not inserted or manufactured to conform to a plan; it is a part of the story itself and has all the marks of genuineness. It has the beauty of self-consistency. In Genesis 14 Chedorlaomer and Amraphel, leaders of a Mesopotamian punitive expedition, wage war in the remote Transjordan country and, after successful combat, are routed by Abraham and his Amorite confederates at Hormah beyond Damascus. As is now well established, the chronological framework in which the Amorites, Amraphel (Hammurabi), and Abraham are thus brought together is in full keeping with historical development. This is not accidental; rather, it is a faithful recording of a contemporary event. If the author were concerned with facts, there was no occasion to design or to invent imaginary circumstances having no basis in reality. We now believe that the account is trustworthy and that it is in accord with historical facts.

Again, the shadowy forms of the sons of Heth are grouped together in the city gate of Hebron agreeing with Abraham on the purchase price of the cave of Machpelah in which to bury his dead. It was easy, of course, to dismiss the whole account as a pure invention of creative art, since nothing was known of any sons of Heth (Hittites) from any other body of ancient literature or from any other source known to the scholarly world. When they did actually appear under another name, as, for instance, the Kheta on the temple records at Karnak, they were not recognized. However, with the revelations following in the wake of Winckler's phenomenal excavations at Boghaz-koi, the Hittites live again and are found properly related to the chronological setting of the Old Testament narratives.

But it is not necessary to multiply illustrations to support this contention regarding chronological accuracy. Beginning with Abraham and continuing through the humiliating experiences of Egyptian servitude; following the emergence of the nation under the leadership of Moses down through the periods of exiles and restoration, the history of Israel unfolds, its events are definitely set in the framework of surrounding peoples (Babylonians, Egyptians, Hittites, Assyrians, Medes, and Persians) with the astounding result that the Hebrew records are shown to be in accord with the chronology as recorded in other documents of the same periods. It is clear that for the later phases of Hebrew history when Assyrian, Babylonian, and Persian records enlarge the field of historical information, we can get a fuller view of contemporary developments, but this is merely a relative matter. The older records, appearing only occasionally and limited in scope, are none the less reliable and their chronological data accurate and appropriate.

The foregoing considerations regarding the possibility and probability of written narratives among the early Hebrews have been advanced solely on the basis of results recently achieved in the field of archaeology. The presence of admitted writings dating between the fifth and ninth centuries B.C. has contributed somewhat to the solution of critical questions bearing on the Pentateuch, or Hexateuch, but, just as certainly, has raised additional questions and problems with particular reference to the extremely low dates assigned to these writings.[13] It is now definitely claimed that, whether in whole or in part, a higher antiquity must be assigned to them than has usually been the case. But it is equally clear that, in contending for earlier composition of these narratives, archaeology must become involved with the conclusions advanced by Higher Criticism, particularly the current views with regard to the date and authorship of the Pentateuch, or Hexateuch, as well as the widely accepted theories concerning the several documents designated *J, E, D,* and *P.* While these and similar questions may be definitely considered as belonging primarily to literary criticism, they are necessarily bound up in matters of historical fact, and archaeology is entitled to set forth its own opinions and conclusions. This is clearly admitted in the following: "Of the main literary position of the critics, however, namely the composite origin of the Pentateuch and the identification of the original documents, all that can be said is that 'while archaeology has not overthrown the critical position, it is in some details tending to modify it. Sellin in Germany and Welch in Britain, though avowedly critical in their methods, represent a movement to date the documents earlier than the Wellhausen school has done.' "[14] "There is a tendency, too, to suspect the existence of very early written sources where hitherto the theory of a merely oral tradition had held the field."[15] These admissions expressed by North, Caiger, and many others, would seem to justify at least a re-examination of the problem of the Pentateuch in the light of the new archaeological evidences concerning its probable sources and approximate date of composition. To this we now turn in the following chapter.

CHAPTER NINE

ARCHAEOLOGY AND CRITICISM

THE WEIRD AND IMPOSING
SPHINX AT GIZEH. SENTINEL
TO THE TOMBS OF CHEOPS,
CHEPHREN, AND MENKAURE.

THE EGYPTIANS ACHIEVED
DISTINCTION IN THE FIELD
OF RELIGIOUS ARCHITECTURE.
SOME OF THEIR MOST BEAU-
TIFUL CREATIONS ARE FOUND
IN THE TEMPLES AT KARNAK,
LUXOR, PHILAE, EDFU, AND
OTHER SITES. THE LOTUS-
BUD AND FLUTED COLUMNS
ARE AMONG THE MOST GRACE-
FUL. THE ENTRANCE HERE
PICTURED IS MARKED BY ITS
DELICATE LINES AND SIM-
PLICITY.

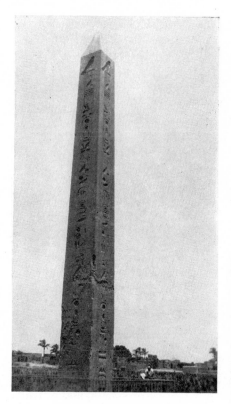

THE OBELISK OF ON, HELIO-
POLIS, ERECTED BY SENUSERT
I (SESOSTRIS) ABOUT 2760
B.C. THE SHAFT OF THIS
OBELISK MEASURES 68 FEET,
OF WHICH A PORTION, 7
FEET, IS SUBMERGED BY THE
ACCUMULATION OF NILE AL-
LUVIAL DEPOSITS THROUGH
MANY CENTURIES.

IN THE SAKKARA ROYAL
CEMETERY ARE FOUND TOMBS,
MURAL DECORATIONS, AND
BOOKS OF THE DEAD, ALL RE-
LATING TO THE FIFTH
DYNASTY OF EGYPTIAN
PHARAOHS. SHOWN IN THIS
VIEW IS THE FALSE DOOR
(DESIGNED TO MISLEAD ROB-
BERS) CONTAINING A STATUE
OF THE DECEASED MERRUKA.
ON EITHER SIDE IS A LIFE-
SIZE PORTRAIT THE COLORS
OF WHICH ARE MARVELOUSLY
PRESERVED.

CHAPTER NINE

ARCHAEOLOGY AND CRITICISM

THE archaeologist is first of all a fact-finder, an investigator in the field of antiquities, whose principal business is the salvaging of ancient civilizations. As a miner, he digs into the remains of the past and, having recovered certain evidences, proceeds to orientate them in the light of their original environment and relation to the then contemporary life. It is in this latter respect that the archaeologist must become an interpreter; but he must previously have come from the mounds with the data which now demand an adequate and faithful explanation. As he handles these evidences his interests might run along many lines. If, for example, the dominant motive of a Near East archaeologist pertains primarily to interest in the history of human culture, the reactions and interactions of competing civilizations, his explanation of recovered evidences will be confined to that particular province, though other interests are not thereby excluded. But if, as is the generally prevailing motive, he is intent on relating his explanations to the great redemptive movement which found its culmination in the history of Israel, the Chosen People, then his horizon is broadened, and the science of archaeology becomes definitely related to the Scriptures both of the Old Testament and the New, and its findings placed under tribute to explicate and illustrate biblical references and claims. It is at this point that archaeology and biblical criticism meet on common grounds and with mutual interests.

It is well known that a great deal of the work now being done in the field of excavations in Palestine, Syria, Egypt, Asia Minor, and Mesopotamia is inspired by religious interest, and that the principal objective is to set in sharper relief the contents of the biblical narratives. The work is prosecuted by societies, institutions, and individuals whose concern is that archaeology shall continue to serve the cause of truth, and in its operations shall provide still wider space where the Bible may stand unencumbered and unfettered. If there are those who are disposed to question the uniqueness of Israel's historical and religious development, they will derive little comfort from the results of archaeological investigation. Scientific research tends consistently to elevate the Scriptures in modern critical opinion, and the Old Testament at present occupies a far higher position than formerly among scholars in various quarters. This development is heartily welcomed and should serve as a deterrent to any effort to misrepresent archaeology and criticism in their relation to each other. In the following statement we get the expression of a fair and judicious attitude: "It is unfortunate that the recent discoveries in Palestine which have shed so interesting a light on the earlier history of the Hebrew invasion, have at times been misused in the interest of an unscholarly prejudice against the work of those who are vaguely called 'the higher critics,' or even 'the so-called high critics': and we have been treated to such statements as that 'archaeology has disproved the higher criticism.' It is a serious mistake thus to set archaeology and criticism against one another [each other]. Both are needed as helps to understand the Bible story. Without higher criticism, Old Testament history would still be largely a chaos: criticism has introduced order and development into the story. Archaeology does not disprove criticism: it only contributes additional data for the problems which criticism has to solve; and the finds of the excavator have to be set side by side with the literary evidences of the Bible itself, in order to obtain what every student, critic, or archaeologist desires, a trustworthy account of the way in which the history and religious growth of the Hebrews prepared for the coming of Christ.'"[1] It is clear, therefore, that criticism and archaeology are both concerned with a fair solution of biblical problems and that, in their search for explanations, they may be mutually helpful. The Bible claims no special immunities from any just canons of the literary, historical, or archaeological approach to its contents, and lends itself willingly to all legitimate efforts to determine and to purify its text. As a consequence, it may be confidently said that the history of the Hebrew people is today far better understood than formerly, not only in its internal development but also as to the framework of contemporary events in which it moved, and that the text of the Old Testament is receiving explication and confirmation from sources hitherto unavailable and unexpected.[2] The recoveries from the mounds have contributed largely to this result and will continue to shed light on perplexing problems.

Now archaeology, while relatively a newcomer in the field of biblical criticism, has gone a long way toward winning its spurs as a science of the first order, and has rather consistently kept to its original province and function. But the history of Higher Criticism of the Old Testament, while properly concerned with authorship, sources, periods of origin, and kindred matters, indicates a steady tendency to include areas of investigation in no sense involved in its inception and original province, and to widen into regions where exact science cannot follow. Driver's pointed reference to this special tendency and enlarged field of critical interest, though advanced several years ago, is still valid both as to the idea of delimitation and propriety in this particular field: "The term 'higher criticism' is often misunderstood, and, consequently, misapplied. It may be worth while, therefore, to explain that 'higher criticism' is not, as seems sometimes to be supposed, an intensified and exaggerated form of ordinary criticism: it is a particular branch or department of criticism, which is so called, simply because, as compared with 'lower,' or textual, criticism, it deals with higher and more difficult problems; and its province is exclusively to determine, with the help of all the data available, the origin, date, and (if they are composite) literary structure of books, or parts of books. It is a mistake to suppose, as is sometimes done, that questions relating to history, the credibility of narratives, the origin and growth of religious beliefs, the influence of Babylonia upon Israel, etc., fall within the province of 'higher criticism.' "[3] That is obviously a fair statement. Had the provisions of such a scheme been respected or adhered to in critical procedure and technique, a vast amount of confusion would have been avoided and the tasks of the critics simplified if not made easier. In that event we should now be regarding the whole province of criticism under three aspects, namely, *Textual Criticism, Source Criticism,* and *Interpretation.* Even now there would probably be no objection to an arrangement of that kind, but Higher Criticism since Eichhorn has had a long history, and its progress has been toward an increasing expansion of, rather than a rigid adherence to, its legitimate field of interests.

As a consequence there is now an insistent demand that the whole scheme of Old Testament reconstruction be re-examined in the light of the new knowledge. This demand is strongly voiced by Marston in one of his recent contributions to biblical archaeology: "About a century and a half ago, men began to use the knowledge then current as a standard for the criticism of the Old Testament; and each succeeding generation adopted similar methods. Thus it comes about that, today, we are able to survey the efforts and conclusions of several generations of critics based solely upon the current knowledge of their time. . . . It was a generation or so after the critics had commenced their work that men began to dig into the mounds of ancient ruins in Bible lands in order to learn about their past history. Thus archaeology asserted itself, and began to unravel the evidence that relics of Bible civilizations had to tell of their own times. During the last eight years a clearer background of the earlier books of the Old Testament has been revealed to us. But in the meanwhile progress is impeded by a residuum of learning—an inchoate mass of critical conclusions—which, being originally based upon incorrect assumptions, have become serious obstacles to the ascertainment of the truth."[4]

While some will probably consider that a pointed condemnation, the author made it with great seriousness and with deep conviction of its truthfulness. But it should not be thought for a moment that he stands alone in that strong reaction to some of the negative conclusions of contemporary criticism of the Old Testament. Indeed, with regard to several of these positions, originally and until lately accepted as "assured results," archaeology has provided quite a bit of evidence which has seriously questioned their validity. One cannot but sense the wholesome effect of recent discoveries on the drift of critical opinion as expressed in the following statement by Meek when introducing the Haskell Lectures of 1933-34: "In these later days of Old Testament research the older documentary hypothesis is being seriously questioned. I occasionally use the documentary symbols J, E, D and P, but in no instance

133

have I used an argument that is dependent upon the documentary hypothesis. I am not committed to any particular point of view, but in these Lectures I have attempted with completely open mind to ascertain the facts of Hebrew origins in so far as these may be revealed in the Hebrew documents themselves and in the excavations."[5] That is a frank recognition of the increasing weight of archaeology in evaluating the early narratives of the Old Testament, but more important in the present discussion is the sweeping claims of Kenyon: "It is therefore legitimate to say that, in respect of that part of the Old Testament against which the disintegrating criticism of the last half of the nineteenth century was chiefly directed, the evidence of archaeology has been to re-establish its authority, and likewise to augment its value by rendering it more intelligible through a fuller knowledge of its background and setting."[6] That is also a frank recognition and a sincere tribute to the contribution of archaeology. But, specifically, what is the critical analysis of the Pentateuch or Hexateuch concerning which there is such serious doubt on the part of scholars that they are reluctant to use its technique? What is the contribution of archaeology in creating this distrust of critical procedure hitherto, on the one hand, and providing correctives for its extremes, on the other? Answers to these questions will be attempted in the following sections.

CRITICAL ANALYSIS OF THE HEXATEUCH

The critical analysis of the early sections of the Hebrew Scriptures has a long and interesting history. Its inception may be attributed to Baruch Spinoza (1632-1677), an excommunicated Jew and father of modern Pantheism, who published in 1671 an opinion that Ezra, not Moses, was the author of the so-called books of Moses, the Pentateuch, a pronouncement that

134

was distinctly revolutionary, since it ran counter to traditional views as held both by Jews and Christians. Jean Astruc, a French physician of Jewish descent and a Roman Catholic in faith, in 1753 called attention to *Elohistic* and *Jehovistic* sections in the book of Genesis, and, on the basis of this, announced his theory as to two distinct documents from which the book was composed by Moses. In quick succession Eichhorn and others began to weigh the Old Testament in the critical scales, examining it not only from the standpoint of the source materials which lie back of the documentary theories, but also including in their critical survey the evaluation of practically every aspect of the development of Israel's religion and institutions. Eichhorn contended that the E and J sections in Genesis are distinguished not simply by the use of the divine names, but by certain literary peculiarities, thus preparing the way for a different hand. Hupfeld observed marked peculiarities in the JE sections and proposed a third writer to account for the differences. DeWette argued that the book of Deuteronomy is to be regarded as a composition struck off during the reign of Josiah to centralize worship in Jerusalem and, furthermore, that the Pentateuch contains no history at all, only legend and poetry. Again, it was argued that the book of Leviticus is simply a partisan production whose interest is centered on the priesthood and its various function in connection with the religious life of the Hebrews, and that its composition is exilian or post-exilian. Finally, the book of Joshua, in which we have the graphic narratives dealing with the conquest of Canaan, is described as pure romance without genuine historical value. Following in the wake of other critics, particularly Reuss, Graf, and Keunen, Wellhausen took up the cudgels for the hyper-critical approach to the Old Testament with such apparent success that the whole movement has largely

135

revolved around him together with Graf. These are the views which largely dominate the field of Old Testament criticism today, and it is to these that archaeology submits convincing evidences at least in partial refutation of the most destructive aspects of the critical analysis.

Now, for the sake of clearness, and without going into the minutiae of the critical analysis, the principal results are indicated in the following general statement: Pentateuchal criticism relates to the first division of the Hebrew Old Testament which consists of Genesis, Exodus, Leviticus, Numbers, and Deuteronomy. By the addition of the historical chronicles of Joshua we get the problem of the Hexateuch. These narratives, though containing some extra material, have as their distinctive purpose the description of the Hebrew people as regards their historical development and relations, on the one hand, and the laws which undergirded their religious and social life, on the other. It is held that both history and law are so intimately interwoven throughout the course of these narratives, particularly in the Pentateuch, that they now appear as a unified work, but their supposed unity is merely artificial, for back of these writings are many sources, authors, and eras. These narratives should not be encumbered with the weight of any Mosaic connection, for it is extremely doubtful that Moses had anything to do with them. On close examination, four distinct sources or documents appear, their probable origins and dates being determined in the following order: During the ninth century (i.e., 900-800 B.C.) there was current in Judah (the Southern Kingdom) a complete written history of the Hebrew people from the period of the Patriarchs through that of Moses, a history that was definitely characterized both by the use of the divine name Jahweh (J) and by its partial or peculiar interest in the affairs

136

of the Southern Kingdom. Corresponding to this Southern document, there was in existence in Ephraim (the Northern Kingdom) as early as the eighth century (i.e., 800-700 B.C.) a similar narrative, which was distinguished by the use of the divine name Elohim (E) and by its peculiar interest in the affairs of the Northern Kingdom. Though the process is not known, it is probable that during the seventh century (i.e., 700-600 B.C.) certain portions of these narratives (J and E) were combined to form what is now specified as the Jahweh-Elohistic account (JE). About the same time (i.e., 621 B.C.) another writer, or school of writers, regarding these documents of J, E, and JE from a national and religious standpoint, proceeded to bring them together, and to interpret them in the interest of the sanctuary at Jerusalem. This work is referred to as the Deuteronomist (D) and is now represented by the book of Deuteronomy. The final step in this Documentary evolution was taken during the Exile or after (i.e., 500-400 B.C.), when a Priestly writer, or school of writers, amplifying and supplementing the older narratives of J, E, and JE, finally brought them together, using his own document (P) as a framework for the whole. The work of the Priestly writer, like that of the J, E, and D writers, must be regarded as a document of specialized interest whose main purpose was the defense of the priesthood and the cult at the sanctuary. The hand of the Priestly writer is seen in all sections of Genesis, Exodus, Leviticus, Numbers, and Joshua, whereas in Deuteronomy only eleven verses, dealing mainly with Moses on Mt. Nebo, are ascribed to him. Thus Deuteronomy becomes a source within itself though its material is regarded as being based on J, E, and the JE combination passages in other portions of the Pentateuch. Now, as an illustration of the framework idea, we give here an analysis of the sections of the Hexateuch usually attributed to the Priestly writer:

Genesis 1:1–2:4a; 5:1-28,30-32; 6:9-22; 7:6,11,13-16a, 17a,18-21,24; 8:1,2a,3b-5,13a,14-19; 9:1-17,28,29; 10:1-7,20,22,23,31,33; 11:10-27,31,32; 12:4b,5; 13:6,11b,12a; 16:1a,3,15,16; 17:1-27; 19:29; 21:1b, 2b-5; 23:1-20; 25:7-11a,12-17,19,20,26b; 26:34,35; 27:46–28:9; 29:24-39; 31:18b; 33:18a; 34:1,2a,4, 6,8-10,13-18,20-24,25,27-29; 35:9-13,15,22b,29; 36 (mostly); 37:1-2a; 48:3,6,7; 49:1a,28b-33; 50:12, 13.

Exodus 1:1-5,7,13,14; 2:23b-25; 6:2–7:13,19,20a,21b,22; 8:5-7,15b-19; 9:8-12; 11:9-10; 12:1-20,28,37a,40, 41,43,51; 13:1,2,20; 14:1-4,8,9,15-18,21a,21c-23,26, 27a,28a,29; 16:1-3,6-24,31-36; 17:1a; 19:1-2a; 24:15-18a; 25:1–31:18a; 34:29,35; 35:1–40:38.

Leviticus 1:1–27:34.

Numbers 1:1–10:28,34; 13:1-17a,21,25,26a,32a; 14:1,2,5, 7,10,26-30,34,38; 15:1-41; 16:1a,2b-7a,7b-11,16,17, 18-24,27a,32b,35,36-40,41-50; 17:1–19:22; 20:1a,2, 3b,4,6,13,22-29; 21:4a,10,11; 22:1; 25:6-18; 26:1– 31:54; 32:18,19,28,32,33-36.

Deuteronomy 1:3; 32:48-52; 34:1a,5b,7a,8,9.

Joshua 4:13,15-17,19; 5:10-12; 7:1; 8:15b,17-21; 13:15-32; 14:1-5; 15:1-13,20-44,48-62; 16:4-8; 17:1a,3,4, 7,9a-10a; 18:1,11-28; 19:1-8,10-46,48-51; 20:1-3,6a, 7-9; 21:1-42; 22:9-34.

Inasmuch as the analysis just given refers only to the Priestly element in the Hexateuch, it follows that the remaining portions, in so far as they rest on sources and are not editorial, are to be credited to J and E, or to JE when the two cannot be separated, their identification resting mainly on the use of the names Jahweh, Elohim, and Jahweh-Elohim. As already stated, the

138

book of Deuteronomy, regarded later than J and E and generally placed at 621 B.C., is attributed to a writer (or writers) who used the older narratives as a basis for advocating the centralization of worship in Jerusalem. It is difficult to conceive of all these intimate and subtle relations, hence we offer a series of illustrations setting forth the various elements as they now appear in several sections of the Hexateuch:

ILLUSTRATIONS OF DOCUMENTARY SOURCES

Genesis 7				*Exodus 3*		
Verses	1- 5	to J		Verses	1	to E
Verses	6	to P		Verses	2- 4a	to J
Verses	7-10	to E		Verses	4b	to E
Verses	11	to P		Verses	5	to J
Verses	12	to J		Verses	6	to E
Verses	13-16a	to P		Verses	7- 8	to J
Verses	16b	to J		Verses	9-15	to E
Verses	17a	to P		Verses	16-18	to J
Verses	17b	to J		Verses	19-22	to E
Verses	18-21	to P				
Verses	22-23	to J		*Joshua 4*		
Verses	24	to P		Verses	1- 3	to JE
				Verses	4- 5	to E
				Verses	6- 7	to J?
Genesis 21				Verses	8	to J
Verses	1a	to J		Verses	9-10	to D
Verses	1b	to P		Verses	11	to E
Verses	2a	to J		Verses	12	to D
Verses	2b- 5	to P		Verses	13	to P
Verses	6-32	to E		Verses	14	to D
Verses	33-34	to J		Verses	15-17	to P
				Verses	18	to JE
				Verses	19	to P
				Verses	20	to JE
				Verses	21-24	to D

139

It will not be necessary to multiply illustrations of the critical analysis to show the several relationships existing among the documents, nor do we regard it as important to set forth other features of the critical method whereby these sources are further complicated by the addition of secondary sources, revisers, editors, and schools. At this point, however, we seek to examine the critical reconstruction of these sources in the light of contemporary epigraphic materials as these may affect the possibility and probability of early written records of Israel's history and religious institutions. Attention will be focused on each section of the Hexateuch with a view to showing how the results of archaeology demand a re-examination and restatement of the whole problem.

ARCHAEOLOGY AND THE HEXATEUCH

GENESIS—HEBREW BACKGROUNDS

In the Genesis narratives there is set forth in orderly progression the conviction of the Hebrew people regarding three great beginnings affecting all human life, namely, the dawn of creation, the dawn of sin and its results, and the dawn of a unique people for redemptive ends. Now, whatever objection might be brought against these historical traditions, either as to their form or content, it seems obvious that one of the prime requisites in handling them should be the assumption that they are serious attempts to describe those convictions, written with no purpose to deceive, but rather to enlighten. Here we have marshaled in orderly manner the religious history of mankind and the gradual unfolding of the part the Hebrew people were to have in redemptive history. It is clear, therefore, that if the requisite of serious intention be granted, we eliminate at once the negative appraisal which represents these

140

records as the wholesale manufacturing of events and alleged personal experiences which have no actual relationship to the historical order.

Generally stated, the documentary theory applied to the contents of Genesis by the Graf-Wellhausen school, claims *J, E,* and *JE* as the basic narratives for the traditions of the Patriarchs, while *P* provides supplementary details according to any information which he might have possessed. Though admitting that these basic narratives might have been *relatively* early—i.e., as compared with exilian or post-exilian writings, they are certainly not to be regarded as of high antiquity since they all fall within the period of the Monarchy, and merely represent the written records of traditions previously of the *oral* type and subject to variation, corruption, legend, and imagination. This view is stated by Wellhausen in frankest terms: "From the patriarchal narratives it is impossible to obtain any historical information with regard to the Patriarchs; we can only learn something about the time in which the stories about them were first told by the Israelite people. This later period, with all its essential and superficial characteristics, was unintentionally *projected back* into hoary antiquity, and is reflected there like a transfigured mirage.'" It follows, of course, that any accounts bearing on pre-patriarchal times are even more unreliable and are to be treated purely and simply as products of the imagination. Among these latter traditions dogmatically rejected are the familiar accounts of Creation, Garden of Eden, Deluge, Confusion of Tongues, etc.

Now, it is obvious that the substantiation of this destructive analysis of the pre-patriarchal and patriarchal narratives would prove subversive of the whole Old Testament, a fatal blow at every claim of its credibility. Fortunately, however, this negative appraisal

141

is no longer permitted to go unchallenged, but in the light of numerous contemporary documents it is shown to be untenable. These documentary evidences have been recovered during a comparatively short period of time; one might say the whole process falls within a period of less than three-quarters of a century. While the order of the discoveries has had no direct bearing on the establishment of any particular point, the nature of these finds has served to provide the scholarly world with many jolts on several points. For, viewed from any era of their history, whether nomadic, semi-nomadic, or national, the Hebrews may be presumed to have had the resources to produce the literary remains ascribed to them. This is the testimony of the monuments with reference to the *Pre-Patriarchal* and *Patriarchal* eras, both of which fall within the limitations of Genesis.[8]

First, out of the *Pre-Patriarchal Era* have come epigraphic materials which are nothing less than phenomenal. The records of the Nile area, made available by the decipherment of the Rosetta Stone, show a period of cultural development of hoary antiquity and provide us with all information necessary to reconstruct the political, social, and religious life of Egyptians who lived more than a millennium before Abraham. Then, with the decipherment of the Behistun inscriptions, the Tigris-Euphrates sector began to yield its age-long secrets. Beginning with the excavations by Botta at Kuyunjik (Nineveh) in 1842, Layard at Nineveh in 1845, Rassam and Koldewey at Babylon, and continuing through to the present period with the startling results witnessed at Kish, Ur of the Chaldees, and Tepe Gawra, the discoveries have simply been revolutionary. These are the discoveries which convinced Woolley that there was no period of Hebrew history, Patriarchal or later, when they could not have had at hand written records

142

of events described in their sacred literature. But more specifically: Out of the Pre-Patriarchal period come the priceless cuneiform tablets of the Creation and the Flood, in which are set forth the Mesopotamian versions of these events in the garb of an extreme polytheism. Learned dissertations have been written on the similarities and dissimilarities between the Babylonian-Sumerian traditions and the Hebrew; various theories have been proposed in explanation of claimed relations. Obviously no theory of mutual dependence can be adequate, either for the Mesopotamian or the Hebrew point of view, since neither of these accounts reveals any actual proof of derivation from the other. With the rejection of the theory of dependence, the more probable explanation may be found in the idea of *cognateness* which is based on the unbroken historical connection of the Hebrew people with Mesopotamian life and traditions from earliest times. This view makes room not only for the early traditions current among Sumerians, Babylonians, and ancestors of the Hebrew people, but also for the unique idea of a revelation based on an exalted conception of God attributed to Abraham, the father of the Hebrew peoples. "The Babylonian narratives (Creation and Deluge) are both polytheistic, while the corresponding biblical narratives (Gen. 1 and 6-9) are made the vehicle of a pure and exalted monotheism; but in spite of this fundamental difference, and also variations in detail, the resemblances are such as to leave no doubt that the Hebrew cosmogony and the Hebrew story of the Deluge are both derived ultimately from the same original as the Babylonian narratives, only transformed by the magic touch of Israel's religion, and infused by it with a new spirit."[9] In harmony with that estimate is the following significant statement: "On this view, *the Biblical stories* are not late and purified versions of the Babylonian, but represent an independent related version, going back to a common origin with the Babylonian, but preserving their monotheistic character in the line of revelation, when the others had long sunk under the corrupting influences of polytheism. Or, if purification is to be spoken of, it is purification on the basis of an older and less debased tradition. Such a view harmonises with the Bible's own postulate that the light of a true knowledge of God has never been wholly extinguished among men, and that from the first there has been a line of pious worshippers, a seed of blessing and promise, on the earth.''[10]

Now, the point at issue here is not the question of relationship between the Babylonian and Hebrew traditions, but rather the establishment of the contention that epigraphic materials bearing on Creation, Deluge, and other subjects appearing in the Old Testament, were already in existence among the Sumerians and Babylonians approximately one thousand years before the age of Moses and likewise before Abraham. For example, the Nippur Tablet, which contains a combination of the Creation and Deluge stories, though produced in 2100 B.C., is now regarded as a copy of a Sumerian original written in 3000 B.C. As a citizen of Ur, Abraham could have been conversant with the literature of his own day and, unless we are to deny all the evidence, he could have had access to a stream of Sumerian tradition antedating him by a millennium. With such material available, he doubtless appropriated some of the tablets and brought them with him on his trek to Canaan. This view is suggested in the following: ''The tenth chapter of Genesis raises difficult questions in reference to original authorship. We can understand the Hebrews having preserved the tradition concerning the creation of the world, or that of mankind. Even the flood may be one of those popular narratives handed on from father to son, through many generations.

144

THE ALABASTER SPHINX UNEARTHED BY PETRIE AT MEMPHIS, LEFT IN
ITS ORIGINAL PLACE AS A PUBLIC MONUMENT. DESCRIBED BY PETRIE
AS A PERFECT LIKENESS OF AMENHOTEP III.

GREAT COURT OF AMENHOTEP III, IN TEMPLE AT LUXOR. NOTE THE
ARCHITECTURAL BEAUTY OF THE LOTUS-BUD COLUMNS. THE FAMOUS
HYPOSTYLE HALL AT NEIGHBORING KARNAK WAS GRACED WITH SIMILAR
COLUMNS.

FACE OF THE GREAT BEHISTUN ROCK WHERE RAWLINSON ACHIEVED THE SIGNAL SUCCESS OF COPYING AND LATER DECIPHERING THE MYSTERIOUS CUNEIFORM CHARACTERS OF EARLY MESOPOTAMIAN WRITINGS. THE RECORDS HERE PRESERVED SET FORTH IN OLD PERSIAN, SUSIAN, AND BABYLONIAN CUNEIFORM THE MILITARY TRIUMPHS OF DARIUS V. THE DECIPHERMENT OF THE TRILINGUAL INSCRIPTION THREW OPEN THE LITERARY RECORDS OF ALL PREVIOUS MESOPOTAMIAN PEOPLES, INCLUDING ASSYRIAN, BABYLONIAN, AND SUMERIAN.

THE BLACK OBELISK OF SHALMANESER III, KING OF ASSYRIA 859-824 B.C., WAS SET UP AT NIMRUD. IT IS SCULPTURED ON ALL FOUR SIDES WITH TWENTY SMALL BAS-RELIEFS, AND 210 LINES OF CUNEIFORM INSCRIPTIONS. IN THE SECOND ROW OF RELIEFS JEHU OF THE NORTHERN KINGDOM IS SEEN DOING HOMAGE TO SHALMANESER. THE TRIBUTE OF JEHU IS DATED IN THE EIGHTEENTH YEAR OF SHALMANESER'S REIGN, 841 B.C.

Nearly all nations have traditions of that kind which are put down in writing, sometimes very long after they originated. It is not at all impossible that the Israelites had these traditions before Abram left Mesopotamia."[11] It is clear also that these Pre-Patriarchal accounts rest upon a fact basis as over against a legendary origin, as frequently alleged. The startling results of excavations by Langdon at Kish and by Woolley at Ur of the Chaldees, particularly with regard to the Flood, astonished the scholarly world. The story of the Deluge thus finds specific confirmation in the eight feet of clay deposit at Ur of the Chaldees which formed a definite stratum between earlier and later civilizations as indicated by the pottery.[12] Such spectacular discoveries are not very frequent, but each one represents strong corroboration of ancient tradition based on facts.

Secondly, out of the *Patriarchal Era* come equally convincing evidences regarding the literary capabilities of the Hebrew people. Wellhausen and his school took for granted that the traditions of Genesis regarding the fathers of Israel reflected conditions in the time of the Monarchy, a good millennium later than the traditional date. The continued excavation and publication of documents from the second millennium have proved, time after time, that the historical, topographical, social, and even linguistic background of these stories is very much earlier than the time of the Monarchy (tenth to seventh centuries B.C.). Of particular interest is the discovery by Speiser and Gordon of many striking social and legal parallels between the stories of the Patriarchs and the Horite documents from Nuzi in eastern Mesopotamia, dating mainly from the fifteenth century B.C. But earlier than these is the Code of Hammurabi with its summary of Sumerian and Babylonian legal procedure so faithfully reflected in the patriarchal narratives,

145

particularly in the experiences of Abraham and, subsequently, in relation to the laws of Moses.[13]

In addition, there have been recovered thousands of tablets bearing on subjects of first-rate importance to Abraham and other citizens of Ur in the twentieth century B.C. The Spartoli Tablets[14] come to the surface to attest the historicity of Genesis 14, in critical opinion one of the most flagrant products of inventive or imaginative genius, and to bear witness to outstanding men who were contemporaries with Abraham.[15] To these may be added the inscriptions of Serabit el-Khadim in the Peninsula of Sinai, whose discovery by Petrie in 1905 threw the proto-Hebrew script and alphabet almost eight hundred years beyond even the most sanguine views of conservative scholars.[16] And now the astounding discoveries by Woolley at Muqayyar (Ur of the Chaldees) whereby the native city of the great Patriarch is reconstructed and its opened tombs, temples, schools, business houses, and residences made to yield their buried treasures of the ages.[17] Indeed, one excavation project is hardly completed before some other site commands attention. "The sensational discovery by Parrot in 1935-7 of nearly 30,000 cuneiform tablets at Mari on the middle Euphrates, belonging to the twentieth century B.C., promises even more remarkable results, especially since the inhabitants of Mari were closely related to the early Hebrews, as we know from their personal names, though the documents are written in Babylonian. M. Dossin's first announcement (summer of 1937) of the contents of these tablets shows that they will completely revolutionize our knowledge of the period."[18] But, even now, our knowledge of the Patriarchal Era represents a great advance over the meager details in our possession only a few years ago. Today this period stands before us in bold outlines, an age that witnessed remarkable literary activity on the part of all

146

people who were contemporaries with the Hebrews. In the light of surviving records, some of which are reflected in the Old Testament, we are fully justified in attributing to the Hebrews their own distinctive traditions which they certainly handed down in written form to succeeding generations. It will be recalled that we have argued for an early composition of these records on the ground of their minute correspondence with original setting and with geographical, ethnographical, and chronological details. In the light of all the evidences the following conclusion appears completely justified: "It is safe to say that the general affect [effect] of the discoveries of the last decade has been to confirm the substantial accuracy of the picture of life in Canaan in the second millennium B.C., as described in the patriarchal narratives of Genesis, and to provide some ground for the view that *written sources for this period may have existed at a much earlier date than has been commonly supposed.*"[19]

Exodus—Birth of the Nation

"The great fact in which the consciousness of Israel ever rooted itself, as that which first gave the nation its freedom, and *made* it a nation, was the Exodus, with which is constantly associated the deliverance at the Red Sea . . . When we turn, accordingly, to the poetical and prophetical books of the Old Testament, we find that, amidst all the vicissitudes of their fortunes, the memory of the Exodus, with its attendant circumstances, never was obliterated, but remained fresh and green in the minds of the people as long as their national life lasted."[20] "No nation ever gratuitously invented the report that it had been ignominiously enslaved by another; none ever forgot the days of its deliverance. And so through all the centuries there survived in

Israel the inextinguishable recollection that it was once delivered out of Egypt, the house of bondage, by Jahweh, the God of its fathers, with a strong hand and outstretched arm; that specially at the passage of the Red Sea it experienced the mighty protection of its God.'"[21] It is clear, therefore, that, whatever the critical evaluation of these narratives, from the standpoint of the Hebrews they assumed an importance in full keeping with the significant events with which they are associated. On any score, they are not to be lightly regarded, certainly not to be dismissed as the wholesale manufacturing by late scribes of incidents which never occurred and conditions which actually never existed. For, on the contrary, there is the highest probability that the narratives in Exodus are based on original documents which were contemporary with the events recorded.[22] It is now no longer possible to rule out the Exodus records on epigraphic grounds—i.e., on the assumption that literary facilities were simply not available at this early date (1400 B.C.), for, as in the case of the Patriarchal Age, the discoveries bearing on the Mosaic era, particularly on these Exodus accounts, confront us with an amazing situation.

Out of the Mosaic period come the significant Tell el-Amarna Letters which represent the official correspondence of Palestinian and other Near East kings with their Egyptian overlords, Amenhotep III and Amenhotep IV (Akhnaton). These letters (or tablets) numbering more than four hundred, are written in the Babylonian cuneiform system (wedge-shaped characters) which was the common medium of communication in the fifteenth century B.C. It is generally admitted that the Amarna correspondence is to be regarded as contemporary with the era of Moses, and that, in all probability, it sets forth the progress of the Hebrew invasion of Canaan from the Canaanite point of view. If this is a correct assumption, these letters should be placed alongside the Old Testament narratives as supplementary and complementary to each other. In that event it is not necessary to demand that there should be perfect uniformity between the two sources. The period covered by the Amarna Letters is roughly 50 years—i.e., 1412-1362 B.C.; the Hebrew narratives, including the Transjordan and West Jordan campaigns, up until the era of the Judges, require a similar period. The general movement described in both sources corresponds as to directions, i.e., northern, southern, and eastern approaches to Canaan, and a remarkable correspondence exists between the two summaries of cities affected and conquered. The difficulty regarding lack of conformity between the king lists is not insuperable, primarily in view of the disturbed conditions following in the wake of war, perhaps frequent assassinations or usurpations produced by political changes. In the matter of time, the Amarna Letters synchronize perfectly with biblical chronology, the Hebrew invasion of Canaan occurring at the beginning of the fourteenth century. Finally, the people described in the Amarna correspondence are the Habiru, the term itself being a perfect equivalent for Hebrews.

Now the principal consideration regarding the Amarna Letters is found in the ability of Palestinian rulers to produce current records of events transpiring in their country, to inform a distant overlord of political developments affecting a part of his empire. Granting that the Hebrews had equal facilities at hand for producing records affecting their progress in establishing themselves as a nation, it is reasonable to believe that they would have made such records and, likewise, would have preserved them. "So long as it was believed that writing was unknown to the Hebrews until about the ninth century it was easy to throw doubt on the trustworthiness of the narratives which purported to go back five hundred years or more before that date. Either they were inventions of an altogether later period, or, at best, they rested only upon oral tradition, the accuracy of which could not be taken for granted. When, therefore, literary criticism declared that the books of the Pentateuch are made up from a combination of once separate works, the earliest of which cannot be placed earlier than the ninth century, the authority of those books was brought into question, and the basis of the moral teaching contained in them was altered, if not shaken. The position is, however, totally different when once it is established that these books, whatever the date of their composition in their present form, may rest upon written records contemporary or nearly contemporary with the events which they describe.''[23] That discerning statement is extremely significant in its bearing on the records of Exodus. For it now seems perfectly obvious, after the exhaustive studies of Yahuda, Jack, Knight, and others, of the distinct Egyptian background reflected in the Exodus narratives, that we are dealing with a composition that must be regarded as an original account or based on written sources contemporary with the events.[24] Certainly such a requirement is legitimate; an original document should reflect not only vividness of description but also minutiae of details in strict conformity with environment or locale. Duncan presents the matter in a convincing manner: ''If the Old Testament narratives are historically accurate, therefore, we have a right to find traces of Egyptian influence in the Hebrew documents; and if these are distinctly manifest in the narratives dealing with Egypt, their presence establishes the historical accuracy of the Old Testament. It may even go further, and prove that the original Hebrew documents were written when the author's knowledge of things Egyptian

150

was still fresh and vivid; or, in other words, were written by one who knew Egypt thoroughly, and written, too, near to the time when the events recorded actually happened.''[25]

LEVITICUS—HEBREW RELIGIOUS LIFE

According to the critical analysis of the Hexateuch, the book of Leviticus must be regarded as the latest section, its production being assigned to the Priestly writer in the exilian or post-exilian period—i.e., 500-400 B.C. In all probability the author was Ezra, who is described as a priest and scribe, one versed in the law of Moses. It is generally held that the linguistic and stylistic characteristics of Leviticus reflect unity of authorship, whatever may have been the period of its composition. Professor Orr has argued convincingly for its unity in connection with the general problem of the Hexateuch.[26]

The view now widely held is that, about one hundred and fifty years after the fabrication of the book of Deuteronomy in 621 B.C., the following events took place in Babylon: ''Ezra and other priests in Babylon forged the priestly code, as chiefly contained in the book of Leviticus, and claiming it to be the book of the law of Moses, brought the people of Jerusalem to swear obedience and loyalty to it in the belief that they were renewing the lapsed covenant of their fathers. These laws, when given such shape as the priests desired, were finally infolded in a historical writing made up from divergent sources in the manner already indicated. Where these 'sources' did not cover the lacunae of the enveloping record, that record was interpolated and additional sections were shaped out of hand to harmonize with the forged laws and ceremonials.''[27] Among these laws and ceremonials were the burnt, meat, peace, sin, and trespass offerings; the consecration of Aaron and his sons to the priesthood; laws relating to eating of holy things and of dealing with leprosy; sundry laws and ordinances followed by requirements for the feast of Pentecost, in particular, and less specifically the day of atonement; and, finally, full details regarding the year of jubilee. All these specifications regarding sacrifices, ritual, and feasts were actually formulated in the exilic period, but they are here represented as being prescribed by Moses and issued under his name and authority. But, according to critical conjecture, the whole set-up of Leviticus, particularly with reference to its sacrificial and ritualistic requirements, is obviously post-Mosaic by a considerable period of time. This obvious anachronism might be resolved by applying the Levitical requirements more or less to the late developments of the second temple.

In answer to this critical appraisal of Leviticus we have some pertinent archaeological evidences which will probably modify the whole picture. The Ras Shamra Tablets, discovered by Claude Schaeffer and Georges Chenet at ancient Ugarit about ten miles north of the city of Latikiyeh on the Syrian coast, are providing astonishing revelations. These tablets, written in the cuneiform characters (now developed into an alphabetic system), and dating from the period 1400 B.C., represent for us the cultural, religious, and historical annals of a polyglot people contemporary with Moses and Joshua. "They afford us valuable evidence as to the nature of religion in Syria and Palestine several centuries before the Israelite monarchy, and constitute a new revelation for the student of the Old Testament. Among other things, they contradict one of the principal assumptions of the Reuss-Graf-Wellhausen school, namely, *that the Israelites could not have had documents at their disposal written before the epoch of the kings.*"[28] They

152

also provide us with priceless contemporary evidences that religious services described in Leviticus were actually, many of them, in operation at Ras Shamra a thousand years before the Leviticus records are said to have been composed. We do not here raise the question as to the vast differences held by the Ugarit people and the Hebrews with reference to these sacrifices and feasts, but specifically mentioned in the Ras Shamra Tablets are the following: Offering without Blemish, Peace Offering, Sin Offering, Offering of Birds, Trespass Offering, Tribute Offering, Wave Offering, Offering of First Fruits, Offering Made by Fire, etc. The tablets also give intimations of sacred feasts such as the Hebrew Feast of Unleavened Bread, Feast of Tabernacles, and the Feast of Weeks.[29] "But there is no need to describe further the similarities existing between the ritual of the dwellers at Ras Shamra and that of the worshippers of Jahweh. The examples given show that much of it was common to both peoples, and consequently that the Jewish Pentateuchal Codes embody cultural elements of a pre-Mosaic nature. The explanation of this parallelism doubtless lies partly in the fact that the Phoenicians and Israelites belonged to the same Semitic race, and inherited the same ritual and religious customs. . . . Israel possessed a different conception of God, for Yahweh had little in common with the Phoenician and other deities. In Israel's view he was not only the God of the whole people and the whole country, but his influence extended to the development of justice and morality among the people."[30]

NUMBERS—THE MOVEMENT TOWARD CANAAN

It will be recalled that the critical analysis of Numbers makes room for three distinct sources in its composition, namely, the Jehovistic, the Elohistic, and the

Priestly, with the bulk of its contents being derived from the Priestly source. Regarded from the standpoint of the newly founded nation, the narratives in Numbers offer distinctive sources for a great deal of information concerning Israel's history, otherwise unavailable. Its contents describe the people as still in the shadows of Mt. Sinai, the numbering of the tribes, particular details regarding the tribe of Levi and the Levitical priesthood, religious offerings, consecrations, the order of Nazarites, and sundry matters. Beginning with Chapter 10, we have the removal from Mt. Sinai, followed by arrival in the wilderness of Paran, the establishment of the tribes at Kadesh-Barnea, report of the spies regarding Canaan, and events of the next thirty-eight years of enforced sojourning. The closing sections deal with the resumption of the journey to Canaan, the route followed being south by way of Edom and Mt. Hor to the headwaters of the Gulf of Akabah, thence north through the Valley of Arnon to the encampment in the Plain of Moab. Other details and events are set forth in these records and all of them go to form an original source for much of our knowledge concerning these particular matters. Apart from our inability to identify specifically every place name and region, the conditions reflected in Numbers are in complete accord with the general geographical framework of the regions involved. It was probably in view of this unusual correspondence in topographical and geographical details, together with the specific claim of Numbers 32:2, that Moses wrote the journeys of the Children of Israel, that Duncan expressed the following conviction: "I do not know why that statement has ever been disputed or the fact regarded as impossible. I believe the author of Numbers is speaking the truth, and all the evidence of archaeology goes to confirm it."[31]

154

It will probably be observed in connection with all of these discussions dealing with extremely early sources that the tendency is always to get back to Moses as the responsible author of these works which Hebrew and Christian traditions have steadfastly attributed to him and to him alone. But, as we have reiterated, our aim here is not the defense of Mosaic authorship; rather, it is to show that the information herein provided is so full and detailed, its fidelity to locale so perfectly in keeping with actual conditions reflected in archaeological discoveries, that no scribe of the eighth or ninth century could possibly have invented the records. The claim for fifth century authorship would thereby fall under its own weight. It may be granted that all of these works have been subjected to the process of editorial and scribal handling through many centuries and that, as shown in the manuscripts of the New Testament, some interpolations have crept in together with a few lacunae, but it remains that the narratives before us rest ultimately not on oral tradition but upon written documents long prior to the period of the Monarchy and practically contemporary with the events which they recount.

DEUTERONOMY—REPETITION OF THE LAW

"Deuteronomy is the one book of the Pentateuch which might seem on the face of it to make claim to direct Mosaic authorship. 'Moses,' it is declared, after the rehearsal is completed, 'wrote this law.' This view of its origin modern criticism decisively rejects; will hardly allow even to be discussed. It was DeWette's achievement in criticism, as we saw, that he relegated Deuteronomy to the age of Josiah; and in this judgment the great majority of critics now follow him, only that a few carry back the composition of the book a reign or two earlier—to the time of Manasseh or of

Hezekiah. Views differ as to how the book is to be regarded—whether as a pseudograph ('forgery'), or as a free composition in the name and spirit of Moses without intention to deceive; but it is generally agreed that, in its present form, it is a production of the prophetic age, and has for its leading aim the centralizing of worship at the sanctuary at Jerusalem.''[32] Wellhausen, Reuss, Graf, Keunen, and others of the older critics had no hesitation in characterizing Deuteronomy as a Fraus Pia (Pious Fraud), and held that it was produced with a deliberate intention to deceive. ''About the origin of Deuteronomy there is still less dispute; in all circles where appreciation of scientific results can be looked for at all, it is recognized that it was composed in the same age as that in which it was discovered, and that it was made the rule of Josiah's reformation, which took place about a generation before the destruction of Jerusalem by the Chaldeans.''[33] It is claimed, furthermore, that the composition and publication of Deuteronomy was a mutual affair between priests and prophets and that the account in the Scriptures describing the discovery of the Book of the Law relates to this particular event and alliance.[34] Finally, ''Deuteronomy is universally allowed to presuppose, and to be dependent on, the laws and history contained in JE, and, these writings being brought down by general consent to the ninth or eighth century B.C., a later date for Deuteronomy necessarily follows.''[35] But, as Orr adds, ''we decline to bind ourselves in starting by this or any similar assumption. It may well be that the result of the argument will rather be *to push the date of JE further back, than to make Deuteronomy late.*''[36] Orr's refusal has been amply justified, and the implications of his statement regarding an earlier date both for JE and Deuteronomy are now finding strong supporters among archaeologists of outstanding ability.

156

The marked change in critical attitude and opinion regarding these and other early narratives has been necessitated by recent discoveries, and with this modification of opinion there has followed a corresponding overhauling of theories. Albright, one of the most competent and versatile archaeologists of the modern period, states the question of Deuteronomy as follows: "The publication of Deuteronomy in 621 B.C. is a fixed date in the uncertain field of Torah chronology; nearly all scholars adopt it, with more or less reservation with regard to the bearing of this fact upon the age of the different parts of the book. However, a careful perusal of it in the light of Chapter 2 will certainly convince most students that Deuteronomy sounds *curiously archaic to have been* written as a whole in the late seventh century B.C. On the other hand, it represents quite another period from that reflected by JE, since there is no trace (except in the historical introduction and in other similar reminiscences scattered through the book) of the nomadic or semi-nomadic period of Hebrew life. The civil code pre-supposed by Deuteronomy belongs to a stage before the development of the royal power, before the great commercial expansion of the eighth and seventh centuries, and consequently before the collapse of the ancient tribal and clan organization, which was gradually replaced during the royal period by a system of administrative districts and trade-guilds. . . . It is not our purpose to enter into the vexed problem of the unity or composite origin of the book; it is our judgment it was written down, substantially as a unit, *in the ninth century* B.C., and was edited in the reign of Josiah or later."[37] But regarding its unity—the point not discussed by Albright in this connection—"no book in the Bible, it may be safely affirmed, bears on its face a stronger impress of unity than the Book of Deuteronomy."[38] Even if editorial

157

revision and work of redactors be admitted for later centuries, the original Deuteronomy was substantially the same as the book now before us. Again, if the critical contention that Deuteronomy is based almost exclusively on materials reflected in the JE documents, be granted, then an early date for Deuteronomy (ninth century) compels still earlier dates for J and E. And if, in the light of previous arguments deduced from epigraphic remains, these documents must be regarded as exceedingly early (probably, for the most part, contemporary with the events described), we have approached the borders of the Mosaic period where they profess to belong, and where they may belong so far as our present knowledge is concerned. This conclusion involves the question of Moses and the laws of Israel, including the Decalogue, the Book of the Covenant, and other laws, but to this matter we will come later. For the present it is important that we recognize the full implication of an early date for Deuteronomy. If in the heyday of critical opinion it was the Ariadne thread, the Achilles heel of the Pentateuchal question, it has lost nothing of its significance in the modern period. "If Deuteronomy, in its present form, be even *substantially* Mosaic,—if it conveys to us with fidelity the purport of discourses and laws actually delivered by Moses to the people of Israel before his death,—then we must go a great deal further. For Deuteronomy undeniably rests in some degree on the JE history embodied in our Pentateuch; on the code of laws which we call the Book of the Covenant, incorporated in that history; as well as on priestly laws from some other sources. The effect of the acceptance of an early date for Deuteronomy, therefore, is to throw all these writings back practically into the Mosaic age, whatever the time when they were finally put together. We should like to be more sure than we are that it is not the perception of this fact which is at least one motive in leading the critics to put down Deuteronomy as far as they do, in the age of the kings.''[39]

JOSHUA—CHRONICLES OF CONQUEST

The narratives of this historical section of the Old Testament are now included by the critics in the general problem of the Hexateuch. Early critical appraisal of these records was content to leave them in the classification of *romance* with no value as historical documents.[40] That evaluation is now completely rejected. In his recent work in this special field of investigation, Garstang states in the Preface: "Of recent years Palestine has been the scene of an unparalleled activity in archaeological investigation, and the results throw light in particular upon the Books of Joshua and Judges. The Bible text contains, as all know, perplexing discrepancies. None the less, the historic sites and walled cities which the writer had the privilege of visiting repeatedly while excavation was in progress, during the seven years that he directed the British School of Archaeology in Jerusalem and the Department of Antiquities in Palestine, impressed him deeply with a sense of material reality underlying the historical narrative. The impression, however, eluded definition, until at last he decided to examine separately the archaeology of those passages which are now generally recognized by scholars as the oldest elements. The result was so full of promise that he returned to Palestine in 1928 to examine the problem further in this light. Every identified site mentioned in the oldest sources J, E, and JE of the Books of Joshua and Judges was revisited; while three selected cities, Jericho, Ai, and Hazor, were examined more thoroughly with the spade. The impression now became positive. *No radical flaw was found at all in the topography and archaeology of these docu-*

ments.''[41] Furthermore, in the light of his thorough investigations, Garstang concludes "that not only were these records in general founded upon fact, *but they must have been derived from earlier writings, almost contemporary with the events described, so detailed and reliable is their information.''*[42] In complete agreement with that statement is the following conclusion reached by Duncan: "When the writer of Numbers or of Joshua refers to the 'Book of the Wars of the Lord' or the 'Book of Jashar' as *documents from which he has drawn information, there is no strain on our credulity if we accept these documents as records kept at the time of the events.''*[43]

Now over against these claims of possible contemporary records for this period, and with the critical analysis of the Pentateuch (or Hexateuch) in view, the theory of the origin of Joshua may be stated as follows: "Early narratives (J, E) written perhaps in the ninth and eighth centuries B.C. respectively, carried down the history of God's guidance of his people to the point at which it culminated in the settlement of the people in the land that God has promised them; a later work (P), written about 500 B.C., carried down the history to the same point.''[44] Furthermore, regarding the sources of J and E, there is little modification in critical opinion, viz.: "The early material utilized by J and E was *probably in the main oral tradition of indefinite antiquity,* though there exist some few indications of the employment of older written sources.''[45] It now appears, however, in the light of Garstang's investigations whereby J and E are adjudged almost contemporary documents of the events they describe, that little or no room is made for "oral tradition of indefinite antiquity," but that we are handling accurate chronicles of current history. This, of course, is a matter of tremendous importance and lies at the basis of

160

FRAGMENT OF A BAKED CLAY TABLET INSCRIBED WITH THE BABYLONIAN
ACCOUNT OF THE DELUGE. WRITTEN IN THE BEAUTIFUL CHARACTERS OF
THE EARLY CUNEIFORM. THE DISCOVERY OF THE FLOOD TABLETS AT
NINEVEH AND NIPPUR CREATED A SENSATION IN BIBLICAL AND SCIENTIFIC
CIRCLES.   TO THESE WRITTEN ACCOUNTS IS NOW BEING ADDED THE
FACTUAL EVIDENCE OF THE HISTORICAL DELUGE.

A PORTION OF THE CREATION TABLET SETTING FORTH THE EARLY MESOPOTAMIAN ACCOUNT OF THE BEGINNING OF THE WORLD. AT PRESENT WE HAVE IN OUR POSSESSION SEVERAL NARRATIVES OF CREATION CURRENT AMONG ANCIENT PEOPLES.

THE DOG RIVER INSCRIPTIONS, EXPOSED TO THE ELEMENTS THROUGH MANY CENTURIES AND DEFACED BY HUMAN HANDS, PROVIDE LITTLE INFORMATION. HERE, AGAIN, EGYPTIAN AND ASSYRIAN JOIN IN THE PROCESSION OF THE NATIONS. THE PORTRAIT IS PROBABLY THAT OF SHALMANESER III, WHO FOUGHT AGAINST AHAB AND CONFEDERATES AT KARKAR AND RECEIVED TRIBUTE FROM JEHU.

widespread reaction against the old views, particularly with regard to the low dates at which they are said to have been produced.

Here, again, the results of recent archaeological investigation have compelled restatement of critical opinion, re-evaluation, and, most of all, reorientation to the age which witnessed the birth of these historical narratives. The testimony of epigraphic remains, contemporary with the era of Joshua and the Elders, is both cumulative and convincing. Indeed, it is now possible to reconstruct the genealogy of ancient Hebrew writings from the period of the final destruction of Jerusalem in 586 B.C. back to the period of Moses and even beyond. This claim may be briefly illustrated as follows: The later epochs in the Bible story, particularly the later monarchy and the period of the great prophets whose messages were sharply directed against the incursions of Israel's great enemies on the north and on the south,—these have for some time been set in sharp relief by epigraphic remains of capital importance. The *Moabite Stone,* for example, discovered by Klein, in 1868, is contemporary with Ahab of the House of Omri and supplements at many points the relations subsisting between Israel and the Moabites about 850 B.C. This recital of Mesha, written in a script very similar to the old Hebrew, reads like a chapter from 2 Kings. Again, the *Samaria Ostraka,* recovered from the wine cellar of Ahab's ivory palace at Samaria, are so suggestive of historical conditions then obtaining that Jack has been able to reconstruct the political and geographic conditions of the Northern Kingdom.[46] The *Siloam Inscription* provides us not only with a fine specimen of Hebrew writing of the eighth century B.C., but also describes the completion of the defensive measure undertaken by Hezekiah in the face of the Assyrian invasion by Sennacherib about 701 B.C. Finally, out of

161

this same period of the Monarchy are the far-reaching
recoveries of the Starkey excavations at Tell ed-Duweir,
the ancient Lachish, which provide us not only with
some details concerning the period of the Monarchy,
but place in our hands an archaic Canaanite script which
Starkey himself would assign to the early thirteenth
century, while Professor Langdon puts it in the fifteenth century B.C.[47] To these early epigraphic remains
reflecting the genealogy of Hebrew script we may add
the *Gebal Inscriptions* of Akhiram which refer to the
period of the Judges in Israel, and the epochal inscriptions of *Serabit el-Khadim* in the Peninsula of Sinai,
whose discovery by Petrie in 1905 threw the proto-
Hebrew and proto-Phoenician script and alphabet almost eight hundred years beyond even the most
sanguine views of conservative scholars. These evidences, of course, relate only to the genealogy of the
Hebrew writings and not to the additional epigraphic
material in other languages in the same period, including both the hieroglyphic and the cuneiform (syllabic
and alphabetic). Certainly the case is proved not only
regarding the possibility of early Hebrew records such
as these, but also their probability. "Anyone who in
future suggests that the Israelites ever lacked facilities for literary expression, will be betraying his un-
acquaintance with modern discoveries of the first
importance. All the theories of oral transmission, either
of the whole, or of part, of the earlier books of the Old
Testament, have of course ceased to be of account. Reference has also been made to archaeological evidence
which suggests that events were recorded in writing
about the time of their occurrence."[48]

CHAPTER TEN

OLD TESTAMENT CHRONOLOGY

OLD TESTAMENT CHRONOLOGY

BEFORE we proceed further in our investigation of the great eras and events of Israel's history as they now appear in the context of archaeological discoveries, it is important that we determine, as far as possible, the *Chronological* setting of these eras and events both with reference to Israel's internal developments and her association with contemporary nations. It is readily agreed that this is an extremely difficult subject and that, generally regarded, there is no uniformity of opinion among Old Testament scholars with reference to any specific chronological framework in which all the events of Hebrew history can be definitely fixed. This fact should occasion no surprise, however, for hitherto Old Testament students simply have not had at hand a body of historical information which would compel uniformity. Theory and supposition played a vital role both in the evaluation of certain events and in the determination of certain epochs. Of course, one could always generalize or, as in the case of Archbishop Ussher, proceeding on the basis of specific years stated in the early narratives of the Old Testament, arrive at conclusions of relatively concordant dates, and it is remarkable that, regarded from the standpoint of subsequent discoveries, in some particulars he was marvelously successful. But the modern student of the Scriptures is in a far better position than Ussher ever was, richer in information regarding Hebrew developments, and possessed of a multitude of ascertained facts of which his predecessor never dreamed. Even so, present-day students have not solved all the problems of the Old Testament; nor have they reached uniformity of opinion on a score of vital questions which remain to be answered. That progress is being made, no one will deny; indeed, relatively speaking, there is more agreement among critics today than at any previous period, and the historical narratives of the Old Testament occupy a far higher position in critical opinion because of their established credibility. This change in evaluation, of course, is the result of recent archaeological discoveries which are compelling a new approach to the Scripture records and a truer appraisal of their accuracy. In the field of Old Testament chronology, this tendency is particularly in evidence, with the result that great events and epochs in Old Testament history now stand out prominently and fairly well defined as to their exact dates.

That we cannot be more specific regarding these outstanding events and less conspicuous happenings in Hebrew history, is no fault of the Old Testament writers; they were not attempting any exhaustive history either of their own nation nor the course of events among neighboring peoples. Their purpose was purely religious, not political. In the accomplishment of that purpose they centered all events on the progressively unfolding plan of redemption in which full historical detail was not a requisite but purely incidental. They recorded those facts which set in sharper relief the gradual realization of the Messianic mission of Israel. Furthermore, it will not do to quarrel with Hebrew historians that they were not more explicit in those historical notations that they do give; they simply did not have the chronological helps which are so freely at the disposal of modern writers. The Egyptians, probably more precise in their chronology than other ancient peoples, never attained the exactness in historical data required by modern scholarship. Early Babylonians and Assyrians made some strides along the line of definite historical reference, but never attained precision. It is true that the Greek and Roman systems, based on dates assigned to the inauguration of the Olympic games and the founding of Rome respectively, offer some advance in definiteness, but every student of ancient history knows how much is still desired. But, as we now know, the Hebrews were not entirely deficient in this requirement of accurate historical reference. Although he did not definitely set his history into the framework of contemporary life among the nations, the Hebrew historian had accurate understanding of internal developments in their relation to one another, and this understanding is reflected continually in the records. He certainly had a religious calendar based on lunar changes, and a civil calendar based on the solar year together with recognized divisions of the day, weeks, and months. It is also probable that the reference in 1 Kings 6:1 indicates the acceptance of the Exodus as marking the year One of Hebrew national history, and that reference was made to it in a manner similar to the custom of the American people in dating state documents in the year of American Independence.[1] At any rate, it is reasonable to assume that the Hebrews had some idea about the periods of their history and that the references which are made may be accepted as approximately correct. This assumption is specially urged in connection with the eras and events falling within the framework of Babylonian and Assyrian chronology, and from these we may deduce approximate dates for those eras stretching from Solomon to Moses, and from Moses to Abraham. Now, in view of the fact that the most difficult problems of Old Testament chronology

167

appear in the middle phases of Hebrew history—i.e., the period immediately preceding the founding of the early monarchy—the establishment of an exact date in this epoch would provide a point from which we could work back with confidence to the beginning of Hebrew history, on the one hand, and to its culmination in the Exiles and Restoration, on the other.

1. *The Battle of Karkar*, 854-3 B.C.

From the standpoint of Biblical chronology, the discovery of the Monolith of Shalmaneser may be regarded as among the most important contributions made by archaeology.[2] Though not within itself a biblical monument, the Monolith is so tied in with biblical events as to provide us with the one certain date in Old Testament history from which we may work with relative confidence in determining other dates. Erected by Shalmaneser to commemorate the outstanding military achievements of the first four and one-half years of his long reign, this monument gives us political and social data of incalculable value. Furthermore, if the Monolith be studied in connection with the Black Obelisk of the same king and the Bronze Gates of Balawat, we will derive geographical and historical information of unsurpassed importance.

The particular section of the inscription in which we are now interested is the following:

> "Karkar, his royal city I destroyed, I devastated, I burned with fire. 1200 chariots, 1200 cavalry, 20,000 soldiers of Hadad-ezer of Damascus . . . 2000 chariots, 10,000 soldiers of Ahab the Israelite . . . thousands of soldiers of Baasa son of Ruhubi the Ammonite . . . (the twelve kings he brought to his support) I defeated."[3]

168

As indicated, the Battle of Karkar was fought in the environs of Karkar on the middle Orontes between Hamath and Aleppo. The date of this crucial struggle, though involved, is determined on the basis of the Assyrian Canon which contains a chronological list of civil officers designated as *limmi* or eponyms.[4] "Lists of eponyms drawn up in their chronological order were carefully kept, as well as other lists in which notice was taken of the principal events occurring during their time of office. Fragmentary copies of these lists have been preserved, thus enabling us to restore the chronology of the Assyrian Empire during the most important period of its existence. The copies were first brought to light by Sir Henry Rawlinson, who gave them the name of the Assyrian Canon, and pointed out their character and bearing on the vexed questions of chronology."[5] "These lists of eponyms can be compared with a list of the Babylonian, Assyrian, and Persian rulers of Babylon which is given by the Greek geographer Ptolemaeus. His record tells how many years each king reigned; it also records eclipses which occurred under the various kings, and the exact dates of these eclipses can be determined astronomically. Thus an exact chronology of late Assyrian history is made possible."[6] In addition to the Assyrian Canon we are also in possession of a different version containing eponym titles and principal events which distinguished their terms of office. We may call this latter version the Assyrian Chronicle.[7] The Canon extends from 909 B.C. to 647 B.C., while the Chronicle includes the period 858 B.C. to 704 B.C., the two thus being concurrent for about 154 years. It is to the Chronicle that we are indebted for the notation that during the eponym year of Isid-Raki's-rabe of Gozan, and in the month Sivan, the sun was eclipsed. On astronomical grounds this particular eclipse, which was

169

visible at Nineveh on June 15, can be definitely determined as having occurred in 763 B.C. By a strange coincidence, Shalmaneser III, on his accession to the throne, was also designated Eponym during his first year and again in the thirtieth year of his reign. Calculating then from the fixed eponymy of 763 B.C., Shalmaneser III began to reign in 859-8 B.C., the thirtieth year of his rule falling thus in 829-8 B.C. Now the crucial Battle of Karkar is definitely stated on the Monolith of Shalmaneser as having occurred in the Eponym year of Dan-Assur (i.e., 854-3 B.C.),[8] to which may be added also the corroborative passage which places the battle in the sixth year of his (Shalmaneser's) reign.[9] Now, as already stated, the Battle of Karkar is not mentioned in the Bible, but the Monolith inscription includes a prominent biblical character, Ahab of Israel, as a member of the defeated coalition opposing Shalmaneser. On the other hand, the narratives in 1 Kings describe two other engagements which obviously occurred about the same time—i.e., Ahab's victory over Benhadad of Syria,[10] and Ahab's death at the hands of the Syrians at the battle of Ramoth-gilead.[11] The Battle of Karkar comes between these two engagements. Ahab's death must have occurred in the early part of 852 B.C., a date which would allow for the reigns of Ahaziah and Jehoram and for the accession of Jehu together with his tribute as described on the Black Obelisk. This latter event took place in the eighteenth year of Shalmaneser, 841-0 B.C., which was probably the first year of Jehu. Accordingly, on the basis of the Monolith and Black Obelisk of Shalmaneser, both monuments being supplemented by the Assyrian Canon and Chronicle, and by the historical narratives of the Old Testament which set forth the reigns of the kings of Judah and of Israel, we are able to determine rather accurately a chronological framework for these kings during the period from 931 B.C. to 841 B.C.:

JUDAH	YEARS	B.C.	ISRAEL	YEARS	B.C.
Rehoboam	17	931-914	Jeroboam I	22	931-910
Ahijah	3	914-911	Nadab	2	910-909
Asa	41	911-870	Baasha	24	909-886
Jehoshaphat	25	870-849	Elah	2	886-885
Jehoram	8	849-841	Zimri	7 (days)	885
Ahaziah	1	841	Omri	12	885-874
			Ahab	22	874-852
			Ahaziah	2	852-851
			Jehoram	12	851-841
			Jehu	28	841

It will be observed that, beginning with the Division of the Kingdom in 931 B.C., the two lines of kings run along rather closely for about 90 years and that they coincided in 841 B.C., a date which is supported by both the Hebrew and the Assyrian records. Furthermore, the Hebrew accounts for this specific period 931 B.C. to 841 B.C., may be regarded in great part as contemporary annals and therefore entirely trustworthy.[12] The apparent discrepancy in which the sum of years attributed to the various kings—Judah 94 years and Israel 98—is not serious and, in the light of overlapping reigns through a considerable period, may be readily resolved. It should be remembered, also, that in the case of the Northern Kingdom the throne was not as steady as in the Southern Kingdom, and that there were repeated upheavals. In the Southern Kingdom affairs were on a more even keel and, with fewer rulers, the reigning periods could be more accurately stated. On this basis, accordingly, and attributing to Solomon the generally accepted period of 40 years, the death of David and the accession of Solomon may be placed with great confidence at 970 B.C. Adopting this date, we are therefore provided with a pivotal point for estimating the period between Solomon and Moses.

2. *From the Construction of Solomon's Temple to the Exodus*

The Temple program inaugurated by David and carried out by Solomon was one of the high points in Hebrew religious history. It made a tremendous appeal to all the tribes of Israel. For four centuries the Tabernacle, which was the meeting place of Jehovah with his people, had been located at various places, Gilgal, Shiloh, probably Gibeon, and at Jerusalem. It was a portable construction, capable of being removed with ease, as during the Wilderness experiences. But it was not regarded as a permanent place for the worship of God. On this account Solomon probably regarded the building project as the most important undertaking confronting him at his succession and proceeded to accomplish it without delay. Every student is familiar with the almost limitless detail concerning this Temple, its actual construction, its ritual, its priesthood, and its system of sacrifice. From a religious and political point of view, the completion of the Temple marked the unification of Israel, a movement which had been in progress since the conquest and settlement in Canaan. The determination of the date of this outstanding event, therefore, was a matter of extreme importance not only for that particular generation, but for those who would come later. And, it is interesting to observe that the Hebrew historian, not having before him the relatively fixed dates in Israel's subsequent history, was compelled to fix the Temple project in the light of Israel's previous history, and that he chose for its determination the most important event in

172

Hebrew life, the Exodus of Israel from Egypt. According to the statement in 1 Kings 6:1: "And it came to pass in the four hundred and eightieth year after the children of Israel were come out of the land of Egypt, in the fourth year of Solomon's reign over Israel, in the month Ziv, which is the second month, that he began to build the house of the Lord." That is a very definite statement. We will not hold it in suspicion on the ground that it is merely an approximation, or that, expressed in multiples of 40, it is only a general reference, and that it has no real value as a definite or fixed date. No scholar has ever found any objection to this passage on textual or critical ground; it is not an insertion by a later scribe, but the specific statement of the original historian.

On the basis then of Hebrew contemporary historical narratives, supplemented by the Assyrian monuments, Solomon began his reign in 970 B.C. The building program which, according to 1 Kings 6:1, was inaugurated in the fourth year of his reign, can be definitely fixed at 966 B.C. in the month of May (Ziv). But no such exactness was at the disposal of the Hebrew historian when referring to this significant event in the life of Israel. It is reasonable to suppose, however, that if there was any event in the history of Israel up to that point whose date was known and permanently preserved, he would have made use of it. The greatest event in the life of Israel was the Exodus from the land of Egypt; practically all the prophets of the Old Testament revert to it in one form or another. It was not only securely fixed in the thought of the people, but, according to the clear statement in 1 Kings 6:1, its chronological setting was accurately defined and subsequently employed as a recognized point in Hebrew historical reference. The explicit statement that 480 years had intervened between the Exodus and the fourth year of Solomon's reign, when the Temple program was inaugurated, must therefore be accepted at its face value and with utmost confidence. On critical grounds there is no justifiable reason for rejecting or even questioning its trustworthiness and accuracy. Accordingly, if we may accept it as a credible statement, then the date of the Exodus is also accurately fixed—i.e., the month of Abiv, 1446 B.C.[13] It will be observed that between these two fixed dates, 966 B.C. and 1446 B.C., there must come four years of Solomon's reign, the whole of the reign of David, of Saul, the long period of the Judges, the rule of the Elders after Joshua, the period of conquest and settlement under Joshua, the overrunning of Transjordan, the forty years at Kadesh-barnea, and the sojourn at Mt. Sinai, but it will be found that the 480-year period thus specified is in substantial agreement with the total number of years required for these various events and careers.[14]

3. *From the Exodus to Abraham*

Accepting 1446 B.C. as the date of the Exodus from Egypt, we may proceed on biblical chronological statements to a series of outstanding persons and events leading back to the phenomenal career of Abraham and his departure from Ur of the Chaldees. This we propose to do. There is no particular reason why these biblical narratives should be eyed with suspicion nor that any of their data bearing on assumed dates and periods should be discounted. It should be remembered that this is their history and that the Hebrews certainly knew and recorded the principal points in their national development. Furthermore, if the persons and events therein recorded appear within a chronological framework of concordant dates and are consistent, then we are under further obligation to accept them without prejudice.

174

The procedure is relatively simple. At the time of the Exodus, Moses was eighty years of age. His birth can be reckoned, then, at approximately 1526 B.C., his death forty years after the Exodus, at 1406 B.C.[15] Again, dating the Exodus at 1446 B.C., the Hebrew people had been in sojourn and bondage in Egypt for 430 years, this particular period being reckoned for the descent of Jacob into Egypt with his sons. Jacob's descent and the beginning of Egyptian sojourn occurred therefore in 1876 B.C.[16] On the basis of the same reckoning Joseph, who was thirty-seven years of age when Jacob descended, was born in 1913 B.C., his death occurring when he was 110, 1803 B.C.[17] Jacob was one hundred thirty years of age when he arrived in Egypt.[18] His birth was therefore in 2006 B.C. Jacob lived in Egypt seventeen years, his death occurring in 1859 B.C.[19] At the time of Jacob's birth in 2006 B.C., his father Isaac was sixty years of age.[20] Isaac's birth was accordingly in 2066 B.C. According to the definite statement in Genesis 21:5, Abraham was one hundred years old when Isaac was born thus determining the date of Abraham's birth in 2166 B.C. Abraham was seventy-five years of age when he left Haran for the journey to Canaan,[21] which makes that event to have fallen about 2090 B.C., with the departure from Ur of the Chaldees probably in 2116 B.C. The fact that we have no Assyrian Canon or Chronicle to corroborate all these dates in the Mosaic and Patriarchal Eras should not be used as an argument against their accuracy, for, as we shall see, they are consistent from a biblical point of view, and also are in accord with known phases of Babylonian and Egyptian history.[22]

4. *From the Battle of Karkar to the Restoration*

Now the acceptance of the Battle of Karkar 854-3 B.C. as a pivotal date for Hebrew history will enable us to work with confidence to the outstanding persons and events appearing in the later phases of the national life, including the Restoration of the Southern Kingdom. Happily, for this period we are in possession not only of the copious historical narratives of the Old Testament, but of contemporary data from the Assyrian, Babylonian, and Persian records. It is reasonable to assume that dates determined in the light of these contemporary documents should have great credibility and that they should be readily accepted.

The period stretching from the Battle of Karkar to the Fall of Samaria includes a total of 132 years— a relatively short period—but for these years on the basis of Assyrian annals we have four fixed dates: *Battle of Karkar* 854-3 B.C., *Tribute of Jehu* 841-0 B.C., *Tribute of Menahem* 739-8 B.C., and the *Fall of Samaria* 722-1 B.C. From the standpoint of Hebrew historical development each of these dates is of great importance, not only in determining specific events, but also in reconstructing the general framework in which all events can be harmoniously related. As for example: The Battle of Ramoth-gilead, at which Ahab was killed, must be placed immediately after the Battle of Karkar to allow for the reign of Ahaziah (2 years) and the reign of Jehoram (12 years) to the accession of Jehu 841-0 B.C. On this basis, counting the two reigns as approximately two and twelve years, respectively, they fall within the period demanded by the Black Obelisk of Shalmaneser, which fixes the Tribute of Jehu in the eighteenth year of Shalmaneser's reign— i.e., 859-8-18=841-0 B.C. This latter date may accordingly be regarded as correct for the accession of Jehu and, likewise, for the beginning of the reign of Ahaziah over Judah.

For the century immediately following the accession of Jehu and Ahaziah—i.e., 841-741 B.C., we have no

THE FORTUNATE DISCOVERY OF THIS BROKEN TABLET MADE A GREAT CONTRIBUTION TO THE PAGE OF OLD TESTAMENT CHRONOLOGY. THE BABYLONIAN CHRONICLE No. 21,901 DEFINITELY FIXES THE DATE OF THE DESTRUCTION OF NINEVEH AT 612 B.C.

THE MARVELOUS TAYLOR PRISM. BAKED CLAY CYLINDER OF SENNACHERIB. THE CUNEIFORM TEXT REFERS TO EIGHT OF HIS MILITARY CAMPAIGNS AND DESCRIBES THE CONQUEST OF THE BABYLONIANS, MEDES, KASSITES, AND ELAMITES. THIS RECORD ALSO SETS FORTH THE SIEGE OF JERUSALEM WHICH TOOK PLACE IN SENNACHERIB'S THIRD CAMPAIGN IN 701 B.C.

ONE OF THE GREAT ACHIEVE-
MENTS OF ARCHAEOLOGY HAS
BEEN THE REDISCOVERY OF
THE HITTITES. IN 1906-1907
WINCKLER DISCOVERED AT
BOGHAZ-KOI, IN ASIA MINOR,
THE ARCHIVES OF THESE
MYSTERIOUS PEOPLE.
THROUGH THE DECIPHER-
MENT OF THEIR RECORDS THE
FULL STORY OF THE HITTITE
IS BEING UNFOLDED. THIS
IS AN INSCRIBED PORTION OF
A STONE DOORWAY FOUND AT
CARCHEMISH.

direct help from Assyrian or other contemporary records. The absence of such records does not appear as very serious, however, for the historical records of the Old Testament dealing with this period are rather complete with details regarding kings both of the Southern and Northern Kingdoms and their relations to one another. On the basis of these narratives, the following reigns may be set forth as highly satisfactory:

SOUTHERN KINGDOM	NORTHERN KINGDOM
Ahaziah .....841-840 B.C.	Jehu ....841-813 B.C.
Athaliah .....840-834 B.C.	Jehoahaz ....813-796 B.C.
Jehoash .....834-794 B.C.	Joash ....796-780 B.C.
Amaziah .....794-765 B.C.	Jeroboam II..780-747 B.C.

Now it will be observed that in connection with the reigns of the kings mentioned, both of the Southern and Northern Kingdoms, we have allowed the number of years claimed for each by the historical narratives of 2 Kings and 2 Chronicles (the latter being a later composition and frequently supplying additional information). There is no ground for rejecting these specific statements as to the duration of reigns in both Judah and Samaria, nor their relations to each other, particularly when they are found to be in substantial agreement. On the other hand, for the succession of kings after Amaziah of Judah, and also after Jeroboam II of Samaria, no such precision is possible. These latter rulers appear in a framework of overlapping reigns and successions that seem almost insoluble on the basis of information now in hand. Strangely enough, however, it is for this very period that the Assyrian and other contemporary records begin to mention the political developments of the Hebrew Kingdoms and thus offer some help in approximately dating these rulers down to the close of the eighth century. Before we attempt to harmonize the reigns of the rulers of both kingdoms appearing in this period—i.e., 739-700 B.C., we must consider the limitations which seem to be required by the testimony of the Assyrian records. The statement of the problem will probably be simplified if we begin with the latter phase of the period, where we are on comparatively firm ground, and then work back to the beginning.

Proceeding on this basis, the *Fall of Samaria* in 722-1 B.C., a fixed date, becomes the pivotal point. This great event is determined for us by the Khorsabad Inscription of Sargon II, 722-705 B.C., which definitely places it in the first year of his reign.[23] Now the siege of Samaria, according to the biblical narrative, began in the fourth year of Hezekiah and, after a duration of three years, fell in his sixth year. This statement offers no real difficulty, assuming that it began in the beginning of the fourth and closed at the end of the sixth, a full three-year period. In any event the reign of Hezekiah cannot be reckoned earlier than 729 B.C., nor later than 728 B.C., the proper designation being 729-8 B.C. If we grant him the full twenty-nine years specified in the biblical record (2 Kings 18:2), the close of his reign would then fall in 799-8 B.C., a satisfactory date.

Furthermore, in this connection three perennial problems of Hezekiah's reign might appear in a more harmonious relation. *First,* the Cylinder of Sargon II, recovered from the Royal Library of Ashurbanipal at Nineveh, recounts the first of these invasions of Southern Palestine when Sargon assaulted and conquered Ashdod and Gath, the ancient cities of the Philistines, which had appealed to neighboring states, including Judah, for help in throwing off the Assyrian yoke. Apparently the appeal to Hezekiah to join in the rebellion was instantly rejected, nor is there any evidence that Sargon attacked Judah during this campaign. That such an incursion into Southern Palestine was

178

made is plainly stated in Isaiah 20:6 where Sargon, Ashdod, and Tartan (Sargon's governor-general) are all mentioned in the same passage. This invasion, whose date is definitely fixed at 711 B.C., did not involve any siege of Jerusalem and is not the same incident as that so fully described in 2 Kings 18:13-19:37. Now in view of this seeming contradiction, the disposition has always been to reject the biblical statement completely and to count it as a poor calculation on the part of the Hebrew historian. But before we throw aside this reference to Hezekiah as an obvious error in computation, let us examine the incident in the light of the Assyrian records themselves. It is clear, of course, that any assumed invasion of Judah in the year *714* B.C., for which there is no confirmation either from Assyrian or Hebrew sources, must have occurred under Sargon II, 722-705 B.C., and not under Sennacherib, who did not succeed to the throne until after the assassination of Sargon II in 705 B.C. There were accordingly two separate invasions occurring at different times and under different kings.

Secondly, it is extremely interesting to note that the *Display Inscription* of Sargon throws the search-light on one of the Babylonian kings, Merodach-baladan, 720-710 B.C., a contemporary of Hezekiah, who, after the recovery of Hezekiah, sent letters and a present to Hezekiah, perhaps in an attempt to involve Judah in a revolt against Sargon.[24] Now if we assume that the death of Hezekiah occurred about 699/8 B.C. (on no account could it have been far removed from this date), and accepting the record of his illness and the addition of fifteen years to his life, his sickness would have occurred approximately 715 or 714 B.C. That it occurred before Sennacherib's siege of Jerusalem in 701 B.C., may be implied in Isaiah 38:5-6. In any event, allowing the credibility of the Merodach-baladan reference and reign in 721-710 B.C., the sickness of Hezekiah cannot be placed *after* 710 B.C. when Merodach-baladan was deposed. Of course, it is possible that the Babylonian monarch regained his throne after the death of Sargon in 705 B.C., and that the overtures to Hezekiah were made in the early part of Sennacherib's reign, but that is hardly probable.

And, *finally*, the unsuccessful siege of Jerusalem begun by Sennacherib in the third year of his reign, together with the overrunning of forty-six other cities of Judah and the assault on Lachish, is recounted on the Taylor Prism which fixes the date at 701 B.C. The parallel passages in 2 Kings 18:13f and in 2 Kings 19:1-37 may be taken in corroboration of the Assyrian records, but the biblical narrative specifically refers the event to the fourteenth year of Hezekiah, a statement which cannot be harmonized with the Assyrian date if the fourteenth year of Hezekiah be reckoned from 729/8, or 729/8–14=715 B.C. or 714 B.C., for the latter date falls not within the period of Sennacherib but during the reign of his predecessor, Sargon II, 722-705 B.C. We may be certain that the biblical historian knew the difference between Sargon's invasion of Judah and Sennacherib's threat to Jerusalem. If, then, this is a correct assumption, the reference in 2 Kings 18:13 to the fourteenth year of Hezekiah's reign may refer to 700/1 B.C., which would be the fourteenth year of his recovery, his additional reign. This would be in strict conformity with the biblical records and also in agreement with the Taylor Prism of Sennacherib, which requires 701 B.C. for the great invasion of Judah and the siege of Jerusalem described in 2 Kings 18:13 to 19:37. The reign of Hezekiah, then, may be reckoned from 729/8 to 699/8 B.C., a total of twenty-nine years.

Proceeding on the basis of this relatively assured date for Hezekiah, Ahaz, his predecessor and father, died in 729 B.C. From the Assyrian monuments we know that Ahaz was living in 734 B.C. The general period is therefore in accord with the Assyrian records of Tiglath-pileser, 745-727 B.C., and also with the biblical narratives in 2 Kings 16:5-10. Granting sixteen years for his reign, Ahaz was king during the period 744-729 B.C.

In the line of Judah's kings, Ahaz succeeded his father Jotham. For Jotham's reign sixteen years are required—i.e., 760-744 B.C. It is clearly stated in 2 Kings 15:5, however, that Jotham was co-regent with his father Uzziah (Azariah), though the number of years of his co-regency is not specified. And, strangely enough, it is just here in connection with the fifty-two years of Uzziah that we have our most involved problem. Even if we counted all of Jotham's reign as a co-regency—i.e., from 760-744 B.C., about sixteen years, Uzziah's rule must go beyond Jotham's death and into the reign of Ahaz. In any event Uzziah would have to begin his reign about 785 B.C.—i.e., near to the beginning of Amaziah's reign, 795/4 B.C. We know from 2 Kings 19:19 that a conspiracy was made against Amaziah and that Uzziah reigned in his stead, but there are no details regarding the time of the conspiracy nor the crowning of Uzziah. Furthermore, on the basis of 2 Kings 14:17 Amaziah died fifteen years after the death of Joash, 780 B.C.—i.e., in 765 B.C., a date which is apparently correct. Again, there are so many references to the long reign of Azariah, of actual contacts between him and other rulers during that period, that we are not justified in arbitrarily reducing the number of years to a lower figure nor dismissing the fifty-two years as fictitious. Do the Assyrian or other contemporary records offer any assistance in this problem?

In the Assyrian annals of the great Tiglath-pileser III (Pul), 745-727 B.C., there are three dates definitely fixed. The first of these, 738 B.C., marks the year in which Menahem of Israel paid tribute unto Tiglath-pileser together with Rezin of Syria and other kings of the westlands.[25] It is held by Luckenbill and Hall that Azariah of Judah was also among these rulers bringing tribute.[26] As we shall see, this possibility is not to be ruled out. The second of the dates fixed on the basis of Tiglath-pileser's annals is the campaign of 734 B.C., when Israel was brought under the yoke of Assyria and when Rezin of Damascus was vanquished. The third date, 733 B.C., marks the year when Pekah of Israel was deposed and Hoshea was established on the throne of the Northern Kingdom. This particular change in Israel is fully corroborated by the record of 2 Kings 15:29-30. Hence, on the basis of these correspondences we can determine the beginning of Hoshea's reign about 733 B.C., or a little later, since his rule terminated with the fall of Samaria in 722-1 B.C., after a duration of nine years—i.e., from 732/1 B.C. This would correspond with the twelfth year of Ahaz as stated in 2 Kings 17:1. On the same basis the reign of Pekah ended in 733 B.C., the duration of which extended through twenty years, according to 2 Kings 15:27. Here, however, we are confronted with an apparently insoluble problem since Pekah's reign is said to have *begun* in Uzziah's fifty-second year. Also on the same biblical reckoning, Pekahiah, the predecessor of Pekah, began his reign in the fiftieth year of Uzziah —i.e., 735 B.C., and reigned for 2 years, 733 B.C.[27] Now on the basis of Uzziah's kingship the reign of Menahem must fall within the thirty-ninth year, together with the one-month rule of Shallum which preceded it. Zechariah's reign would therefore come immediately before Shallum's, or, according to 2 Kings 15:8, in the thirty-eighth year of Uzziah. Expressed in terms of these requirements, the Northern Kingdom rulers appear as follows:

Zechariah, 6 months, 38th year of Uzziah=785–38= 747 B.C.

Shallum, 1 month, 39th year of Uzziah=785–39= 746 B.C.

Menahem, 10 years, 39th year of Uzziah=785–39= 746-735 B.C.

Pekahiah, 2 years, 50th year of Uzziah=785–50= 735-733 B.C.

Pekah, 20 years, 52nd year of Uzziah=785–52= 733 B.C.

Hoshea, 9 years, 733/2/1—722/1 B.C.

The kings of the Southern Kingdom for this parallel period appear as follows:

Amaziah, 794-765 B.C.

Azariah, 785-733 B.C.

Jotham, 760-744 B.C.

Ahaz, 744-728 B.C.

Hezekiah, 728-698 B.C.

After the death of Hezekiah in 698 B.C., seven kings reigned over the Southern Kingdom for a total period of 111 years. The narratives of 2 Kings and 2 Chronicles describing these reigns are rather detailed both as regards the internal affairs of the Jews and their external relations to contemporary nations, particularly the Assyrians, Egyptians, and Babylonians. It is interesting to note, also, that the lengths of the reigns claimed for these several kings can be shown to be correct from biblical reckoning and from contemporary foreign documents. A few isolated events also stand out in clearer relief in the light of the monuments.

The reference in 2 Chronicles 33:11, in which Manasseh is described as being bound with fetters and carried to Babylon, is probably corroborated by inscriptions of Esarhaddon dated in 679 B.C. and 678 B.C., especially the latter, which specifically mentions Manasseh, king of Judah, as among those summoned to appear before Esarhaddon.[28] Significantly, also, Manasseh, king of Judah, is mentioned in the historical annals of the Assyrian Ashurbanipal (668-627 B.C.), as one of his tributaries. This is the same king who is referred to as "the great and noble Osnappar" in Ezra 4:10.

Regarding the most outstanding event of the early sixth century, the destruction of Jerusalem in 586 B.C., the monuments are relatively silent. The records of Nebuchadnezzar, though rather full in many respects, do not feature the fall of Jerusalem together with its tremendous reaction on the Jews. But its story is comprehensively described in the historical narratives of the Old Testament and in the works of Jeremiah, the prophet. The archaeological evidence finds its chief significance in the general illumination of the social and political background, with which it is in full agreement. Similarly, the periods of the Exile and the Restoration, though not fully documented from the Babylonian and Persian points of view, are nevertheless rather well defined and their generally accepted dates may be regarded as correct. On the basis, therefore, of these considerations, the following summary of all the eras discussed in this chapter may be viewed as relatively accurate and satisfactory. Future references to these dates and periods will be based on the results of this particular investigation and summary.[29]

CHAPTER ELEVEN

THE ERA OF THE PATRIARCH ABRAHAM

THE ERA OF THE PATRIARCH ABRAHAM

FROM the Hebrew point of view, Genesis is the book of beginnings. In the early sections we have the exalted narratives regarding the creation of the world, the creation of man, the appearance of sin in human experience, and the age of the great flood. The dignified recital of these events, together with the gradual unfolding of the redemptive purpose, is in full keeping with the Hebrew view of the world and is based on their abiding conviction concerning the sole sovereignty of God and his purposes of salvation. These Hebrew records for the most part fall within a chronological framework considerably later than the great Sumerian and Babylonian tablets recently recovered, but still may be regarded as pre-patriarchal. However, there is no comparison between these records as one passes from the gross darkness of a degraded Mesopotamian idolatry into the emerging radiance of a clear monotheism which held at its center a great purpose of grace for all the families of the earth. Now, in the accomplishment of that purpose, at least from the human standpoint, we are immediately brought face to face with the patriarch Abraham, the man of Ur, who introduces not only his own age but a better age for all mankind.

Regarded from the standpoint of his unparalleled spiritual mission, the Patriarch stands as the most pivotal and strategic man in the course of world history, greater than Egyptian pharaohs, Babylonian or Assyrian monarchs, Alexander the Great, or any other.

It is not incidental nor accidental that the three appellations applied to him were never spoken of any other man, viz., Abraham, the Friend of God; Abraham, the Father of the Hebrew people; and Abraham, the Father of all believers. It is not incidental nor accidental that from this man comes the most rigid conception of monotheism the world has known, nor that the only monotheistic peoples yet to appear in the world course, namely, Hebrews, Mohammedans, and Christians, trace their lineage, either through flesh or faith, to Father Abraham. But who was this man, the lengthened projection of whose shadow was to be at the foundation of the highest civilization and the most exalted views of ethics and morals that the world has yet known? We are asked to believe that he was an imaginary hero, postulated to assure the essential unity of the Hebrew people, a pure creation of unconscious art, a legend, a tradition, and moving about in a world that in its ultimate was but the baseless fabric of a dream! Did such a man as Abraham ever live? Can we possibly recover anything of his environment, his world, or recapture the spirit of the time in which he lived, and moved, and had his being?

One of the fascinating experiences of a traveler in the Near East is the phenomenal passage from the green of a refreshing oasis into the barrenness of scorched and sterile sands; or, after a difficult journey through the great and terrible wilderness east of the Dead Sea, to arrive in the upland pastures of Moab, to view the Land of Promise big with hope and assurance of peace. The same kind of an experience will come to the serious and sensitive student of the Old Testament when he is ushered from the difficult narratives of Creation, Eden, Flood, and complicated genealogies, into the presence of an imposing character who gathers up into himself the numerous strands of redemptive history from which he is inseparable. At any rate, with Abram, the man of Ur, we suddenly realize that the narratives become intensely personal, significantly characterized by details and conditions in contemporary life which could never have been manufactured nor even suspected by a writer fifteen hundred years removed from the Patriarch and his world. Now, quite positively and directly, are these statements about Abraham true?

For many years we have been desperately hanging to royal robes of the great Hammurabi of Babylon to secure fully the age of Abraham. In the king list of Genesis, chapter 14, Chedorlaomer, Amraphel, Arioch of Ellasar, and Tidal, king of the Goiim, appear. Opposed by the five Amorite sovereigns in the Vale of Siddim, in the region of the Dead Sea, the Mesopotamian coalition wins a complete victory which included not only the chastisement of the revolting cities of the Jordan area, but also the capture of Lot, the nephew of Abraham. When *Abram the Hebrew* was informed of the fate of his kinsman, he went out from the Plain of Mamre (Hebron) with his Amorite confederates to overtake the Mesopotamian rulers at Hormah, northwest of Damascus. Here he defeated them in a surprise attack, rescued Lot and his possessions, and returned by way of Salem (Jerusalem) where he offered spoils of battle as a tithe to Melchizedek, priest of God Most High.[1] It was obvious, of course, that in this account there was a most attractive field for firsthand investigation. Who were these Mesopotamian rulers among whom Abraham was placed not only as contemporary but actually as conqueror? The deciphering of the Spartoli Tablet offered to some the long-desired data, and by a series of ingenious deductions found not only Chedorlaomer in Kudur-lagumal, Arioch in Eri-aku of Larsa, and Tidal in Tudhala, leader of the mercenary

189

troops, but found them as contemporaries.² It is clear also that the leadership of the Mesopotamian coalition vested in Chedorlaomer, king of Elam, is in strict consonance with all that we know of political conditions immediately preceding the revolt of Hammurabi and the establishment of early Babylonian supremacy in the Tigris-Euphrates region. It is true that not all scholars are agreed in equating Amraphel with Hammurabi, but the preponderance of critical opinion does. At any rate it is unquestionable that it was the purpose of the biblical writer to make Abraham contemporary with Hammurabi. The generally accepted date for the great Babylonian lawgiver, 2123-2081 B.C., may be accepted on the scriptural account as the exact period for Abraham.³

Now, concerning this remarkable man we have several items of information to which we attach great importance. Abraham is the first person in the Old Testament to be called a Hebrew, but there is no reason to dissociate him from *Eber*, the sixth in the line of patriarchs, from whom it is generally thought the Hebrews derive. It is of course known that the name Hebrew is of very early origin. In contemporary secular literature in Southern Babylonia we find mention of a people called *Habiru*, Aramaean nomads who had come in from the surrounding desert, some of whom had enrolled themselves as mercenaries in the Sumerian army. "Now the name 'Habiru' is the same as 'Hebrew'—the philological equivalence is perfect. About this there can be no doubt at all."⁴ Here then is definite evidence. And Professor Burney makes a further point; discussing the Hebrew language, he remarks that there is a distinction in the verbal form between two types of the past tense which is peculiar to Babylonian and Hebrew and is otherwise unknown in Semitic; 'it is reasonable,' he concludes, 'to explain the connection as

190

due to the influence of the older civilization upon the younger at a specially formative period in the history of the latter.' That 'formative period' was surely the youth of the Hebrew people, and the opportunity for Mesopotamian influence to be exerted on its speech was afforded by the residence in southern Mesopotamia of Terah and Abraham and by no other phase in its history. The philological argument—that 'Hebrew' and 'Habiru' are the same word—is in itself almost conclusive; when we find that the history of the Hebrews accords with what we can learn of that of the Habiru, and when the identification of the two alone enables us to account for the peculiarities of the Hebrew language, then we can regard the case as proved.'"[5]

But the evidence for the existence of such a man as Abraham does not hang on the slender thread of correspondence between the two terms Habiru and Hebrew though, as will be seen later, that correspondence has great significance. The point of first consideration here is the perfect agreement of these early records with their own times and conditions. The local coloring that may be seen on the face of these patriarchal narratives is true only of the age out of which they come; at no other period of Hebrew development can they be understood. The references to Abraham's procedure in family difficulties, for example, reflect legal practices which no writer of the fifth and sixth centuries B.C. could possibly have invented or even imagined, but which were strictly in accordance with the patriarchal age. We are referring to the unfortunate conditions existing between Sarah and Hagar, her Egyptian handmaid, who became the mother of Ishmael, Abraham's first-born. It has been customary to deal harshly with Sarah, to picture her as an oversensitive and jealous mistress who was unable to face the result of her own suggestion to Abraham regarding the hope of seed by the Egyptian, and who, in the end, thought of herself as occupying an inferior position with reference to her lord. On the other hand, Abraham himself has also appeared in a rather unfavorable light and has been regarded as complying without protest to the unfair demands of a jealous and vindictive woman. Now, without trying to absolve either Sarah or Abraham of guilt, and recognizing the fact that both should have acted more graciously, in the final count the trouble here is not with Abraham and Sarah, but rather with Hagar. According to Sumerian and Babylonian legal practices, familiar alike to Sarah and Abraham, if a mistress gave one of her slaves to her husband and "she has borne children and afterwards the maid has made herself equal with her mistress, because she has borne children, her mistress shall not sell her for money, she shall put a mark upon her and count her among the maidservants."[6] It is suggestive that, when Sarah complained to Abraham regarding Hagar's deportment, his only reply was, "Thy maid is in thy hand; do to her that which is good in thine eyes."[7] In other words, it was the law under which they had been brought up. Sarah was wholly within her rights from a legal standpoint; as a matter of fact, she might be regarded as showing a certain amount of mercy in *not* reducing Hagar to slavery. On the other hand, there was another turn to this family squabble in which Sarah demanded, "Cast out this handmaid and her son: for the son of this handmaid shall not be heir with my son, even with Isaac."[8] According to the Scripture narrative, this ultimatum was very grievous to Abraham, and it is clear that he would not have acceded had it not been for divine interposition and command. In the first instance, Sarah was properly invoking the law on her side, with Abraham acknowledging her rights and respecting them; but in the second instance

192

IN COMMUNICATIONS BETWEEN THE EAST AND THE WEST, ARMIES USUALLY FOLLOWED THE COAST ROAD ALONG THE EASTERN MEDITERRANEAN. THE FAMOUS PASS AT DOG RIVER SLOWED DOWN THE PROGRESS OF TROOPS AND ARMOR. THE VIEW SHOWS DOG RIVER IN THE FOREGROUND, THE MODERN HIGHWAY, AND THE ANCIENT NARROW PASS IMMEDIATELY ABOVE. ON THE FACE OF THIS MOUNTAIN APPEAR THE INSCRIPTIONS AND THE PORTRAITS.

IN THE DOG RIVER GALLERY OF ANCIENT INSCRIPTIONS AND PORTRAITS, FRIENDS AND FOES STAND SIDE BY SIDE. EGYPT'S RAMESES THE GREAT, 1292-1225 B.C., IS HERE JOINED BY ASSYRIA'S ESARHADDON, 681-668 B.C., WHOSE PORTRAIT IS ON THE LEFT.

THE FAMOUS MOABITE STONE, WHICH WAS DISCOVERED AT DIBON IN 1868. THE INSCRIPTION IS SUPPLEMENTARY AND COMPLEMENTARY TO THE NARRATIVE IN THE BOOK OF KINGS. DATE ASSIGNED TO THIS MONUMENT IS ABOUT 850 B.C.

she was going counter to the same laws which Abraham continued to respect. Through the selective principle and the plan of redemption continuously pursued by the God of all mercy, Sumerian, Babylonian, and tribal practices were put aside according to the purpose of God. "Only in the light of Hammurabi's Code does the conduct of Abraham towards Hagar become intelligible. Taken by itself the story can only prove a callousness and a lack of justice strangely at variance with the high character which piety assigns to the Patriarch. But the case is very different when we regard Abraham not as a free agent but as bound in allegiance to Sumerian law, striving to rule his actions by it; and in every detail of the Old Testament narrative the working of that law is indeed unmistakable. There can be no doubt but that in the nomad tents the life of the Patriarch was guided and controlled by principles which Abraham had brought with him from his home in the civilized East."[9]

Again, the story of Abraham moves forward in a geographical environment perfectly in keeping with conditions now known to have characterized the patriarchal age. No late writer or editor could possibly have invented these places, investing them with local coloring and actually localizing the places in relation to contiguous territory. For example, Shechem, Bethel, Ai, Jerusalem, Hebron, and Beersheba—all of which are among the oldest communities in Palestine—every one of them is now known to have existed long prior to the age of Abraham and to have been in the processes of life during his era. But the appearance of Ai in this list provides us with an item which betrays an early source for these historical records. Though an inhabited center in the age of Abraham, Ai was destroyed by Joshua and the children of Israel in 1400 B.C., and never rebuilt.[10] We are asked to believe that a thousand years after this time a ready scribe in Israel knew not only that a town by the name of Ai had existed but actually knew its location—east of Bethel; and that Abraham pitched his tent between the two cities.[11] But one of the most interesting geographical notices is the case of Ur of the Chaldees, the town from which he migrated.[12]

Eupolemus, an Alexandrian historian, preserves for us an item of historical interest which he attributes to the chronicler Berossus, who flourished in Babylon during the third century B.C., as follows: "In the city of Kamarina of Babylon, which some call the city of Urie (that is, being interpreted, city of the Chaldaeans), there was born in the thirteenth generation (after the Flood) Abraham, who surpassed all in birth and wisdom." It is clear, of course, that the historian made a bad guess when he interpreted *Kamarina* as meaning the city of the Chaldaeans, for it does not mean that at all, but is the Arabic for *moon*. On the other hand, in assigning Kamarina to Babylon he was geographically correct. A literal interpretation of the phrase would be the moon-city in the vicinity of Babylon, or the moon-city of Babylonia, since there was only one. It is of interest to note here that the Hebrew tradition regarding Ur persisted in the biblical narratives in spite of the fact that the city had long ceased to exist, even its location had faded from the memory of man. To say that Abraham came from Ur was just about as definite as saying that he came from Uz. As a consequence, when Christian writers of later centuries felt the necessity of more exact knowledge of the geographical setting of these early narratives in Genesis, to recover, for example, the city of Ur of the Chaldees, nobody had the slightest idea where it was, though it was believed that such a city once existed.

194

In the upland region of Aram-Naharaim, that is, the Aram of the twin rivers, there is a town called Urfa, whose chief distinction lies in the fact that during the Middle Ages it became the capital of the first Christian kingdom. "The similarity between the names Ur and Urfa could not be overlooked by writers whose etymology was of the simplest and most unscientific sort, and actually legend did connect the site with Abraham. Nor was this all; close to Urfa was Haran, so intimately associated with the beginnings of Hebrew history, the place to which Terah went from Ur, at which Abraham and Jacob lived; for an uncritical age nothing more was needed to confirm the identification, and accordingly for many years 'Ur of the Chaldees' was placed on Biblical maps at the spot where Urfa stands today."[13]

But this was an impossible identification, if one cared to respect the biblical references, for Ur was located in the Chaldees beyond the great river Euphrates and, according to Berossus, it was in the region of Babylon. Today, through the accurate work of Taylor, who found cuneiform cylinders of Nabonidus of Babylon commemorating the rebuilding of the Ziggurat of Ur, and through the magnificent recoveries made by Sir Leonard Woolley in connection with the British Museum-University of Pennsylvania Expedition from 1922 to 1934, the student of the Old Testament is shown the actual town where Abraham was born and where he lived for a half-century. The recovery of Ur has completely revolutionized our conceptions of Abraham. He was no Bedouin sheikh camped somewhere along the fringes of the burning Arabian sands, but was an urbanite of first-rate culture who caught somehow the gleam of the upward calling and struck out for the free and open spaces on his trek of faith. In Abraham's day, Ur of the Chaldees was beyond the river, as the biblical statement implies; today the majestic ruins of the Sumerian metropolis lie in the midst of desert sands more than ten miles west of the Euphrates. There is no difficulty involving its identification, however, for air photography shows the ancient river-bed running from Al-Ubeid in the north, past the western wall of Ur, towards the great city of Eridu in the south, thence turning to the great marshes at the head of the Persian Gulf. We cannot go into any description of Abraham's native city except to say that it was a metropolis of approximately 250,000 inhabitants, the chief Babylonian center of moon-god worship, and that its museum of antiquities would have shown a civilization that reached its apex exactly one thousand five hundred years before Abraham was born.[14]

Finally, in addition to the local coloring and geographical accuracy reflected in these patriarchal narratives, one is impressed with the first-hand knowledge of Abraham's neighbors shown by the composer of these records. The great Patriarch was no imaginary figure moving across the landscape from Ur to Canaan, wandering hither and thither with no personal contacts to mark the progress of his journey, or to set forth his successes and failures. The picture now drawn in sharp relief represents Abraham as associating with well known people of his own native area, Mesopotamia, but coming into vital relations with contemporary peoples of other areas far to the west. It is hardly of any consequence that modern historians, even up until recent years, held that some of these neighbors, particularly the Hittites, were just as fictitious as Abraham; that the biblical references were entirely worthless. It was bluntly stated that no people by name of Hittites ever existed, that they were legendary or mythological. There was no occasion to rethink the problem of the Hittites; any claim regarding their actual existence was without foundation. Meanwhile, the early records of the Old Testament spoke of Heth the son of Canaan,[15] of the land of Canaan as a country of the Hittites,[16] of the sons of Heth as owners of the burial cave at Machpelah in Hebron,[17] and of other events connected with these mysterious people. Of particular interest are those references which bring them into direct association with the era of Abraham and with the Patriarch himself. Furthermore, if it could be shown that such passages had no relation to any factual basis, then the reality of Abraham would also be subject to serious challenge. Happily, however, in the light of the recoveries at Boghaz-koi, and our increasing knowledge both of the Hittites and their civilization, we may still cling to them and to their contemporary Abraham. Actually, the emergence of the Hittites, after two and a half millennia of perfect obscurity, has contributed largely to the re-establishment of the authority of the early narratives of the Old Testament. There is no occasion here to enter into a lengthy discussion of the marvelous development associated with the kingdom of the Hittites, particularly their beginnings in the Cappadocian area of Asia Minor, their expansion east, west, and south to include even the southern reaches of Canaan in Abraham's day, nor the culmination of their power when they were able to stop the powerful Egyptians under Rameses II at Kadesh on the Orontes in 1288 B.C. Our claim is established in their presence at Hebron as early as 2000 B.C., where Abraham dealt with them not as nomads or mercenaries but as actual owners of the land which the Patriarch purchased for a family burial ground. It might be of interest to add that the cave of Machpelah is still in Hebron, the traditional burial place of Abraham, Isaac, and Jacob, together with their wives, and that the place might be regarded as an authentic site.

197

But there were other contemporary peoples with whom the Patriarch is said to have had dealings. Among those prominently mentioned are the Amorite confederates who accompanied Abraham on his expedition against the Mesopotamian kings and who contributed to their decisive defeat at Hormah near Damascus.[18] These, of course, are echoes of far-off times and events, antedating, in fact, by a full millennium the earliest date allowed for any portion of these narratives. Obviously, a later author would have laid himself open to grave errors in specifically referring to peoples unless he had possessed some accurate information. In the case of the Amorites this was particularly true, for hitherto we have generally confined these outstanding Semites to the upper and lower regions of Syria, especially to the great Lebanon and Anti-Lebanon areas and not to southern Canaan where Abraham accepted their aid. But our knowledge of the Amorites has been vastly increased during recent years, particularly with reference to their relation to Canaan approximately 2500 B.C., with the result that the patriarchal narratives are completely corroborated. In common with all Semitic peoples, and as one of the principal branches of that great race, the Amorites originated in the Peninsula of Arabia at a very early date. Successive migratory waves from the peninsular area witnessed the emergence of the Amorites in southern Mesopotamia, then in northern Aram, and subsequently in Syria, and Canaan to the borders of Egypt.[19] Their arrival in Canaan occurred about the middle of the third millennium B.C., at which time, both in the west and east Jordan highlands, they largely displaced the resident population and began to establish themselves in cultural centers of great strength. Five hundred years before Abraham arrived, the Amorites were dwelling in fortified cities and developing that culture which

198

was to challenge the faith and loyalty of Abraham's descendants one thousand years later.[20] Their presence at Hebron and their confederacy with Abraham are now seen in their proper setting, and are found to be in perfect accord with the author's claims in these early accounts of Abraham and his neighbors.

Now it is interesting to observe that these great neighbors of the Patriarch, the Hittites and the Amorites, owe their literary preservation to the early records of the Old Testament. If other ancient historians were acquainted with them, such information as they might have given was unknown prior to the recovery of recent archaeological evidences. Even when standing alone, the narratives of the Old Testament persisted in calling attention to these remote peoples and claiming close relations between them and the father of the Hebrews. Clearly, therefore, these records were not "exaggerations" nor fictitious; they rested upon sober fact, upon information which later writers could not possibly have imagined or invented.[21] But the list is not exhausted with the Hittites and the Amorites. References are made to the Horites,[22] a people of fabulous antiquity generally confined by early scholars to the caves of Mount Seir, but who appear in recent investigations as one of the most important peoples of the second millennium B.C. These are the Hurrians whose dramatic story is just beginning to unfold.[23] Then there are the Amalekites who are now well known;[24] the Rephaim both of east and west Jordan areas begin to take historical form;[25] the Jebusites, particularly of Jerusalem, who probably represent an early amalgam of Amorites and Hittites;[26] the Hivites who dwelt at Shechem, under Mount Hermon, and in the vicinity of Jerusalem;[27] and the Philistines, pursuing their grain export business in the Plain of Philistia, are now allowed in Canaan long before the mass invasion of the coastlands by the men of Caphtor.[28] So the story goes. "It is this unique and profoundly significant character which the revolutionary criticism would dissipate into unsubstantial myth and legend. But the thing cannot be done. What legend can effect for the life of Abraham is sufficiently evidenced by the fables of and stories in Jewish, Mohammedan, and Persian sources. The history of Abraham in the Bible stands, from internal evidence alone, on an entirely different footing from these. In its simple, coherent, elevated character, its organic unity with the rest of revelation, its freedom from the puerility and extravagance which mark the products of the myth-forming spirit, it approves itself as a serious record of important events, the knowledge of which had been carefully preserved— possibly at an early date had been written down—and the essential contents of which we may safely trust."[29]

Thus with each new grip on Abraham's contemporaries and patriarchal times, the great Patriarch himself stands before us as a definite historical person, touching elbows with the men and nations of his day while following through his venture of faith. We may therefore conclude with Woolley: "The Old Testament evidences supported by the independent testimony of secular literature, justifies us in holding that there was such a person, that he was an Aramaean or Amorite, the founder and head of a clan that later developed into the Hebrew nation, that he lived originally at Ur in Mesopotamia, that he and his people moved thence into Northern Syria and subsequently into Palestine, and that he lived in about the twentieth century before Christ."[30]

200

CHAPTER TWELVE

THE MOSAIC AGE

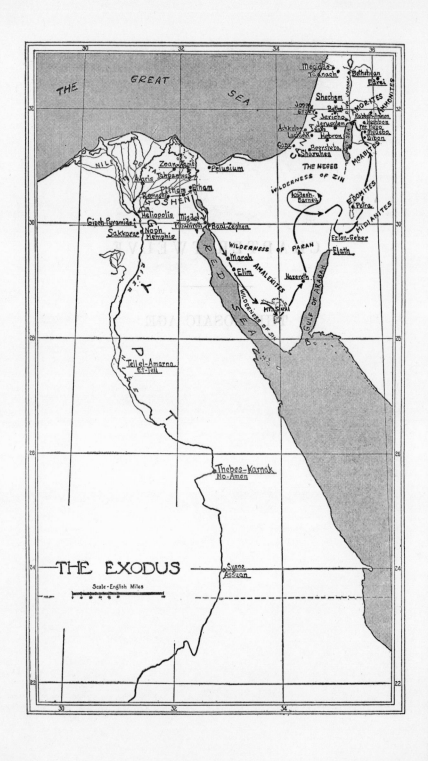

THE EXODUS

Scale-English Miles

THE MOSAIC AGE

FOR a long period now the Mosaic Age has been under the close examination of the critical eye as one of the most inviting fields for speculation and, at the same time, regarded as one of the most vulnerable from the standpoint of biblical accuracy and integrity. It was held that the whole arrangement of the narratives bearing on the era of Moses presented chronological and literary difficulties which, in all probability, could never be solved, particularly the approximate length of the Sojourn in Egypt, the date of the Exodus, the arrival at Mt. Sinai, and the adoption of the laws of Moses in covenant relations between Jehovah and the people of Israel. These were the focal points around which the subsequent historical development of Hebrew life and thought revolved. Indeed, the events here referred to, together with the results flowing from them, were rightly regarded as the most important in Hebrew history. Consequently, to the student of the Old Testament, it was a matter of primary concern that the narratives of the Mosaic Age be examined in the full light of archaeological investigation with a view to ascertaining their historicity and trustworthiness. As is well known, during recent years the investigation has been accelerated by additional evidences from the excavations, with the result that the issues have not only been more clearly defined, but an enlarged measure of agreement has been reached on several disputed points. We may ask, therefore, what is the present state of our knowledge regarding the biblical accounts of Moses and the epochal events of the Mosaic Age? Have we ever been justified in discounting these narratives or rejecting them as historical and reliable records, in looking upon them as the wholesale manufacturing of national traditions from the standpoint of some writer who was first of all a propagandist? In answering these and similar questions, our main interest must always lie in our approach to the Scriptures themselves that they may be allowed to present their own point of view. The Sojourn in Egypt, for example, was a definite period in the experience of Israel, their subsequent deliverance in the Exodus was the great event that marked the beginning of their national life: What do the Old Testament narratives have to say regarding these turning points in Hebrew history?

I. SOJOURN OF ISRAEL IN EGYPT

Apart from Abraham's enforced visit to Egypt in the days of the famine referred to in Genesis 12:10, there is no record of Hebrew-Egyptian relations until the period of Jacob and Joseph. That there were to be the most intimate relations after Abraham's days is clearly foreshadowed in the following: "Know of a surety that thy seed shall be sojourners in a land that is not theirs, and shall serve them; and they shall afflict them four hundred years; and also that nation, whom they shall serve, will I judge: and afterwards shall they come out with great substance."[1] If it be objected that Egypt is not definitely named in this passage as the place of Israel's serfdom, it will be agreed that all subsequent writers understood the statement as applying to Egypt as the house of bondage, and to Egypt alone. But the point of emphasis here is not the place of serfdom but the *period of time* involved. In making his

204

defense before the Jewish Sanhedrin, about A.D. 33, Stephen uses practically the same phraseology employed in the Genesis passage and mentions definitely a period of four hundred years.[2] But more emphatic is the chronological note in Exodus 12:40, in which the period of bondage is given as four hundred thirty years: "Now the sojourning of the children of Israel, who dwelt in Egypt, was four hundred and thirty years." It is known, of course, that the LXX rendering of Exodus 12:40, supported also by the Samaritan Pentateuch, adds, "The sojourning of the children of Israel and their fathers, who dwelt in Egypt *and* in Canaan, was four hundred and thirty years."[3] Now if we were to assume the correctness of this interpolation, we would be compelled to reject not only the repeated statements of the Hebrew biblical text regarding the Sojourn, but run counter to the whole course of recent archaeological evidences which obviously support it. In other words, the acceptance of the LXX rendering would necessitate placing Abraham's date about 1650— exactly 400 years after Hammurabi—the descent of Jacob and his sons into Egypt about 1435 (actually ten years later than the Exodus from Egypt, according to biblical statements), and the whole of the Mosaic period from about 1275 to 1150 B.C.—i.e., during the reign of Rameses II, Merneptah, Rameses III, IV, and V. Indeed, the case is worse than that because it involves the whole of the period of wilderness wandering, conquests in Transjordania and Canaan, the settlement of the tribes, the era of the Judges, and the reigns of Saul and David, and four years of the reign of Solomon—all of which must be reduced to a period of 249 years. The biblical reckoning gives for this period exactly 480 years. In the light of recent developments the accuracy of the biblical reckoning is strongly supported and critical opinion accepts it as having a factual basis. We may hold with confidence, therefore, that the intent of the biblical writers demands a period of 400 or 430 years for the sojourn of Israel in the land of Egypt. It is obvious, of course, that if we can determine when the Sojourn *began,* we will thereby be able to fix definitely the period of Hebrew history lying between Abraham and the Age of Moses.

With reference to the period lying between Abraham and Moses, there is admittedly a problem raised by Paul's statement in Galatians when comparing the Abrahamic and Mosaic covenants, as follows: "Now this I say: a covenant confirmed beforehand by God, the law, which came four hundred and thirty years after, doth not disannul, so as to make the promise of none effect."[4] There is clearly no difficulty regarding the date when the Mosaic covenant was made, for if the Exodus occurred in 1446, then the establishment of the law and the founding of the nation at Sinai must be synchronous. But to whom is this covenant of faith to be referred? to Abraham only, or to Isaac and Jacob, also? Restricting this covenant to Abraham, we must be prepared to accept a late date for the Patriarch—i.e., about 1876 B.C., which is two centuries after Hammurabi, his contemporary. If, on the other hand, we are justified in interpreting the covenant as successively renewed in the case of Isaac and of Jacob—particularly in the case of Jacob whose paternal relation to the twelve tribes of Israel was not only determinative in covenant relations, but whose descent into Egypt actually marked the beginning of the 430 years of sojourn in a strange land—if we are justified in this interpretation, then there is no insoluble difficulty involved; the passage perfectly harmonizes with the Exodus date given in 1 Kings 6:1. It is significant that the psalmist stresses the successive nature of God's covenant with Abraham in this definite manner: "which covenant he made with Abraham, and his oath unto Isaac; and confirmed the same unto Jacob for a law, and to Israel for an everlasting covenant."[5] Now on biblical reckoning we can determine Jacob's descent into Egypt with his sons about the year 1876 B.C.; four hundred thirty years after that date brings us to 1446, the date of the Exodus and the Mosaic covenant at Mt. Sinai.

II. The Exodus of Israel from Egypt

The historicity of the Exodus as an event of tremendous importance in the life of Israel is willingly granted in the following: "It is impossible to deny either the fact of the Exodus or the historicity of Moses. An event which stamped itself so deeply on the consciousness of the people as to control all of its later thinking, to ratify its religion, and to dictate its theory of history, can by no possibility have been a mere invention."[6] Or to refresh our minds with the double assurance left by the late Professor T. Eric Peet: "That an exodus occurred need not for a moment be doubted. It has already been pointed out that the whole incident of the sojourn in Egypt is bound up so closely with the revelation of Jehovah that it is hardly likely to be a pure invention. If, then, some of the ancestors of the later Israelites were once in Egypt, they must at some moment have come out of it, and therefore there must have been an exodus."[7] But such concessions, however freely given, hardly do justice to the event which actually marks the culminating point of Egyptian servitude and the beginning of Israel as a nation. "Deeply embedded in the historical narratives of the Old Testament is found the account of four centuries of humiliating bondage visited upon the sons of Jacob in the land of the Pharaohs. Inseparably connected with these

207

records is the memory of a great deliverance at the Red Sea,—an event unparalleled in the experiences of any other people,—which was followed by a series of miraculous interventions to preserve the Hebrews through a period of forty years of wilderness wandering, and, finally, to conduct them into the land of Canaan. The whole story, including serfdom and liberation, is told with the utmost simplicity. There is not the slightest effort to exaggerate divine interposition, nor to embellish it with unnecessary occurrence. Nor, on the other hand, is there any disposition to remove the stigma of an humble lot which found the Hebrew people sorely oppressed and crying out in anguish of heart for deliverance. It is reasonable to suppose that no people ever manufactured stories of a national beginning on this order. Furthermore, it is obvious that the satisfaction and inspiration derived from the recital of these traditions pertained solely to the memories of an outstretched arm working in wondrous ways in behalf of the seed of Abraham, Isaac, and Jacob.''[8] Now, as we have repeatedly insisted, whatever may be the critical appraisal of these traditions, it is perfectly obvious that, from the viewpoint of the Hebrew people, these narratives reflect their convictions regarding their national beginnings and are accordingly placed in the very forefront of their sacred literature. Consequently, any attempt on our part to evaluate these records should certainly be based on a full knowledge of their contents and claims.

Immediately we are confronted with the one clear statement in biblical tradition regarding the date of the Exodus, as follows: "And it came to pass in the four hundred and eightieth year after the children of Israel were come out of the land of Egypt, in the fourth year of Solomon's reign over Israel, in the month Ziv, which is the second month, that he began to build the house

AN OSTRAKON, OR BROKEN PIECE OF VESSEL, CONTAINING AN INSCRIPTION IN EARLY SEMITIC WRITING. THESE OSTRAKA AND OTHER POTSHERDS ARE PRACTICALLY IMPERISHABLE. THE SAMARIA OSTRAKA AND THE LACHISH LETTERS ARE SIMILAR TO THE ABOVE IN APPEARANCE.

THE MOUND OF ED-DUWEIR IS NOW IDENTIFIED WITH THE LACHISH OF THE OLD TESTAMENT AND THE ASSYRIAN RECORDS. SCENE OF THE WONDERFUL RECOVERY OF THE LACHISH LETTERS AND THE LACHISH EWER.

MODERN REPRESENTATIVES OF AN ANCIENT PEOPLE WHO HAVE CONTINUOUSLY RESIDED IN PALESTINE SINCE THE DAYS OF THE HEBREW CONQUEST AND SETTLEMENT. PRIESTS OF THE SAMARITAN GROUP AT SHECHEM STAND BY THE SAMARITAN PENTATEUCH, THE MOSAIC LAW.

THE SITE OF GEBAL IN PROCESS OF EXCAVATION. FROM THIS CITY COME THE STARTLING EPIGRAPHIC MONUMENTS OF THE THIRTEENTH CENTURY B.C. GEBAL PROVIDED BOTH ARTISANS AND SHIPBUILDERS TO THE KINGDOM OF THE HEBREWS UNDER DAVID AND SOLOMON. THE CITY IS ALSO IMPORTANT AS THE SCENE OF THE EXPERIENCES OF WEN-AMON, AN EGYPTIAN ENVOY, WHOSE TRAVEL-LOGUE WAS RECENTLY DISCOVERED.

of Jehovah.'"⁹ "This tradition, it is true, has been generally assigned by the critics to a late source and treated with mistrust, as the round figure of 480 years is found not to agree with the summary of details recorded in the received text of the Book of Judges. Nonetheless it will be found on re-examination in fresh light to be based exclusively on the oldest sources, while the elements of disagreement will be seen to have been introduced by the later insertions.'"¹⁰ "Now we can date Solomon's reign very accurately, for the battle of Qarqar, at which Ahab was present in alliance with Hadad-idri of Damascus, the Benhadad of I Kings 20:33, as related by the Assyrian account of it, can be fixed astronomically to 854 B.C.¹¹ This alliance seems to have been made in Ahab's twenty-first year, and by reckoning backward over a period the documentary sources for which are in part at least contemporary and should therefore be worthy of considerable credit, we get 970 B.C., for Solomon's accession, and 966 for the building of the temple. Adding 480 to this we obtain 1446 B.C., for the traditional date of the exodus.'"¹² It should be pointed out that in the quotation just given from Professor Peet's *Egypt and the Old Testament,* the reference to 1446 as the traditional date of the Exodus is from the standpoint of Hebrew tradition, and not the usually designated traditional and conservative school of present-day critics whose views of the Exodus are in reality unscriptural and antitraditional. Now, without going into the minutiae of argument, we may accept the statement in 1 Kings 6:1 as a credible historical notice referring to comparatively recent times, concerning whose genuineness and accuracy there is no justifiable question.

Still, if 1 Kings 6:1 is an authoritative statement, it must be in agreement with other periods of Israel's historical development for which we have biblical statements also, particularly the period of the Judges which stretched from the conquest of Canaan to the installation of Saul as the first king of Israel. Now, happily, the Bible does not leave us here to rambling conjecture to determine the duration of this period; the records are complete and consistent. There are two passages that are pertinently related to our inquiry, and to these we turn for brief examination. In the first passage, Paul gives us a definite statement regarding the period that followed immediately in the wake of Joshua's conquest in Canaan: "And when he had destroyed seven nations in the land of Canaan, he gave them their land for an inheritance, for about four hundred and fifty years: and after these things he gave them judges until Samuel the prophet."[13] It will be recalled that the rendering of this passage in the Textus Receptus and the King James English version requires that the 450-year period of the Judges shall follow immediately on the conquest and settlement in Canaan. In all probability that is the correct view. But the Textus Receptus construction of the text is not permitted by the oldest manuscripts ABC, etc., though the change in phraseology by a later scribe indicates that he was confronted with a problem of Old Testament history. That he was familiar with 1 Kings 6:1 seems clear. Even now all the difficulties of this passage are not removed, but it certainly was not the design of Paul nor of the writer in Acts to apply this period of 450 years to any particular interval *preceding* Joshua's conquest of Canaan. If, therefore, we have the correct text, it is obvious that our problem remains unsolved. Whether it is insoluble or not, the future will reveal. If the passage means that after God destroyed the seven nations in the land of Canaan, he gave Israel their land for an inheritance for about 450 years, and that during this period the Elders and Judges ruled until Samuel the prophet, that would fit in perfectly with 1 Kings 6:1, thus allowing sufficient time for the conquest of Canaan and the forty years of wandering in the wilderness.

The second passage bearing on the era of the Judges is found in the book of Judges 11:25-26, where Jephthah reproaches the Ammonites for their unprovoked attacks on the children of Israel: "And now art thou anything better than Balak the son of Zippor, king of Moab? did he ever strive against Israel, or did he ever fight against them? While Israel dwelt in Heshbon and its towns, and in Aroer and its towns, and in all the cities that are along by the side of the Arnon, three hundred years; wherefore did ye not recover them within that time?" Now here is a statement of great significance, but it has been rejected by certain critics "who ascribe the words 'three hundred years' to the post exilic priestly hand, though the body of the text belongs to the early source E. The words are admittedly an insertion, being ungrammatical in the Hebrew text; but the reason usually given for their rejection is itself fallacious.[14] It is based on the assumption that the figure 300 was mistakenly obtained by adding together the preceding chronological data in the book of Judges, down to but not including the Ammonite oppression, which happen to amount to 301 years. But it is clearly stated that the 300 years is to be reckoned from the sojourn in Heshbon, and therefore must include the period of Joshua's leadership and that of the Elders."[15] If one will take the trouble to divest himself of any preconceived notion as to what the biblical narratives must say and commence to weigh the evidence which they actually give, the results will be astonishing. Even the period of the Judges with its tangled mass of chronological difficulties will begin to stand out as a definite era in the history of Israel and will appear in duration of time approximately as the Scriptures define it. The difficulty here, and in several other places as pronounced, is that we have started with a mistaken view of Israel's arrival in Canaan—i.e., about 1190 B.C.—and being unable to disregard the monumental evidences of Solomon's accession and reign in 970 B.C., we have been compelled to press within the period lying between the Exodus and Solomon's accession the whole mass of biblical detail relating to the wanderings, the east Jordan conquests, Joshua, Elders, Judges, Saul, and David. Clearly the undertaking was doomed to failure, but, meanwhile, in order to make room for the relatively certain events associated with Joshua and the Elders, and with Samuel, Saul, and David, we have continually whittled down the period of the Judges until a bare fragment of about 150 years is left. Now we are not defending the proposition that the reign of every judge was an independent rulership, absolutely detached from the rule of every other judge—for it is clear that in two cases at least we have concurrent reigns—but we are defending the proposition that we have had no critical or moral right to mutilate this historical period until it is only the barest skeleton. Jephthah's statement is literally correct, and on the surface of the narrative in Judges his assertion can be mathematically proved. Furthermore, remembering the probability of concurrent reigns and the unknown period of the Conquest, the chronological notice here given is in almost uncanny agreement with 1 Kings 6:1—i.e., the 480 years from Solomon to the exodus from Egypt.

III. Theories of the Exodus

In the foregoing summary of biblical statements bearing on the epochal events of the Mosaic Age, particularly the Sojourn, the Exodus, and the total period leading up to the accession of Solomon, we have not sought to introduce definitely any of the modern theories which have been proposed in explanation of these matters. Rather, the approach has been entirely from the Hebrew point of view, thus permitting the Old Testament to present its own claims. After all, these historical events refer primarily to the Hebrew people, and it is assumed that they were fairly well informed regarding their past, and that they inserted the outlines of their history into a chronological framework which, to them at least, was satisfactory and harmonious. Reverting to our previous discussion on Old Testament chronology, the early and middle phases of this framework now appear as follows: Based on astronomical calculations determining approximately the Battle of Karkar, 854 B.C., Solomon's accession is reckoned at 970 B.C. Accepting the accuracy of 1 Kings 6:1, the Exodus occurred in 1446 B.C. The period immediately preceding this event, including the descent of Jacob into Egypt and the bondage of 430 years, determines Abraham's date as approximately 2166 B.C. Thus, from the biblical point of view, there is at least uniformity in detail and, likewise, consistency. Now, from the standpoint of current criticism, what are the explanations offered for these outstanding events, particularly the Exodus, which is the focal point of the whole controversy?

Reviewing the field of discussion regarding the exodus of the Hebrews from the land of Egypt, three principal theories have been proposed and defended with great learning. During the more recent years of the controversy, when scientific investigation entered the debate with its astounding archaeological discoveries, the early views have been seriously challenged while the latest theory has steadily appeared as the most reasonable. The final answer is perhaps not yet available, but definite progress is being made in the solution of the problem. Inasmuch as the backgrounds of the Bondage and the Exodus are Egyptian, the theories proposed are all designated in terms of Egyptian eras, namely, *Period of Hyksos Domination and Expulsion,* *Period of the Eighteenth Dynasty,* and *Period of the Nineteenth Dynasty.* The order of discussion will set forth the *Eighteenth Dynasty Theory* as the final consideration.

1. *Period of Hyksos Domination and Expulsion*[16]

Under this view the exodus of the Hebrews is regarded as synchronous with the expulsion of the Hyksos from Egypt and was probably a part of that movement. Though it is an interesting theory from many angles, it has never been vigorously championed. Strangely enough, the view is derived from Josephus, the Jewish historian who, at the close of the first century A.D., sought to give a connected account of the history of his people based on the records of the sacred Scriptures and supplemented by additional information derived from the writings of the Alexandrian historian Manetho, about 300 B.C.[17] Though Josephus does not explicitly state that the Hebrew descent into Egypt began with the Hyksos invasion about 2080 B.C., it is assumed that such was the case since the Hyksos are referred to as "the ancestors of our people." Incidentally, it is clear that, on this theory, the identification of the Hebrews with the conquering and ruling Hyksos leaves no room for a bondage and an oppression in Egypt described in the early portions of the book of Exodus.[18] But, apart from this, it is held that the bitterness engendered by the foreign dynasty in Egypt was so intense that when the native princes succeeded in throwing off the Hyksos yoke in 1580 B.C., the Hebrews were involved as a part of the general expul-

214

sion. It is hardly probable, however, that if the connection between the Hyksos and the Hebrews had been so intimate, this fact would have escaped the Old Testament historians, who make no mention of them. On the other hand, the willingness of Josephus to concede racial connections between the two peoples might throw light on the favorable reception extended to the Hebrews in Egypt as recorded in the experiences of Abraham, Jacob, and Joseph.[19] But Josephus was mistaken about the Exodus, just as he was in attributing the founding of Jerusalem to the Hyksos as an aftermath of their expulsion from Egypt.[20] It is likely that the Hyksos became a part of the early inhabitants of Jerusalem, but the history of the city can be definitely traced 1500 years before the Hyksos expulsion and may be regarded originally as a settlement of cave dwellers subsequently displaced by an amalgam of Hittites and Amorites. Furthermore, historically, the Hyksos did not proceed to Jerusalem after their expulsion, but made their final stand at Sharuhen in southern Canaan.[21] From this point they become a forgotten people. Finally, the theory is wholly unsatisfactory from a chronological standpoint. The approximate date of 1580 B.C. for the Hyksos expulsion is accepted by Egyptologists as a fixed point in Egyptian history, but to place the Exodus at this date would do violence not only to the implications of Exodus 1:7-14 regarding intensified persecution of the Hebrews, but also would run roughshod over 1 Kings 6:1 to lengthen the period from Solomon to the Exodus to 612 years instead of 480 demanded by the biblical statement.[22]

2. *Period of the Nineteenth Dynasty*[23]

The general period of the Nineteenth Dynasty, which incorporated the reigns of only a few rulers, is usually defined as stretching from about 1350 B.C. to

1200 B.C. In view of the wide agreement with reference to 1580 B.C. as the date of Hyksos expulsion, the dynastic period can be reckoned with relative accuracy. The Rameses-Merneptah theory of the Bondage and Exodus of Israel sets forth the latter phases of Israel's intense persecution as having occurred under Rameses II, 1292-1225 B.C., while the Exodus followed under his thirteenth son and successor Merneptah, 1225-1215 B.C. The acceptance of this theory by the great majority of biblical scholars is now of long duration, a fact to be attributed, perhaps, not only to the great desire to localize the events in definite dynastic terms, but also to the conspicuous absence of any other likely explanation or competing theory. With the progress of archaeological investigations, especially in Egypt and Palestine during the latter part of the past century, many erstwhile problems have taken on an entirely different complexion. The astounding recoveries during the past few years have been of the highest significance for Bible study and have definitely created a new spirit and a new approach in biblical investigation and interpretation. No one can tell what the future may disclose, but at present we may have the assurance that we are at last on the right road. This confidence means probably a little bit more than students of our generation can realize, for, where we are amply provided with suitable material on which to ground a sane defense of Bible integrity, the fathers of an earlier generation stood almost helpless in the face of a powerful onslaught of destructive criticism. In all probability, some of the views which they held seemed rather naive to the opposition, but we have witnessed monuments being erected for the prophets whom they stoned. Even so, some of the identifications and views which they advanced are rather puzzling, and among these none more conspicuous than the Rameses-Merneptah theory.

Indeed, who knows why we ever settled on Rameses II to dub him with the everlasting stigma, *The Pharaoh of the Oppression?* From what we now know of that powerful monarch, he could very easily have been spared this additional notoriety! No doubt we found him in that descriptive passage in Exodus 1:11, where it is said, "And they built for Pharaoh the store-cities, Pithom and Rameses." From this we inferred that the city of Rameses was named for the oppressing Pharaoh himself, and thus put Rameses the Great into the dual role of builder and oppressor. On closer examination of the passage, however, it will be observed that neither the name of the Pharaoh nor the dynasty to which he belonged is given. Then through the widely acclaimed excavations of Naville at Tell el-Mashkuteh and Petrie at Tell er-Retabeh, it was thought that we had found the very cities which the Israelites had constructed for Rameses.[24] At this juncture we did not think of the possibility that the cities recovered might have been of more ancient founding and that Rameses might merely have rebuilt them in his own day apart from any reference to the Israelites.[25] Similarly, the much-heralded Stela of Rameses II, recovered at Bethshean in Canaan by Fisher in 1921, "which, when first interpreted was said to recount among other works of Pharaoh, that he built the treasure city, Raamses in Egypt, with the help of Semitic Asiatic slaves."[26] Many accepted this Stela as corroborative evidence of the Rameses II oppression. "But alas! the inscription has been found to be mistranslated, and therefore misinterpreted; Barton frankly admits: 'While it refers to the city of Raamses mentioned in Exodus i.11, it makes no reference, as was at first thought, to the employment of Semitic captives in building it.' This new interpretation of the stele vitiates to a very large degree the proof that Rameses II was the Great Oppressor of Israel.'"[27] In addition, it

217

might be pointed out that any reference to Semitic labor might have referred to a large number of distinct tribes or clans composing that outstanding race of the ancient world. Finally, through isolated bits of supposed evidence here and there we tightened our hold on Rameses, so that even today his supercilious mummy "still frowns over claw-like hands in most of our Bible illustrations" as the oppressor relegated forever to the company of Nero and Herod the Great of later ages. That he was a great Pharaoh is beyond question, the extent and glory of the Egyptian Empire under him are well known; that he reigned for approximately 67 years, thus fulfilling the requirement of the biblical reference concerning "many days" or years, is also historically correct; that he had a son by the name of Merneptah who succeeded him and that under this same successor the imperial organization began to disintegrate, is duly acknowledged; but that he was the Pharaoh of the oppression in Egypt, the merciless tyrant who caused the Hebrews to cry out in anguish of heart for divine deliverance, is vigorously disputed and may be rejected in the light of recent discoveries.

It followed, of course, that having determined Rameses II as the Pharaoh of the Oppression, the dubious title "Pharaoh of the Exodus" naturally fell to Merneptah, his son, though there was not the slightest evidence for attributing to him that distinction. The view persisted, however, and we are told that "as late as 1909 Merenptah's mummified heart was sent to the Royal College of Surgeons to see if it was really 'hardened.' "[28] "As a matter of fact, Dr. Shattock reported that it was—from a disease called atheroma."[29] Accordingly, having fixed Merneptah as the monarch who let the children of Israel go, the Exodus could not be placed either earlier or later than his reign, hence 1220 B.C. became the accepted date. It will be remem-

218

bered, of course, that according to this view the chronological data given in the Bible would have to be entirely rejected. Happily, however, we do not have to resort to this extreme for, thanks to this same Merneptah or to his publicity agent, we now have a slab of stone, recovered by Petrie at Karnak, on which the following information is recorded:

"Devastated is Tehennu
The Hittite land is pacified;
Plundered is Canaan with every evil;
Carried off is Ascalon;
Seized upon is Gezer
Yenoam is made a thing of naught;
Israel is desolated, her seed is not;
Palestine has become a defenseless widow for Egypt;
Every one that is turbulent is bound by King Merneptah,
Giving life like the sun every day."

It is of interest to note that this is the only place on any Egyptian monument that the name of Israel is found, but it is enough; for with one flourish of the chisel the court historian removes the Exodus crown from Pharaoh Merneptah to pass it back to its rightful owner. For it is as clear as a pikestaff that Israel was already a settled people in the land of Canaan at the very time the alleged exodus was taking place. Many ingenious theories were quickly advanced to explain the Merneptah inscription, particularly the following: That the Exodus occurred in the third year of Merneptah's reign, 1222 B.C., while the attack took place in 1220 B.C.; that only the Joseph tribes had actually been in Egypt, thus allowing a conquest of the tribes who remained in Canaan; and, finally, that the attack was made against the Leah tribes who effected their exodus from Egypt under the Eighteenth Dynasty (the Rachel tribes under the Nineteenth).[30]

Now these are undoubtedly interesting theories, but they are thoroughly non-scriptural, and one can hardly believe that they offer adequate explanations. Indeed, the most charitable view regarding these theories is that the more they explain, the more needful is it to explain the explanations, seeing that the Scripture requirements are further violated and carelessly handled. The Merneptah Stela must be accepted on its face value. "It is almost incredible that in some minds the discovery of this new document merely served to clinch the belief in the dating of the exodus to the reign of Merenptah. Cooler heads, however, were much more concerned to note that, so far from confirming the Merenptah date it made it practically impossible, for obviously, if the Israelites left Egypt in Merenptah's own reign and wandered forty years before reaching Canaan, he could hardly have found them settled there as early as his fifth year."[31] Again: "In any case, it is hardly worth while to go to all this trouble to defend the theory of an exodus under Merenptah, for which there is so little to be said on other grounds. Is there no earlier date at which, in view of Egyptian and Syrian history, an exodus might reasonably have fallen?"[32] The answer to that question is probably found in the Eighteenth Dynasty.

3. Period of the Eighteenth Dynasty[33]

In the light of increasing knowledge made available by several outstanding recoveries, it gradually became evident that the Rameses-Merneptah theory of the Oppression and Exodus was inadequate from the standpoint of Hebrew Scripture requirements and also from that of Egyptian history. Slowly the mist enveloping the question was being dissipated, with the result that a more reasonable view was apparently emerging in connection with the Eighteenth Dynasty rulers, the Oppression being attributed to Thutmosis III, 1501-1447 B.C., and the Exodus to his successor, Amenhotep II, 1447-1420 B.C. This change in critical opinion was practically inevitable, for where there was so much concurrent evidence pointing definitely to the same conclusion, it was clear that the evidence could not be laid aside as merely incidental or accidental. A review of the entire problem was strongly demanded on every hand.

As we have seen, the discovery of the Merneptah Stela by Petrie at Karnak in 1896 instantly threw the Rameses-Merneptah theory into utter confusion, for it was obvious that an exodus such as is described in the Hebrew narratives could not possibly have occurred under Merneptah. If his claim is at all genuine, Israel was already settled in Canaan when the Merneptah invasion took place. The objection that we have no corresponding biblical version of this alleged invasion is not a formidable one, particularly in view of the general period of upheaval (period of the Judges) in which the event occurred, and the absence of any organized government among the Hebrew people. Attention has already been called to the fact that at the Battle of Kadesh, 1288 B.C., Palestine had become a buffer state between the Egyptians and the Hittites, being virtually ceded to the Egyptians under the terms of the Treaty then ratified.[34] On this view Palestine was already Egyptian territory, and with no internal government of the newly settled Hebrews strong enough to resist him, Merneptah's account may be regarded as true. But we simply do not have any biblical allusions to this invasion. On the other hand, granting the absence of any corroborative biblical evidence bearing on the Merneptah invasion, in the Tell el-Amarna Correspondence we have reliable records of an earlier overrunning of Canaan by the Habiru which are substantiated by the almost certain contemporary records of the Old Testament relating to the same event. It was immediately recognized that in this correspondence we might have helpful information concerning the problem of the Exodus.

The discovery of the major portion of the Tell el-Amarna Letters in 1887 introduced one of the thrilling chapters in modern archaeology.[35] Through the lowly medium of a peasant woman at Et Tell in the land of Egypt, the scholarly world was provided with the archives of the Egyptian Foreign Office during the period 1412 B.C. to 1362 B.C. The recovered correspondence, now consisting of more than 400 baked clay tablets written in the Babylonian cuneiform, was recognized as very important from the beginning, but no one understood the indispensable role that these tablets would play in all future discussions of Israel's exodus from Egypt and subsequent settlement in Canaan. It is now generally acknowledged that, for the first time, we have in these Amarna Tablets the Canaanite version of the Hebrew invasion under Joshua, the corresponding Hebrew account appearing in the historical narratives of the Old Testament. "This contemporaneous account of the settlement of the Habiru in Palestine so exactly parallels the Old Testament account of the Israelite conquest of Jericho and the invasion of the highlands of Ephraim under Joshua that the two manifestly must have reference to the same episode."[36] This judgment is generally shared by contemporary critics. "That they were the Hebrews is now the almost unanimous conclusion of archaeologists. Zimmern was the first to identify them. Etymologically and philologically their names are identical. Both the likeness of their language, and the part they played in the history of Western Asia at the time of the Exodus make it little less than certain that they are closely related to each other, if not identical.''[37] If it be objected that there is not the close correspondence in detail between the Amarna Letters and the historical narratives of Joshua and Judges—assuming that all of these annals refer to the same movement—in broad outline they are clearly not opposed, and in certain details they may be regarded as being in full agreement.

As we have seen, the designations Habiru and Hebrews are perfectly sound philological equivalents and refer to the same people; chronologically the movement described tallies completely with the biblical requirement in 1 Kings 6:1; the general directions from which the Habiru approached Canaan are in accord with the Hebrew approaches south and east as described in the Old Testament accounts; the cities, particularly Jerusalem, Ashkelon, Gezer, Taanach, etc., are the same as those affected by the Hebrew campaigns and conquests; the political conditions obtaining at this particular time in Canaan are faithfully reflected in both sources. Furthermore, the objection that we do not have correspondence in personal names appearing in the Amarna and biblical narratives is not insuperable in view of the critical upheaval gripping the Canaanite strongholds, resulting in rebellion, intrigue, assassinations, and treachery.[38] The argument, however, has not been allowed to go unchallenged.[39] No arbitrary demands for absolute conformity should be made in view of the unsettled conditions obtaining and the uncertainty as to the length of the period involved. On the other hand, Olmstead is willing to allow for the presence of a Joshua in both accounts: ''It is a remarkable coincidence, if coincidence it is, that a historical Joshua actually is mentioned in an Amarna letter; name, place, and time seem to force an identification of this historical Joshua with the Joshua of the epic."[40] But we are not insisting on this particular identification nor on any other probable correspondence; rather, the principal interest is to stress the apparent similarities between the two peoples and movements along general lines which suggest most intimate connections, perhaps even identification. Such an approach will probably result in most cases in the conviction held by Hall: "We may definitely say that in the Tel el-Amarna Letters we have Joshua's conquests seen from the Egyptian point of view."[41]

Now Hall's conclusion that the Amarna correspondence reflects the Joshua invasion of Canaan from the Egyptian point of view, encourages us to examine further the Egyptian connections with the hope of determining, if possible, other probable relations or implications. The discovery, for example, of a contemporary period of weakness in Egyptian political affairs, during which period an overrunning of Canaan might go on virtually unopposed, would lend support to the Habiru-Hebrew identification. Immediately we are introduced to the closing phases of the brilliant Eighteenth Dynasty when Amenhotep IV, 1376-1362 B.C., was in the midst of his religious innovations, having outlawed the ancient state cult of Amon-Ra together with the Theban hierarchy, and established his new capital at Tell el-Amarna 300 miles north of Thebes.[42] It was to this monarch Amenhotep IV (Akhnaton) that most of the Amarna Letters were addressed, though a few received by his father, Amenhotep III, 1412-1376 B.C., at Thebes were brought to Amarna as part of the Foreign Office papers when the capital was removed. It seems that neither monarch was greatly concerned about either the Habiru invasion of Canaan or the charges of defection on the part of native princes

224

THE ROYAL SARCOPHAGUS OF AKHIRAM, KING OF GEBAL, WAS TAKEN TO THE NATIONAL MUSEUM IN BEIRUT. SEVERAL OTHER SARCOPHAGI WERE FOUND BY MONTET IN 1922, ONE OF WHICH IS HERE SHOWN IN SITU AT GEBAL. THE CITY IS MENTIONED PROMINENTLY IN THE OLD TESTAMENT NARRATIVES.

THE STELA OF APRIES (THE HOPHRA OF THE OLD TESTAMENT NARRATIVES) WHO BECAME INVOLVED WITH ZEDEKIAH AGAINST NEBUCHADNEZZAR, KING OF BABYLON, IN THE FINAL STRUGGLE OF JERUSALEM 587-6 B.C. THE STELA STANDS AMID THE RUINS OF OLD MEMPHIS.

EXCAVATIONS AT UR OF THE CHALDEES, CONDUCTED BY SIR C. LEONARD WOOLLEY UNDER THE AUSPICES OF THE JOINT EXPEDITION OF THE BRITISH MUSEUM AND THE UNIVERSITY OF PENNSYLVANIA, ARE BEING REWARDED WITH PHENOMENAL DISCOVERIES. THE CAREER OF ABRAHAM IS NOW BEING SKETCHED ON A RELIGIOUS, SOCIAL, ECONOMIC, AND POLITICAL BACKGROUND OF STARTLING IMPORTANCE.

THE ANCIENT ROYAL TOMBS AT UR OF THE CHALDEES YIELD MATERIAL TREASURES OF UNSURPASSED VALUE IN RECONSTRUCTING THE CULTURE WHICH WAS IN THE MAKING FOR SEVERAL CENTURIES. IT IS NOW BELIEVED THAT THE APEX OF MESOPOTAMIAN CIVILIZATION WAS REACHED AT UR ABOUT 3500 B.C. FROM THESE TOMBS CAME MANY OF THE EVIDENCES OF THAT EARLY AND PHENOMENAL DEVELOPMENT OF HUMAN SOCIETY.

normally subject to the Egyptian crown. In the case of Amenhotep III this indisposition was probably due to sheer impotence of old age, whereas in Akhnaton's case the religious revolution demanded his complete attention. As a consequence the imperial organization bequeathed to the successors of the great Thutmosis III gradually weakened until it became scarcely more than a skeleton of sovereignty over native and subject peoples. Of course the point at issue here is, if the Hebrew conquest of Canaan is in any degree connected with the Habiru movement, the overrunning of the country occurred at a time when definite weakness characterized the Egyptian rule over Canaan as implied in the urgent but futile appeals of Palestinian princes to the Egyptian court. As a consequence, whether due to the indisposition or impotence of the reigning pharaohs, Amenhotep III and Akhnaton, the powerful invaders of Canaan apparently succeeded in conquering the country, displacing the native people and rulers in representative sections of the newly conquered territory. It is interesting to note that there is no official correspondence in the Tell el-Amarna archives later than Akhnaton, who died in 1362 B.C., a date that probably coincides with the final phases of Joshua's campaigns and the rule of the Elders in Israel. All of this fits in perfectly with the general outline of the biblical narratives and points to the complete identification of the Habiru and the Hebrews.

In view of the strong probability that the Hebrew conquest of Canaan was, in some of its phases, identical with the invasion by the Habiru as reflected in the Tell el-Amarna Letters about 1400 B.C., it is reasonable to suppose that an examination of some of the Canaanite strongholds affected would provide further corroborative evidence. Certainly, such a conquest as is here implied would not fail to leave its marks, particularly in cases where the destruction is said to have been complete. Furthermore, if it can be shown that the archaeological evidences submitted refer specifically to the era of the Amarna Letters and that they are also in accord with the historical narratives of the Old Testament bearing on this same period, the conclusion that the two movements are identical is perhaps inescapable. One could hardly expect that there were two movements running along at the same time, affecting the same localities, and issuing in the same results, but with no intimate connections nor in any sense involved. But, to be more specific, let us consider the following examples. In the correspondence of Ebedhepa of Jerusalem definite mention is made of Keilah, Gezer, Ashkelon, Lachish, Ajalon, Rubute (Hebron), Gaza, and Gath, all of which are in Southern Canaan where the Hebrew invasion secured its first foothold. In the northern and middle sections the citadels include Shechem, Taanach, Bethshean, and others. General references are made to affected areas stretching from Mt. Carmel and Esdraelon to the extreme southern portions of the country around Beersheba. It is of interest to note at this point that these are precisely the cities and areas assaulted by the Hebrews under Joshua in his several campaigns. In the southern campaign the biblical records also feature Jericho, Ai, Bethel, and five cities of the Hivite League, but no letters from any of these cities were sent to Akhnaton, probably because they were quickly con-

226

quered by the Hebrews. As suggested by Knight: "For the towns mentioned in the Amarna Tablets do not include the well-known old sites of Bethel, Ai, or Jericho, or Hebron, or Beersheba, or Shiloh, or Gibeon. Why? Was it chance? Was it not rather by the time the other Letters were written, these cities were already captured by the Hebrews, and it was useless to ask for help, for in their case it was too late? Shechem, after Jerusalem the most important city in Palestine, is mentioned only *once* in the Amarna Letters. Why? The answer is that it fell so soon into the hands of the victorious Israelites. Thus the fact that we possess no tablets from the cities just mentioned is a strong indirect verification of the truth of the Biblical narrative."[43]

On the other hand, in the case of cities definitely mentioned as calling for help and their final conquest by the Hebrews, the biblical records and the Amarna Letters are both corroborated by archaeology as seen in the results obtained by Mackenzie in his excavations at Beth-shemesh,[46] by Sellin at Taanach,[47] by Macalister at Gezer,[48] and by Sellin at Jericho.[49] It is perhaps in connection with Jericho that we have the most astonishing results indicating plainly not only the collapse of the city's wall, and the destruction of the city by fire, but the certainty that the conquest of the city occurred approximately 1400 B.C.—the date required by the biblical narratives and the period of the Amarna Letters.[50] "Jericho indeed furnishes us with an overwhelming proof that the Exodus did not take place under the Nineteenth Dynasty. By the time of Merenptah the city had already been in ruins for 147 years, as the

227

archaeological evidence clearly shows. If it be maintained that the Exodus happened under that monarch, then the story of the fall of the walls of Jericho will have to be abandoned, as by that time there were no walls in existence to fall!"[51] Finally, it is hardly necessary to present further evidence on this particular point; the operations both of the Habiru and the Hebrews appear as a unified movement and may be accepted as identical.

It is important, however, to fix definitely this period in relation to the larger question of the Exodus as suggested by Garstang: "The fact that the three important cities which Joshua is said to have overwhelmed in the course of his campaigns, and one other subsequently captured, seem on archaeological grounds one and all to have suffered destruction at about the same time, is of itself sufficiently striking to merit consideration; it becomes of first importance when the approximate date, at the close of the fifteenth century, or in round figures 1400 B.C., is found to tally closely with the one clear indication in Biblical tradition. This is embodied in the statement that the Exodus occurred 480 years before Solomon began to build his temple, that is about 1447 B.C., so that the date of Joshua's invasion of Canaan would fall about 1407 B.C."[52] This conclusion is fully acceptable to Kenyon as indicated in the following: "The most definite contribution comes from Jericho, where the evidence both of its destruction and of its rebuilding harmonizes strikingly with the Old Testament narrative, and also seems to assist materially in fixing the date of the Hebrew invasion of Palestine under Joshua."[53]

Assuming, then, the probability that the Hebrew invasion of Canaan is definitely a part of the Habiru movement described in the Amarna Letters, and assuming the credibility of the biblical narratives regarding

228

a period of *forty years* from the Exodus to the beginning of the invasion under Joshua, we are in a position to approximate the date of the Exodus in terms of Egyptian dynastic chronology. Any correspondence addressed to Amenhotep III would have to be placed during 1412-1376 B.C., thus determining the limit for the beginning of the invasion. In consideration of several factors which will be discussed later, we may with confidence date the beginning of the invasion of Canaan under Joshua at approximately 1407 B.C., and by the addition of the 40-year period preceding arrive at 1446 B.C. for the Exodus. Now this pivotal date of 1446 B.C., which is in complete harmony with the Amarna period plus the 40 years of wandering, and with Solomon's building project plus the 480 years specified in 1 Kings 6:1, falls at the very beginning of the reign of Amenhotep II, 1447-1420 B.C., son and successor to Thutmosis III, 1501-1447 B.C., of the Eighteenth Dynasty. These are the conspicuous monarchs on whom the searchlights of history and archaeology are now focused. On any score, if the conclusions suggested in the previous discussion are justifiable, Amenhotep II must be regarded as the Pharaoh of the Exodus, while his father, Thutmosis III, must assume the stigma of the Pharaoh of the Oppression of Israel through a considerable period of years. The evidence pointing to the correctness of these identifications is both cumulative and convincing.

The emergence of the Eighteenth Dynasty is associated with the successful revolution of native Theban princes against the hated Asiatic Hyksos who, according to Manetho, dominated Egypt for approximately 500 years, their capital city being at Avaris in the Delta. According to this interpretation of the most difficult period of Egyptian history, the Fifteenth and Sixteenth dynasties are to be regarded as distinctively Hyksos, while the Seventeenth represents an era of transition and struggle between the native population and the foreign interlopers, which resulted in the final establishment of the Eighteenth Dynasty under Amosis in 1580 B.C. Though differing in the interpretation of various dynastic details, there is practically unanimous agreement among Egyptologists that the expulsion of the Hyksos and the founding of the Eighteenth Dynasty occurred at the same time. Now this general agreement is extremely important for it enables us to determine positively some essential chronological details, and throws light on the obvious change of Egyptian state policies toward the Hebrews whose servitude was already of long duration—i.e., from 1876 B.C. when Jacob descended into Egypt, to 1580 when the Hyksos kings were overthrown. It will be observed, of course, that this period of 296 years covers neither the entire era of Hyksos domination (500 years according to Manetho) nor the total period of Hebrew bondage (430 years on biblical reckoning). But the matter of prime importance is the clear implication that as long as the Hyksos rule and Hebrew bondage were concurrent, the condition of the Hebrews was clearly not that of a menial and base servitude but, more likely, a tolerable sojourn, the explanation being found in the close ethnological relations between the two peoples. On the same assumption, the expulsion of the Hyksos would have been a clear signal for the inauguration of repressive measures against the hitherto favored Hebrews, the shepherds from Canaan. This view has strong Scripture support in the Exodus statement: "Now there arose a new king over Egypt who knew not Joseph."[54] It is perfectly obvious that, whatever the particular interpretation given this passage, the inference is that prior to the accession of this *new king* the treatment of the Hebrews up to this point had been humane and that it was clearly connected with some distinguished service

230

that Joseph had rendered to the crown. With the new ruler the state policy toward the Hebrews was completely reversed, issuing in active persecution of the Hebrews and, finally, their utter thralldom. Furthermore, the Exodus passage implies not only a new king, but also a new dynasty, and this additional requirement is fully met in the founding of the Eighteenth Dynasty. This view is suggested by the clear inference that the persecution began with the first ruler of the new regime and that it was continued by successive kings until the culmination was reached in a monarch whose oppressive measures were extremely bitter and of long duration. The Scripture support for this conclusion is likewise found in Exodus: "And it came to pass in the course of those many days, that the king of Egypt died: and the children of Israel sighed by reason of the bondage, and they cried, and their cry came up to God by reason of the bondage."[55] The historical circumstances required for the simplest interpretation of this passage are most likely provided in the exceptional career of Thutmosis III, 1501-1447 B.C.

Thutmosis III, generally characterized as one of the really great monarchs of ancient Egypt, came to the throne as the fifth Pharaoh of the Eighteenth Dynasty. His features, as represented by the court sculptors, suggest a man of extraordinary physical strength, culture, and mentality. Though all the details are not known, it was probably in recognition of these unusual gifts that his father, Thutmosis II, made him co-regent for a period of years, during which time he was under the close scrutiny of his Aunt Hatshepsut. After the death of his father, Thutmosis III inherited the throne, but his position as sole monarch was largely nullified by the presence of his domineering aunt, who was virtually the power behind the throne. Her death, probably about 1480 B.C., released Thutmosis from all restraints and as pharaoh in his own right he proceeded to accomplish his own policies for Egypt in relation both to internal administration and foreign possessions. The annals of his reign, carved on the temple walls and pylons at Karnak, set forth details of numerous military expeditions that affected not only the near-by cities of Canaan and Syria, but also included established centers located along the borders of southern Asia Minor and the great Euphrates area. His military prowess was recognized on every hand; tribute, consisting of men, women, and materials, was forwarded to the court of Egypt from Mesopotamia, from Cyprus, and from Crete. Southern Africa, the regions of Nubia, came under his dominion. During a period of approximately forty years Thutmosis engaged in seventeen campaigns of conquest. "Through these expeditions, conducted with such arrogance and inhumanity, Thutmosis III raised the power of Egypt to its zenith. Not only Canaan and Syria, as far as the Euphrates acknowledged his overlordship, but even the isles of the Mediterranean trembled at his name. The ancient supremacy of the Pharaoh over Sinai is attested by steles, sphinxes, and a hall and cave of Sopdu, the god of the East, at Serabit el-Khadim, which were all erected during his reign. The Theban Empire now stretched from Nubia to Asia Minor, and from Libya to Mesopotamia."[56]

On the other hand, while thus engaged in extensive foreign campaigns, Thutmosis was equally effective in promoting domestic undertakings. His public works program was one of the most ambitious of any Egyptian monarch, involving not only unlimited material treasures, but also vast resources of human labor, skilled and unskilled. "Possessed of such vast financial resources, Thothmes III embellished with temples over thirty cities throughout Egypt. One of the cities to which he devoted special attention was Memphis. Although the

232

ancient capital had sunk into a subordinate place relatively to the mighty and magnificent Thebes, such, nevertheless, was her venerable sanctity and prestige, that she retained undiminished her hold on the religious sentiment of the country. In the long centuries during which her southern rival enjoyed the glory of being the seat of royal authority, Memphis is again and again mentioned as a spot honored by the devotion and piety of the Theban sovereigns. But the piece de resistance of Thothmes III was his rebuilding of the famous temple of Amen at Thebes. Before the southern pylon he erected colossal statues of his father and grandfather. Then he began to reconstruct the entire edifice. Little by little he transformed it from common stone to granite, always preserving the old design, and thus he rendered it so imperishable that it has endured to the present day.''[57]

Now it is perfectly obvious that, in the accomplishment of these vast undertakings affecting both foreign and domestic interests, Thutmosis had at hand almost unlimited human resources, native and foreign. The first line of his Egyptian military might would naturally consist of native Egyptians, while the building and rebuilding programs would have been effected by foreign or slave labor. The Egyptian attitude toward subjugated peoples rendered this policy practically inevitable. In like manner, it is clear that the subsidizing of these colossal building enterprises made necessary the exacting of tribute and taxes which became almost unbearable. Amid the outward glory of his temporal rule he had also succeeded in producing unparalleled sorrow for many people through many years. ''The long reign of Thothmes III, however, drew to an end. He had been co-regent for 21 years with Hatshepset, and for 53 sole monarch, in all 74 years on the throne.[58] His scribes interested themselves

233

so much in the ancient history of the country, while at the same time flattering the glory and vanity of their long-lived sovereign, that they drew up a list of 61 of his royal predecessors, and represented him on the celebrated 'Tablet of Karnak' as adoring their majesty. To history, Thothmes III is known as the greatest military conqueror which Egypt ever produced, but to students of Scripture he is again being very generally recognized as the 'Pharaoh of the Oppression,' now that the obsession that that unenviable distinction belongs to Rameses II of the Nineteenth Dynasty is gradually being discarded.'"[59]

Finally, in setting forth the principal facts regarding the reign of Thutmosis III, 1501-1447 B.C., the probable Pharaoh of the Oppression, we have laid the foundation for several inferences which are apparently directly connected with him and with his immediate dynasty as follows: *First,* the establishment of the Eighteenth Dynasty as a result of the Hyksos Expulsion in 1580 B.C. was immediately accompanied by a new ruler of the native Theban royal line and a radical change in the state policy with reference to subject peoples in Egypt, particularly the sojourning Hebrews who had now been in Egypt for a period of approximately 296 years, the entire period being concurrent with the Hyksos domination. The persecution of the Hebrews, which began in 1580 B.C., was continued throughout the first half of the Eighteenth Dynasty, reaching its culmination during the long reign of Thutmosis III. *Secondly,* assuming the substantial correctness of 1446 B.C. as the date of the Exodus—the assumption being based on the arguments advanced in connection with the Tell el-Amarna Letters, the Habiru and the Hebrews, the apparent archaeological confirmation, and biblical chronological data—the career of Moses must be reckoned as beginning at least 80 years before

234

that event, or approximately 1526 B.C. Now this date of 1526 B.C. is not arbitrarily conceived or fixed but is fully in accord with biblical chronological references. It is of great significance, however, to find that it falls within the reign of Thutmosis I, 1545-1514, and that in this specific period we have the appearance of the Pharaoh's daughter, Hatshepsut, who was most likely the princess who rescued the Hebrew child from the Nile and named him after her own father, Thutmosis.[60] If this is merely a coincidence, it is one of the most remarkable in historic annals. It coincides not only with the biblical representations regarding the bitterness of Hebrew sufferings at the hands of the ruling Pharaoh, but provides us with explanatory details regarding the early experiences of one of the world's outstanding figures together with the exceptional preparation which he had for his unique mission.[61] *Thirdly,* the career of the great Thutmosis III as conqueror and builder provides us with appropriate backgrounds on which to project his unparalleled campaigns against foreign peoples, his arrogance and inhumanity in dealing with subjugated kingdoms, his vast public building programs which called for unending supplies both of men and materials, and the certainty that in effecting all his plans slaves in Egypt itself would be reduced to absolute thralldom. And, *finally,* the extraordinary length of his reign corresponds perfectly to the scriptural inference that many years of galling serfdom had been endured: "And it came to pass in the course of those many days, that the king of Egypt died: and the children of Israel sighed by reason of the bondage, and they cried, and their cry came up unto God."[62] Thus the wretched condition of the Hebrew slaves, inaugurated by Amosis, the founder of the Eighteenth Dynasty in 1580, and continued in ever-increasing bitterness during the intervening reigns of Amenhotep I, Thutmosis I, and Thutmosis II, reached its culmination under the great persecutor Thutmosis III, whose kingly career extended through approximately 74 years.

Immediately following the death of Thutmosis III, his son, Amenhotep II, 1447-1420 B.C., succeeded to the throne. It now appears, through the happy coincidence of several lines of converging evidence, that in this conspicuous monarch we have the Pharaoh of the Exodus, and that the great deliverance from Egypt was effected in the early part of his reign. The coincidence here referred to is found in the marvelous correspondence between the Tell el-Amarna Letters and the Hebrew narratives of conquest which would determine the beginning of the Joshua invasion about 1400 B.C. Add to this approximate date the period of 40 years, as the Wilderness wandering following the Exodus, we are brought into the early part of Amenhotep's reign. Furthermore, assuming the correctness of the chronological reference in 1 Kings 6:1 which places the building program of Solomon in his fourth year and in the 480th year after the Exodus, we get the same result— i.e., 966 B.C. $+$ 480 $=$ 1446 B.C. In like manner, the career of Moses, assuming his birth in 1526 B.C., corresponds perfectly with the requirements of residence at the Pharaoh's court and an enforced absence in the Sinaitic peninsula to appear before a new monarch demanding freedom for his people.[63] All of these correspondences converge on Amenhotep II in the beginning of his reign, 1447-1420 B.C. Nor are they arbitrarily conceived. Now, in view of these significant correspondences both in circumstances and in time, it would seem to be almost incredible that there should be no vital or even probable connection. Whatever the details, there is hardly any occasion to conjecture with reference to this monarch as the Pharaoh who let the children of Israel go. This is the great king who

236

refused the request of Moses and Aaron, who denied any knowledge of Jehovah, who stubbornly hardened his heart, and who received in turn the manifestation of divine wrath in the visitation of the ten plagues. This is the sovereign who, in the coming of the tenth plague, was unable to save his own heir, the Crown Prince of Egypt, but witnessed his passing together with the firstborn throughout the land. In probable confirmation of this tremendous tragedy, we have the stela of Thutmosis IV, Amenhotep's successor, set up at the base of the Great Harmachis, the Sphinx, at Giza.[64] "It is clear from this inscription that Thothmes' hopes of succession had been remote, which proves—since the law of primogeniture obtained in Egypt at the time— that he could not have been Amenhotep's eldest son. In other words, there is room for the explanation that the heir apparent died in the manner related in the Bible."[65]

CONCLUSION

In the foregoing discussion regarding both the Sojourn in and Exodus from Egypt, we have sought to set forth the credibility of the biblical narratives which refer to these epochal periods, claiming for the Sojourn approximately 430 years, and for the Exodus a date 480 years before the building of Solomon's Temple.[66] In support of these narratives we have used the one fixed date in Old Testament history, 854-3 B.C., to determine the accession of Solomon and his building program and thus to establish definitely 1446 B.C. as the date of the Exodus. In substantiation of this date we have argued for the period of conquest and the era of the Judges as represented in the biblical narratives. Assuming the credibility of 1 Kings 6:1, no drastic reduction of the era of the Judges can be allowed without a corresponding reduction of the 480-year period demanded by the Scripture. By the introduction of contemporary testimony which we apparently possess in the

237

Tell el-Amarna Letters, we have contended for a limited connection between the Hebrew invasion of Canaan under Joshua and the Habiru invasion affecting the same territory. This identification was justified not only on the philological argument of complete correspondence between the names Habiru and Hebrew, but further supported by archaeological and chronological considerations of prime importance. And, finally, the whole of this reconstruction has been placed in a context of Egyptian history, the Eighteenth Dynasty, where it seems to be in perfect correspondence. As a consequence, and in the light of our present knowledge, we must hold to the view which determines the Sojourn as beginning with the descent of Jacob into Egypt in 1876 B.C., the culmination of the 430-year bondage in 1446 B.C., the extreme bitterness of the persecution inaugurated in 1580 B.C. by the Eighteenth Dynasty rulers being reached in Thutmosis III, the Pharaoh of the Oppression, and the Exodus under Moses occurring during the early part of the reign of Amenhotep II, the Pharaoh of the Exodus. This view will in all probability find increasing support with the progress of archaeological investigation.

CHAPTER THIRTEEN

THE LAWS OF MOSES

THE ISRAEL STELA OF MERNEPTAH WAS DISCOVERED BY PETRIE AT KARNAK IN 1896. THE ONLY MONUMENT OF ANCIENT EGYPT TO MAKE MENTION OF ISRAEL. THE POPULAR THEORY THAT IDENTIFIED MERNEPTAH WITH THE PHARAOH OF THE EXODUS IS SERIOUSLY CHALLENGED BY THE INSCRIPTION ON THIS STONE.

HEAD FROM A RED GRANITE COLOS-
SAL STATUE OF THUTMOSIS III. HE
WEARS THE CROWN OF THE SOUTH
AND OF THE NORTH, WITH THE
URAEUS OVER HIS FOREHEAD. THIS
GREAT PHARAOH OF THE
EIGHTEENTH DYNASTY WAS PROB-
ABLY THE OPPRESSOR OF ISRAEL.

RAMESES II, NINETEENTH
DYNASTY, WAS ONE OF THE
GREAT PHARAOHS OF ANCIENT
EGYPT. RULED FROM 1292
B.C. TO 1225 B.C. UNTIL RE-
CENTLY HE WAS GENERALLY
REGARDED AS THE PHARAOH
OF THE OPPRESSION OF
ISRAEL. FATHER OF MER-
NEPTAH, 1225-1215 B.C., WHO
IS CONSIDERED BY MANY TO
HAVE BEEN THE PHARAOH
OF THE EXODUS.

CHAPTER THIRTEEN

THE LAWS OF MOSES

WITH the progress of excavations throughout the Mesopotamian area during the past half century, some outstanding recoveries have been made which have completely revolutionized all previous conceptions, both with regard to the ethnic movements of early peoples in this area and the cultural conditions under which they lived. We have long been familiar with the startling results achieved in the early excavations at Nineveh, Babylon, Tello, Sippar, etc., under Botta, Layard, Rassam, Loftus, Fusnel, Hilprecht, George Smith, Oppert, Thomas, Taylor, and many others, whereby the ancient cultural centers of the Middle East emerged from obscurity to engage the attention of the scholarly world. But, probably, more astonishing than these early discoveries connected with Mesopotamian life and thought have been the comparatively recent disclosures attending the excavations by J. de Morgan at Susa, Woolley at Ur of the Chaldees, Langdon at Kish, and Speiser at Tepe Gawra. To these may be added the phenomenal results of Winckler's work at Boghaz-koi in Asia Minor which contributed so much to an understanding of Mesopotamian backgrounds in the early part of the second millennium B.C. The effect of all these widely separated excavations has been perfectly astounding.

For our present inquiry regarding the backgrounds of the laws of Moses, the most important discovery was the finding of the Code of Hammurabi in January, 1902.

241

In the light of this specific system of laws we are able to reconstruct the conditions under which Babylonians of the Hammurabi period pursued their daily living in temple, home, and state. This far-off period is regarded as contemporary with Abraham, the father of the Hebrew people, and five centuries approximately earlier than Moses, the great Hebrew lawgiver. It is confidently believed that "this Code of Hammurabi with all its information, will necessitate the re-writing of large parts of all the works that deal with the civilizations that lie back of the constructive period of the history of the ancient Hebrews, and will reassure us of the superiority of the religious and spiritual elements in the Old Testament."[1]

The Stela was set up at Susa, a city located about 250 miles southeast of Babylon, the capital of Hammurabi's Empire. Its presence at Susa has not been fully explained. It is thought by some that a king of Elam carried off the Stela as an act of spoliation, which was then very common, and set it up in Susa as a memorial of his triumph over Babylon. On the other hand, there are those who think that the Stela was set up at Susa by Hammurabi himself, and that it was designed to acquaint the Susians with the standards of living expected of all citizens of the Empire of Babylon. This latter view is perhaps the correct interpretation on the ground that the influence of Babylon was widespread, extending as it did from Elam on the east to Palestine and Syria on the west, and from the southern highlands of Asia Minor to the headwaters of the Persian Gulf. That vast kingdom was effectively administered from Babylon on the Euphrates. Hammurabi was one of the most notable rulers of antiquity and his career is still regarded as unsurpassed among old world sovereigns. His particular glory rests upon the orderliness with which he conducted imperial affairs and the high social standards set for his subjects, both of which are reflected in the marvelous Code now bearing his name. Though drawn from many sources, including Sumerian and early Semitic people of this area, the majority of these laws may be attributed to Hammurabi himself, and definitely set forth the accepted standards of living achieved by the southern Mesopotamians through many centuries of organized society.

In close succession to this unprecedented discovery by J. de Morgan at Susa, Hugo Winckler commenced excavations at Boghaz-koi, the site of ancient Hattusas, capital city of the early Hittite Empire. Here, almost in the heart of Asia Minor, flourished the kingdom of the mysterious Hittites of the Old Testament, the people whose very existence hung by a slender thread through many years. Indeed, to the great majority of Old Testament scholars the Hittites never existed; their appearance in the early narratives of the Old Testament was purely fictitious. But with the advance of Winckler's excavations in 1906-07, the shadowy Hittites commenced to take on substance, they began to live in cities, their society became highly organized, their relations to other people became conspicuous, and, finally, they appeared in a dominant role as one of the three great nations of the Near and Middle East, disputing with and successfully warring against the powerful Babylonians on the east and the imperial Egyptians on the west. In close association with the fact of their political importance, was the discovery by Winckler of the Non-Aggression Pact between the Egyptians and the Hittites during the days of Egypt's Rameses the Great, 1288 B.C., which was likewise duly published by the Egyptian on the temple walls at Karnak. Incidentally, this is the earliest example of any recovered treaty ever adopted by two outstanding peoples of the ancient world. In addition to the text of the Egyptian-Hittite Treaty, there came to the surface about 20,000 other state documents deposited in the Foreign Office at Boghaz-koi, setting forth various aspects of Hittite relations with contemporary peoples. These documents are written in the strange and baffling characters of the Hittite language which appear in the early stage as cuneiform and later as hieroglyphics. Through the stupendous labors of King, Sayce, Hogarth, Cowley, and Hrozny these enigmatic characters commenced to yield their hidden meaning with the result that the Hittite Historical Archives are now known to a great extent. Fortunate, indeed, is the scholarly world that among these deciphered records is now an elaborate Code of Laws which the Hittites adopted for themselves and probably applied to neighboring people. This Code came to the surface during the early excavations by Winckler in 1906-07 but, because of its difficult cuneiform system, was not deciphered until 1922 when Hrozny restored it to the world.[2] Consequently, as now reflected in the Hittite Code, we can see the operations of a highly advanced social structure in the interior of Asia Minor in the early part of the second millennium B.C.

Two other developments should be mentioned at this point. *First,* located approximately midway between the great kingdoms of the Hittites and Babylonians, beginning about the ninth century B.C., Assyria commenced to emerge as a world power and to continue its ferocious sway over the nations for three centuries. Originally descended from Semitic strains coming up from the southern areas of Mesopotamia, to which was added in all probability a highland element from the adjacent regions of the Caucasus and Iranian plateaus, the Assyrians established themselves in their capital city, Nineveh, and from this center made their incursions into near-by and distant countries. Here at Nineveh lived the great Tiglath-pileser, Shalmaneser,

Sennacherib, Ashurnasirpal, Ashurbanipal, and others; here they erected their immense palaces; here they exhibited the unending processions of spoils of war, the streets resounding with the echoes of chariots and machines of war, accompanied by fabulous displays of tribute both of enslaved peoples and materials. But most important for us, here at Nineveh and in suburban areas where they built their stately mansions, the Assyrian monarchs left the historical records of their campaigns and conquests which the excavations have brought to light. Among these startling records of the past is the *Assyrian Code of Laws* found at Asshur by the German Society excavations just before the First World War and published in 1920.[3] From this Code we are able to reconstruct the general outlines of the social structure erected by the Assyrians and to compare that society with the social achievements of other ancient peoples. And, *secondly,* the recapturing of isolated Egyptian laws appearing on the monuments of early Egypt, on tombs, and in the Books of the Dead. Unlike the recovered Babylonian, Hittite, and Assyrian Codes, the Egyptian laws are not codified but, considering the highly developed civilizations of the Nile Valley, we are hardly justified in thinking that no such code was ever in existence. It is likely that, at some future time, an *Egyptian Code of Laws* might become the invaluable possession of the scholarly world. We may be sure that the Nilotic people, who were so marvelously proficient along so many lines, also conducted their society on orderly lines and that in social relations they kept well within the conventions of recognized laws and practices.

Now practically all of these legal developments among the Babylonians, Hittites, and Assyrians, which are set forth in the preceding brief summary of archaeological recoveries, fall within the short period of the

245

past fifty years. The discoveries created a sensation, particularly in critical circles where the records of the Old Testament were under constant scrutiny, for it was immediately recognized that the Code of the Hebrews, or the laws of Moses, must be reckoned among these recovered Codes both as to relative content and age of composition or origin. These are the laws preserved for us in the early sections of the Old Testament, especially in Exodus, Leviticus, and Deuteronomy. For many centuries, both among Jewish and Christian scholars, these laws have been associated with Moses, the great lawgiver, as the responsible author, or mediator to the chosen people of Israel. In modern critical procedure, on the other hand, the Mosaic authorship has largely been discarded with the result that an elaborate analysis, both as to laws and periods of origin, has taken its place, as follows: *First, The Book of the Covenant,* originally produced in the ninth century and now appearing in Exodus, chapters 20-23 (E), and Exodus 34:17-26 (J); *secondly, The Deuteronomic Code,* written in the latter part of the seventh century; *thirdly, The Holiness Code,* contained in Leviticus, chapters 17-26, and composed in the sixth century; and *finally, The Priestly Code,* produced in the fifth century and incorporated in certain parts of Exodus, Leviticus, and Numbers.[4] As will be observed at once, none of these designated groups of laws is in any sense encumbered with Mosaic authorship; on the contrary, with the exception of the Covenant Code, which is granted ninth century composition, all of these laws fall many centuries outside the era of Moses. But, in addition to the groups here mentioned, there are other laws which appear in the early records hitherto regarded as essentially Mosaic but now rejected on critical grounds as extremely late. It should be pointed out, however, that this critical analysis of Pentateuchal laws is not

246

accepted in all quarters and that, particularly, in recent years the results of archaeological recoveries have compelled a new examination of the probable date of composition of these very early narratives of the Old Testament, some of which are now believed to have been contemporary with the events they describe. With this new evidence in view, Price pointedly observes: "The critical views of the origin of many of the laws ascribed to Moses in the Pentateuch, locating them in the ninth, eighth, and seventh centuries, and even later B.C., must not only be modified, but in some cases, entirely rejected."[5] As we proceed, therefore, in our study of the Hebrew Code, or laws of Moses, in relation to the Babylonian, Hittite, and Assyrian Codes, it is the extensive corpus of laws embodied in the early narratives of the Old Testament, particularly in the Pentateuch, which are in view and which will be referred to as Pentateuchal laws.[6]

Immediately upon the discovery of the Code of Hammurabi, attention was focused on possible and probable relations existing between the laws of the Babylonians and the laws of the Hebrew people.[7] This was a perfectly logical development, for where there were so many similarities appearing in the two systems it was quite obvious that there must have been some relation, however remote; but equally obvious were the dissimilarities which no theory of dependence could explain. It was generally accepted that the Code of Hammurabi antedated the Hebrew Code by at least half a millennium, but priority of age carried no conclusive proof regarding either derivation or dependence on the part of the Hebrew laws. Indeed, the age of codification has never been the turning point with reference to the relations existing between these two systems. The fundamental consideration was deeper than a matter of mere chronology, however early or late, and struck at the spirit and ideals as well as the general content of the laws set forth.

On this principle of comparison, based on spirit, ideals, and content, there is hardly any necessity laid upon us for a minute examination of any essential relations between the Hittite Code of laws and the Hebrew system, on the one hand, nor the Assyrian and Hebrew codes, on the other. For, as suggested by Meek, "In the case of the Hittite," a code whose origin antedates the Hebrew by perhaps a century, "we need not expect much contact with the Hebrew Torah, though there was probably some Hittite blood in the Hebrew people. The code reflects a degree of culture for the Hittites in which the agricultural, industrial, and commercial life of the people was far beyond any that the Hebrews ever attained in Old Testament times. The laws are accordingly more advanced than the Hebrew laws, and the penalties are fines rather than penalties based on the *lex talionis*. There is no law strictly parallel to a Hebrew law and none that is particularly close."[8] Similarly, there is practically nothing to suggest relations of derivation or dependence between the Assyrian and Hebrew codes, though the Assyrian is certainly more ancient. "There is kindred legislation in the codes of the two peoples, but there is nothing to suggest that there was borrowing on the part of the Hebrew lawmakers from the Assyrian Code. The two have slight points of contact, but on the whole they are very different."[9] On the point of priority of date, therefore, the Hebrews would have depended on the Assyrian and Hittite codes, and these in turn on the Babylonian, but this has certainly not been the case with reference either to the Hebrew or to the Hittite.[10] The Assyrian is naturally much closer to the Babylonian, the similarities more marked and numerous.

248

Turning now to an examination of the relations existing between the Hebrew and Babylonian laws, several theories have been proposed, namely, *The Theory of Independence, The Theory of Dependence, The Theory of Intermediate Transmission,* and *The Theory of Cognateness.*[11] These views cannot here be elaborated, but a word of explanation should be given concerning each. *First,* the *Theory of Independence* rests on the proposition of possible development of social conventions in the life of two peoples widely separated geographically and with little in common politically. On this view the orderly progress of social changes and usages would naturally have produced a corpus of laws with similar content based on experience. Add to this development the Hebrew conceptions of inspiration and revelation to explain the obvious dissimilarities, the plus elements, the theory is held to be adequate. The view has serious objections, however, particularly the presence of close parallelisms between some Hebrew and Babylonian enactments both in subject matter and viewpoint. If the theory of independence were made to apply to the *immediate* relations between the Hebrew and Babylonian codes themselves, that is, that there was no conscious borrowing, but that both codes derive ultimately from a general Semitic background of common heritage, it would be substantially correct.

Secondly, the *Theory of Dependence* sets forth the formulation of Hebrew laws on the basis of Hammurabi's Code. Clearly, there can be no question of Babylonian dependence on the Hebrew since the former *antedates* the latter by more than half a millennium. "There is no doubt that there is a great similarity between the Hebrew and Babylonian codes. Both are the concrete expression of the same general principles of morality and justice, and a spirit of humaneness pervades both

249

codes, even the Hammurabi Code. There is similarity in content and sometimes in terminology and arrangement. . . . All these similarities and others like them can scarcely be regarded as wholly accidental. There must be some connection between the two codes, but the connection is not such as to indicate *direct* borrowing."[12] "A comparison of the Code of Hammurapi as a whole with the Pentateuchal laws as a whole, while it reveals certain similarities, convinces the student that the laws of the Old Testament are in no essential way dependent upon the Babylonian laws. Such resemblances as there are arose, it seems clear, from a similarity of antecedents and of general intellectual outlook; the striking differences show that there was no direct borrowing."[13]

Thirdly, the *Theory of Intermediate Transmission* sets forth the influence of the highly advanced Cannanite culture on the incoming Hebrews both at the time of the invasion and settlement in Canaan, and for a considerable period thereafter when the two peoples were closely associated. Under this view the culture of the Canaanite, being regarded as superior to the Hebrew civilization, greatly influenced the social and religious developments of Hebrew life, and ultimately determined the forms in which they were expressed. It is clear that the Canaanites themselves were dependent on the Babylonians who, as early as Hammurabi, were masters of the westland, and that in this subordinate position the Babylonian way of life and thought became dominant. Hence, the Canaanite simply transmitted that which he had received.[14] Now this theory of Cannanite influence on the evolution of Pentateuchal laws occupies a very high place in the opinion of not a few scholars. "But," as suggested by Driver, "our present knowledge does not enable us to do more than put forward the conjectures on the subject, any one of which may be shown by future discoveries to be incorrect.''[15] Indeed, that is practically the case now when, proceeding on the assumption of the western origin of the First Babylonian Dynasty (of which Hammurabi was the sixth king), this dynasty not only becomes definitely Amorite (the Amurru of the Syria-Canaan area) but the Code of Hammurabi is given a distinctive Canaanite cast. Such a view, however, while possible, is hardly probable and, furthermore, this theory of Amorite-Babylonian origins has never attained any considerable support among critics.[16] It may be said in general that the theory rests on a sound basis—i.e., with reference to the powerful influence of the Canaanite population upon the incoming Hebrews. The reactions precipitated by contacts between these two opposing groups, Canaanites and Hebrews, are reflected on practically every page of Old Testament history in its early and middle phases. But beyond this it is not necessary to go in search of positive support for the theory; everything else is negative. There is nothing upon which we can base comparisons, for no *Canaanite Code* of any description is known to be in existence, though some Canaanite laws might lie behind fragments of North Syrian, Moabite, and Phoenician laws now in hand. If the Canaanites mediated the Code to the Hebrews, the Canaanites themselves might be presumed to have had such a code in their possession; but of this there is no proof. But a far more formidable objection to Canaanite transmission lies in the assumption that the Hebrews, opposed to the polytheistic Canaanites at every conceivable point, should nevertheless have received from these people the corpus of laws which they put in the very forefront of their sacred literature, the Pentateuch.

Finally, the *Theory of Cognateness* represents both Hebrew and Babylonian laws in general as derived ultimately from a common Semitic background coextensive with the era of Hammurabi and Abraham, which in turn was definitely influenced by the earlier developments which are now attributed to the Sumerians. On this view, which is quite sufficient to explain similarities, the Hebrew and Babylonian laws meet in a common parentage of Semitic usage. Later developments in their respective spheres, together with characteristic growth of social and religious institutions, produced marked differences, especially among the Hebrews who preserved their religious, moral, and ethical values in the line of revelation and under inspiration of the Spirit spoke with a finality unparalleled. "Neither Babylonian, nor Assyrian, nor Hittite laws attain an equal level with Hebrew law in the moral and spiritual sphere. In the field of honesty, social justice, sympathy for the poor, and consideration for foreigners the Hebrew law far surpasses all previous and contemporary law. This was the outstanding triumph of the Hebrews."[17] One might also add that this Hebrew triumph in the field of ethics, of morality pitched upon the highest plane, became one of the great triumphs in the history of the world. Is it possible to grant any connection between these marvelous conceptions of the Hebrew Torah with the system set forth in the Code of Hammurabi and, at the same time, maintain the integrity or originality of the Mosaic or Pentateuchal laws?

Regarded now in the retrospect, it was one of the most remarkable things that advocates of the traditional or conservative school of Old Testament critics never seized upon the Code of Hammurabi in an effort to buttress their own positions with regard to the antiquity of Hebrew laws, on the one hand, and the obvious antiquity of the writings in which they make their appearance, on the other. One of the most convincing arguments concerning this matter must be attributed to S. A. Cook who "assumed the critical view of the Pentateuch as then presented, and made the most successful defense of the originality of the Mosaic Law yet attempted.''[18] Again, when archaeological evidences began to pour in upon us (particularly the evidences of ancient legal systems obtaining among Israel's neighbors), and when cumulative proofs of the actual literary achievements of ancient peoples overwhelmed us, the reaction was almost passive, with little appreciation of the astounding implications which they had with reference to the early narratives of the Hebrew Old Testament. But, to be more specific. Assuming the substantial correctness of the conservative views with regard to Moses and the Mosaic Age, views that are partly outlined in the preceding chapter: ''That a leader in the position to which tradition assigned Moses could perfectly well promulgate a code of laws as full and complete as the whole Mosaic law, even for a people in the primitive state of society in which Israel is often supposed to have been at the Exodus, is obvious. He had only to avail himself of the knowledge of cuneiform, available at that time both in Canaan and in Egypt, and import copies of the Hammurabi Code from Babylonia if they were not at hand where he then was. He could exercise his judgment as to what would be suitable for his people, add what he chose, and reject what he disliked. That he did this or anything like it is not asserted, but it would be so natural for anyone in his position then that we have no excuse for surprise if we should find indications of his having done exactly that.''[19] That is certainly a fair statement of the possibilities of the case, and it is made by an author who in no sense advocates Mosaic authorship for any of the Pentateuchal laws. The implication, however, that the Code of Hammurabi stands in the immediate background of the Hebrew laws and that the latter were clearly dependent on it, is open to serious objection, as we have already seen. That there is an intimate connection between the Babylonian and Hebrew laws in some definite statutes, is freely admitted, but the relation finds a more satisfactory explanation in a common ancestry for both rather than in a direct dependence of the Hebrew on the Hammurabi Code.

In the preceding discussions on Hebrew origins we have laid much stress on the general backgrounds from which the great Semitic tribes have emerged. Their ancestry has been traced to that migratory wave which came out of Arabia to penetrate at an early date the southern regions of Mesopotamia. In this lower section of the River Country we have witnessed the invasion of the mysterious Sumerians, their successful conquests, their superior civilization, their domination for a considerable period, and their final amalgamation with the numerically superior Semites. It is probable that the disappearance of the Sumerians coincided in considerable degree with the phenomenal career of Hammurabi, the great king of Babylonia, and his contemporary Abraham, the father of the Hebrew people. These are the ethnological backgrounds both of Babylonians and Hebrews. Within this historical and geographical framework appear the antecedents of Babylonian and Hebrew social conventions and ethical practices, the practical expressions of daily life and thought. The laws under which these peoples lived were not originally enacted by Hammurabi, though he might have been the responsible author for a considerable portion of them, but were rather the result of a long period of organized or even nomadic life on the part of early Semites, Sumerians, and later Semites. The recovery of actual Sumerian laws outside the Hammurabi Code, but corresponding to those within the Code, shows conclusively that Hammurabi was indebted to Sumerians for certain statutes which now appear in the Code under his own

254

name. Now it is assumed that Abraham was also familiar with these laws and that he acted in conformity with them through his subsequent experiences in Canaan. He could have brought with him actual tablets of laws then known and observed for centuries, and likewise have passed them on to his own people through other centuries. The Code of Hammurabi is not therefore an absolute requisite for Hebrew familiarity with Semitic Babylonian laws and practices. The common source from which both emerged is quite sufficient to account for any similarities or correspondences which might be claimed. But more important than any evident similarities or parallels between the two systems are the clear-cut dissimilarities which no theory of dependence can possibly explain, but which could be harmonized on the view of common ancestry plus the additional elements now characterizing the Hebrew laws.

The first of these additional elements is the presence of a *distinct monotheistic background* radically opposed to the polytheistic setting of the Babylonian laws. While this polytheistic setting is not to the front in the actual code of Hammurabi it is conspicuous in the prologue. This may be explained on the basis that the Babylonian system is primarily a civil and commerical code, that it has no reference to human conduct as defined and determined within the realm of relations with Deity, but this is the fundamental conception of the Hebrew Code, the foundation of acceptable conduct and character. "Hammurapi pictured himself at the top of the pillar on which these laws are written as receiving them from the sun-god. The Bible tells us that Moses received the laws of the Pentateuch from Jehovah. The whole attitude of the two documents is, however, different. Hammurapi, in spite of the picture, takes credit, both in the prologue and in the epilogue of his code, for the laws. He, not Shamash, established

255

justice in the land. Moses, on the other hand, was only the instrument; the legislation stands as that of Jehovah himself.''[20]

The second additional element is found in the high *ethical and moral conception* permeating the entire corpus of Pentateuchal laws. In the last analysis, these exalted views of ethics and morals are based upon the moral character of Jehovah; the plummet line of exemplary human conduct points always to the center of his moral perfection. This is something unique. There is no parallel anywhere else. It is not strange, therefore, that the whole of these laws of the Hebrew people can be summed up in the twofold aspect of right relations with Jehovah resulting in right relations with man. On the two conceptions of ''love to God'' and ''love to man'' hang all the law and the prophetic teaching.

A third additional element is found in the *spiritual content* of the Hebrew laws, the mysterious factor that somehow envisages the other-worldliness, whose ultimate looks beyond the temporal to that which is permanent, everlasting. Obviously the Pentateuchal laws make specific provisions for all social relations based on justice and righteousness, demanding always fullest compliance with standards of noblest living, but in the background the whole system is clearly predicated on the Hebrew conception of God as the supreme force making for holiness, truth, justice, and righteousness now and always.

The fourth element is found in the *universal aspect* of these Hebrew laws, particularly the Decalogue appearing in Exodus 20:1-17.[21] Here is a corpus of laws embedded in the heart of Pentateuchal legislation which not only carries force in the modern world, but in its comprehensiveness includes all human relations under all conceivable conditions of upright living. It is possible, of course, that regarding this ''absolute world-

256

A LETTER FROM TUSHRATTA, KING OF THE MITANNI, ADDRESSED TO AMENHOTEP III, PHARAOH OF EGYPT 1412-1376 B.C. WRITTEN IN THE BABYLONIAN CUNEIFORM, THE MEDIUM OF WORLD COMMUNICATION IN THE FIFTEENTH CENTURY B.C. THE TABLET COMES FROM THE GREAT TELL EL-AMARNA CORRESPONDENCE.

ON THE WEST SIDE OF THE NILE, IN THE GENERAL AREA OF THE THEBAN ROYAL NECROPOLIS, STANDS THE UNIQUE MORTUARY TEMPLE OF HATSHEPSUT, AUNT OF THUTMOSIS III, AND PROBABLE PRINCESS WHO ADOPTED MOSES INTO THE HOUSEHOLD OF THUTMOSIS I.

THE COLOSSAL STATUE OF AMENHOTEP III, AND HIS WIFE TIY, IN THE MUSEUM AT CAIRO. THE REIGN OF AMENHOTEP IS OUTSTANDING IN THE ANNALS OF EGYPT. SOME OF THE TELL EL-AMARNA LETTERS WERE ADDRESSED TO HIM BEFORE HIS HERETICAL SON, AMENHOTEP IV, MOVED THE CAPITAL FROM THEBES TO AMARNA.

THE MYSTERIOUS SPHINX CROUCHING BEFORE THE PYRAMIDS AT GIZEH, THE PYRAMID OF MENKAURE STANDS IN THE BACKGROUND. IMMEDIATELY IN FRONT OF THE SPHINX MAY BE SEEN THE STELA OF THUTMOSIS IV, WHICH SETS FORTH THE CIRCUMSTANCES OF HIS ACCESSION TO THE THRONE OF AMENHOTEP II, PROBABLE PHARAOH OF THE EXODUS.

wide scope of operation" objection could be made, as in the following: "We can hardly suppose that the leader of a group of escaped slaves would be legislating for them in terms of world-wide significance. The problems and conditions which confronted the Hebrew clans at that time were not universal and cosmopolitan; they were rather interclannish and intertribal. The laws required by the situation were such as would enable the clans to live together in amicable relations."[22] Exactly. And in the light of Israel's relation to the world—accepting the teleological principle of divine purposiveness as shown in its history—there is apparently projected through the nation this absolute and marvelous group of laws which would enable all men to live together in helpful and amicable relations. The history of these laws fully justifies any claim of comprehensiveness and application which we could make for them. We may be sure that they were not spoken in a corner nor designed merely for a local need.

And, finally, a fifth element may now be claimed for these Mosaic laws, particularly for those which describe the quality of character and conduct acceptable unto God, and that is *their finality*. Reverting to the principle of divine purposiveness with reference to Israel, we have the right to assume that any revelation which God might make through them concerning the excellencies of moral and spiritual living would be considered as obligatory and final. And, here again, it is not a question with reference to any particular theory regarding this central fact. The Ten Words do carry authority, their implications are still binding, their inhibitions are laden with ethical and spiritual dynamics, and the scope of their application unrestricted by clan or nation. Not a commandment has been rescinded nor modified. On the contrary, these commandments, mediated to the world through Moses and the people of ancient Israel, stand as forever determinative in all human relations and aspirations; in them we find the justification of the ways of God to man, the fulfillment of all laws and all the prophets.

The additional elements which we have summed up in the preceding discussion may be further defined as the *plus elements* in the Mosaic system. They are not present in the Code of Hammurabi either explicitly or implicitly; neither are they in the Codes of Hittites or Assyrians. But they are in the Hebrew Code in an explicit sense; they are also implicit in each respect of the whole context of Hebrew life and thought. They are continually elaborated throughout the Pentateuchal narratives. Now, whatever the explanation of these phenomena, such are the facts. If one were to have the audacity to proffer an explanation which, in view of all the evidences, alone seems adequate and justifiable, he would propose the simple presence of the Spirit of God in *revelation* and in *inspiration*.

The assumption of inspiration with reference to the Hebrew laws is not only a requisite for a proper understanding of their content; it is also required to explain their finality and perpetuity. It is not necessary to demand that these laws shall stand out as *de novo*, with no relation or resemblance to any other laws evolved in the experience of the human race. Inspiration must not be conceived as applying merely to that which is new; there is an inspiration of *selection*, and an inspiration of interpretation as well as an inspiration of new ideas and even new laws. Johns has a statement on this point which is clear and convincing: "It may be remembered in this connexion that according to the author of the Acts of the Apostles Moses was traditionally learned in all the learning of the Egyptians. Taking that statement as literally true, we know from the Tell el-Amarna tablets that that learning included the knowledge of cuneiform at least on the part of some Egyptian scribes before the Exodus. Philo tells us that Moses was also learned in the learning of the Assyrians who were correspondents of Egypt in the same period, of the Babylonians who wrote to the same kings at the same time, and the Chaldeans, who were then known as an independent kingdom in the Southern Sea lands of Babylonia. These and similar traditions are usually dismissed by the critics as mere senseless attempts to enhance the reputation of Moses for wisdom and knowledge, which included that of the wisest nations of antiquity. But in view of what we have seen already, may there not have been a different reason for these claims? Did not these learned men, who themselves knew much of that knowledge, recognize in the Books of Moses many startling parallels to the wisdom of Babylonia? Was it not the only acceptable way to account for such parallels to assert boldly that Moses did know these things, but in such a way that, guided by the Spirit of God, he used them so far as they were in accordance with Divine revelation, independently indeed as exercising his own discretion in selecting from them, but dependently in so far as they had found out already by man's wisdom or the light of nature that which was good and of good report?"[23] That is certainly a judicious view to take of the matter and, on further examination, will be found to be in consonance with the records themselves. There is no attempt to exaggerate the supernatural in these sacred narratives nor to embellish the events and developments therein described with divine interposition. The divine is there, the supernatural and the miraculous, but everything is under the perfect control of the Spirit of God who effects all goals through enlightened inspiration and revelation. Under this leadership room is made for those deep spiritual insights, those exalted standards of character and conduct which continually appear in the great Pentateuchal laws though they have no parallels elsewhere. Thus we may continue to advocate the uniqueness and independence of the Mosaic Law and have genuine confidence that in this corpus of moral and spiritual legislation we have the illumination of divine light and understanding.

"And yet when the most generous recognition of the best features of Hammurabi's Code has been made, the candid scholar must accord to the law of Moses a position far above the ancient Babylonian system. In the Mosaic scheme the first and greatest commandment is, 'Thou shalt love Jehovah thy God with all thy heart, and with all thy soul, and with all thy might' (Deut. vi. 5), and the second is like it in both form and spirit, 'Thou shalt love thy neighbor as thyself' (Lev. xix. 18). All the ethical precepts and legal enactments of the Pentateuch strike their roots down in the fertile soil of these two commandments. Religion and conduct are vitally related in the Bible. A man must do what is just and right because he worships a just and holy God. As his knowledge of God increases, his ethical standards are raised, and the Bible contains a progressive revelation attaining finality in Jesus Christ."[24]

CHAPTER FOURTEEN

THE SETTLEMENT IN CANAAN

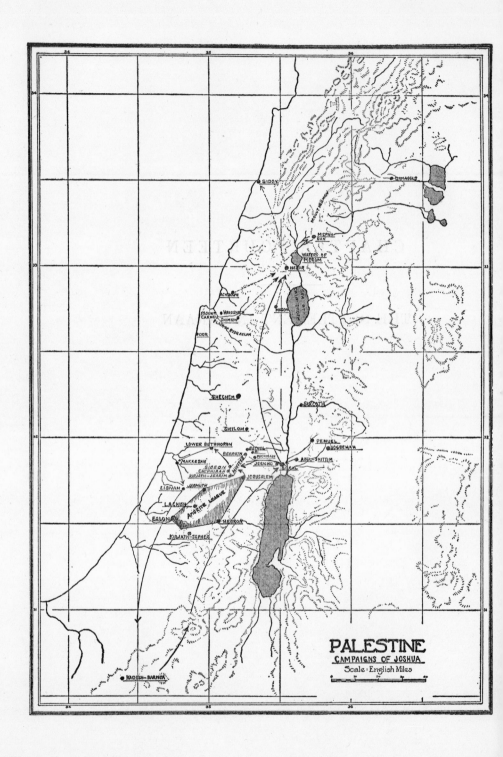

PALESTINE
CAMPAIGNS OF JOSHUA
Scale · English Miles

THE SETTLEMENT IN CANAAN

THE historical narratives of the Old Testament dealing with the conquests and tribal settlements in Canaan are in all probability contemporary records. Information derived from these sources is not only detailed, but characterized by vividness and accuracy possible only to a participant or eyewitness. Slowly but surely these ancient literary monuments of Israel's gradual overrunning of Canaan are being restored to their proper place as authoritative and credible accounts of that extensive movement.[1] Students of the Old Testament are no longer driven to a continuous defense of the records with only a few telling points against the conclusions of erratic criticism; unexpectedly, but thrice welcome, modern scientific investigation has done valiant service for the cause of truth and is constantly providing convincing proofs of the trustworthiness of the Bible in the events which it chronicles. Nor is it accidental nor incidental that where most light was needed in order to understand Israel's experiences in the land of their adoption, we now possess most reliable information enabling us not only to illustrate and corroborate the biblical records, but also to reconstruct on fairly accurate lines some difficult features of Canaanite backgrounds which the Israelites confronted and finally overcame. Particularly interesting in this respect are the Tell el-Amarna Letters recovered from the Egyptian archives a few years ago. Written in the

Babylonian cuneiform language, the common medium of diplomatic exchange during the period, they were addressed to Egyptian rulers by Canaanite petty kings who complain of a formidable people, the Habiru, now invading the country.[2] It seems quite likely that we have in these letters the Canaanite accounts of the Hebrew invasion under Joshua. While no uniformity in details could be expected from these two independent sources of the biblical narratives and the Amarna Correspondence, sufficient is given to enable us to outline with greater clearness and appreciation the numerous problems and difficulties faced by the Israelites in subjugating the territory of the Canaanites. Although these problems were simultaneous with Israel's arrival in Canaan, baffling even to Joshua, Caleb, and others of the invading forces, they were by no means confined to that particular stage. As a matter of fact, they were carried over into the succeeding phases of the struggle, coming to the most crucial point during the era of the Judges.[3]

In our present study of Israel's Settlement in Canaan, we are not primarily concerned with any details of the chronological problems of the period of the Conquest and Judges,[4] but our chief concern is to delineate the general backgrounds in which peerless leaders like Joshua, Caleb, Deborah, and Gideon struggled for Israel's existence and unification. Such a study will throw into sharp relief not only a series of brilliant achievements in battle, but also a continuous heroism on the part of the Israelites as they struggled for a foothold in the Land of Promise. For certainly it was a struggle, critical in every way to the incoming Hebrews. In its early stages it had all the features of a zealous crusade, a youth movement breaking forth from the parched sands of the Arabian desert, but in its middle phases characterized by dangers which foreshadowed dire failure unless checked. It is admitted that there were some external circumstances wholly unfavorable to the Hebrews, but the mainspring of their weakness and ineffectiveness was always within. Conquests in battle were probably essential for a possession of Canaan; retention of the country, however, was based purely on loyalty to Jehovah in all matters of His worship and their mission. These are the pivotal points around which the whole period revolves; any departure from them was followed not only by severe disciplinary measures, but constantly attended by the divine warning that permanent possession of the land was utterly futile apart from loyalty to Jehovah. While it may be granted that the modern student views all of this great process in the retrospective, knowing the actual outcome of the struggle on historical grounds, still no superficial appraisal of the movement should be allowed to remove from the picture the vital factors involved and the distressing experiences attendant thereto. In a word, the conquest of Canaan under Joshua, conceived from any standpoint, was an impossible undertaking apart from divine assistance and direction; settlement in the land was fraught with impending dangers challenging both the fortitude of the tribes and their religious mission; and, finally, retention of the conquered territory was always conditioned by concerted action of the people under aggressive and competent leadership as they struggled for the permanent possession of Canaan.

It is precisely in this transition period that we find most of all the deteriorating influences at work in the heart of Israel, with the consequent effort on the part of the leaders to salvage the unique things in Israelite life. In the initial stages of Israel's struggles, Joshua and Caleb were the agents in breaking the political domination of Canaanite tribes, thus winning at least a nominal foothold in the land though constantly challenged by strongly fortified centers. In the middle and final phases of the period the issue at stake was still the survival of Israel in the face of a strong native resistance and recurrent periods of oppression by bordering peoples. Deborah's struggles were primarily in connection with Semitic tribes in northern Canaan, though even more powerful opposition was being exerted in southern Canaan by the Philistines, the hereditary enemies of Israel. The critical nature of the Philistine oppression and their continuous effort to dominate the whole of Canaan was a major concern to Israel's leaders. To Gideon, on the other hand, was entrusted a mission designed to ward off a foreign invasion coming from the extreme southern portions of the great Wilderness of Paran and the Transjordan Area, and centering on the northern tribes adjacent to the Valley of Jezreel and the Plain of Esdraelon. Thus throughout the period of conquest and occupation, Israel was clearly on the defensive against powerful enemies bent on destruction. As we proceed to examine Israel's success in meeting this opposition, we should not think of Joshua, Caleb, Deborah, and Gideon as the only leaders who wrought valiant deeds in Israel; in reality they were simply representatives of a long line of constructive leaders who sought after and finally attained complete possession of the land and an established government for the Hebrews. The historical narratives dealing with this period are found in the books of Joshua and Judges, but extraneous material is provided in the Tell el-Amarna Letters. For information on the problem of the Philistines we depend not only on the biblical records but also on information coming from recent excavations. Now all of these matters pertaining to the movement of Israel in conquest and settlement will be discussed under the following heads: *First,* the *Military Conquest of Canaan* under Joshua,

266

Caleb, Deborah, Barak, and Gideon; *secondly, Canaan in the Tell el-Amarna Letters; thirdly,* the Hebrews in contact with *Canaanite Culture;* and *finally,* the crucial *Struggle with the Philistines.*

I. THE MILITARY CONQUEST OF CANAAN

The Hebrew invasion of Canaan began under Joshua. The biblical narratives know nothing of a dismembered Israel making independent assaults on isolated strongholds in the land of Canaan. It is a movement in which all the tribes are engaged. With the full complement of tribes, Moses and Joshua quickly subjugated the whole of Transjordania, subsequently encamping a little northeast of the Dead Sea in the Plains of Moab. After the death of Moses on Mount Nebo, the hosts of Israel are found at Abel-Shittim (meadow of the Acacias), east of the Jordan opposite Jericho. The camp was probably six miles from the river. The appearance of this territory today is that of a barren wilderness, but it should be remembered that conditions have considerably changed in the Jordan Valley as in some other parts of the country. From this point the spies were sent out to Jericho to obtain information regarding the great Canaanite stronghold. With the report of the spies in hand, Israel commenced to advance toward the Land of Promise, all the tribes participating. The miraculous passage of the Jordan was made in late spring when the river was in a state of flood. Permanent encampment was made at Gilgal, a site represented by the modern Tell Jiljul, halfway between the Jordan and Jericho. The distance of only three miles to Jericho allowed constant communication between the besieging forces of Israel and those who remained in camp.

The strategic position of Jericho at the very gateway to Canaan converted it into a border fortress

267

designed to ward off all marauding forces from the east. Excavations made at the old site (Tell es-Sultan) indicate that the city must have presented a spectacular appearance with its great walls rising abruptly from the lowlands of the Judean hills. The height of these walls was approximately thirty feet, the foundations being composed of rock, while the superstructure was largely of brick. In early Amorite fashion, the inclosed city was entered only by one gate which, as in the case of Jerusalem, was located nearest to the water supply of the town. The Jericho gate stood immediately opposite the spring of Elisha on the eastern side of the mound. According to the narrative, the spies did not make their escape by way of the town gate but were let down from the wall. The flight of the spies to the mountain suggests that Rahab's house stood on the western side of Jericho looking to the hills of Judea. The whole area of the city consisted of about seven acres, with a population around four thousand. The overwhelming forces of Israel discouraged any counter movement on the part of Jericho, thus giving the unusual spectacle of an investing army unmolested in every phase of its movement around the city. It is clear that Jericho could have been reduced to submission by prolonged siege, but the divine plan called for a miraculous deliverance, and consequent devotement both of the city and its spoil as an expression of Jehovah's judgment against the heinous iniquity of the rejected Canaanites. Startling indeed have been the results of excavations at Jericho in their confirmation of the biblical narratives regarding the fall of the city. Evidences indicate the following items in particular: First, the apparently impregnable walls of the city fell, as stated in the Joshua account, under their own weight. Remains of these walls are now exposed in the midst of complete desolation. Second, in the light of pottery remains, the approximate date of the city's destruction can be fixed at 1400 B.C., the exact period when the Israelite invasion occurred.⁵ And, finally, according to the curse pronounced against the rebuilding of Jericho, excavations disclose that the mound remained deserted until the era of Ahab, when Hiel the Bethelite began to rebuild the city on its old foundations.⁶

With Jericho in ruins, the Israelites were at liberty to proceed into the interior of Canaan. Following the ancient pass by way of Michmash, Joshua chose to advance to the plateau section of southern Canaan rather than to attempt the more difficult route along the Jericho-Jerusalem ascent. By way of Michmash he would come to Ai, two miles east of Bethel, and at Bethel attain an open country with Jerusalem only ten miles to the south. Israel's assault on Ai, however, was disastrous because of the sin of Achan in hoarding the spoil of Jericho, which was followed by severest judgment in the Valley of Achor. In close connection with these events was the visit of the Hivite spies, whose deceptive strategy involved Israel in a defensive and offensive alliance which provoked opposition on the part of five of the most important strongholds in southern Canaan, Jerusalem, Hebron, Jarmuth, Eglon, and Lachish. Your map will show the relative positions of these great centers. You may trace the forced march of Joshua to succor the Hivite allies, Kirjath-Jearim, Chephirah, Beeroth, and Gibeon, before the walls of the last named place. The distance from Jericho to Gibeon was twenty-four miles. Joshua's arrival was a complete surprise to the Amorite kings, who were routed, fleeing down the Ajalon Valley by way of the famous Bethhoron Pass into the Shephelah area and finally into the plains. After this decisive victory, Joshua pressed his campaign in a gradual overrunning of other Amorite and Canaanite strongholds in the vicinity

269

of Beersheba, Kadesh-barnea, Kirjath-Sepher, and Hebron.

In the last phase of his campaigns, Joshua massed his forces in northern Canaan on the southwest coasts of the Waters of Merom (Lake Huleh), to meet a powerful confederacy of Canaanites under the leadership of Jabin, king of Hazor. In all probability the battle was fought south of Hazor, a formidable place about four miles from the lake. Here for the first time Israel fought a battle in the open field, opposed likewise for the first time by powerful horse-drawn chariots of iron. Through brilliant strategy and rapid movement of soldiers, Joshua defeated the confederates, pursuing them under Mount Hermon as far as Dan. Here again recent archaeological investigation helps us in determining the approximate date of this struggle; the pottery remains indicating that Hazor was completely destroyed about 1400 B.C. All of this is in strict conformity with the biblical narratives. With the Canaanites vanquished, Joshua returned to southern Canaan for final allotment of territory to the several tribes. Much territory remained unconquered, many strong cities were still occupied by the enemies of Israel, but Joshua succeeded in breaking the first line of Canaanite resistance to the Hebrews. The full fruits of his military campaigns come to the front during the periods of the Judges and the Kings.

The second phase of the movement of Conquest is set forth in the work of Caleb in the neighborhood of Hebron. The city of Hebron and its environs became the possession of Caleb. It was a reward for his fidelity in spying out Canaan and recommending an immediate advance out of Kadesh-barnea for its conquest. In this recommendation he was joined by Joshua, though the ten spies advised against any effort to take a country where men were giants and cities were walled up to

270

heaven. It is accordingly significant that the two men who were most aggressive and confident regarding the ultimate victory in Canaan should have been most instrumental in achieving that end. In any event, Canaan was more than a promised land; its possession was conditioned by most exacting struggles, tests of Israel's physical endurance, mental discipline, moral courage, and religious loyalty. Upstanding and outstanding in meeting these tests were Joshua and Caleb who, forty-five years after the failure of Israel at Kadesh-barnea, entered into their inheritance in the land promised to Abraham, Isaac, and Jacob. It is fitting that one section of the country, Hebron, so intimately associated with the patriarchs, should have become the possession of Caleb, a valiant and knightly soul.

Hebron stands on one of the oldest foundations in the land of Canaan. Our records state that it was originally called Kirjath-Arva, having been founded seven years before Zoan (Tanis) in Egypt.[7] This note is of considerable importance in showing the antiquity of Hebron, since Zoan is known to have been a flourishing city as early as the Sixth Egyptian Dynasty, or 2600 B.C. The location of the town was practically on the modern site in the Judean highlands, 3,000 feet above the Mediterranean, eighteen miles south of Jerusalem. Hebron stands on the main highway which enters Canaan at the Waters of Merom, extending south through the Plain of Esdraelon to Dothan, Shechem, Bethel, Jerusalem, Bethlehem, Hebron, Beersheba, and the Wilderness of Shur to Egypt. In addition to this main arterial connection, Hebron was at the junction point of a network of roads penetrating every part of southern Canaan. Its position was pivotal in all commercial, social, and military relations. One sees at a glance that the patriarchal residence was correspondingly at the heart of things. The association of the patriarchs converted Hebron into one of the most sacred places in Canaan, an importance which persists through the modern era. Caleb's inheritance accordingly embraced not only a flourishing business center, but also the custodianship of Israel's ancestral tombs in the cave of Machpelah which Abraham purchased from the sons of Heth. There is little question regarding the site of Machpelah; continuous tradition connects it with the sacred area over which the Hebron Mohammedan Mosque now stands. The modern city of Hebron, with a population of about 25,000, is called El-Khalil, or city of the Friend, referring, of course, to Abraham the friend of God. Bedouin fanaticism is usually dangerous in Hebron, as witnessed in recent Jewish-Arab relations when several theological students in the Jewish Seminary were killed. But the town is a delightful place to visit. At Hebron one stands in the steps of a long line of patriarchs and their immediate descendants, of Caleb to whom the city was given, and of David who reigned here for seven years before taking Jerusalem for his capital city.[8]

In connection with the inheritance of Caleb in Hebron must be taken the ancient stronghold of Debir or Kirjath-Sepher, a city given by Caleb to his son-in-law Othniel. Its definite location has always been a matter of dispute, but certainly the biblical narratives call for a site not far removed from Hebron on the borders of the South Country. It seems fairly certain that the modern excavations at Tell Beit Mirsim are reintroducing us to Kirjath-Sepher, revealing a cultural history antedating the period of Abraham. Captured by the Israelites at the time of the Hebrew invasion, the city became one of the most important centers of Israelite culture and influence. The final chapter of the town was written when it was totally destroyed during

AKHNATON OR AMENHOTEP
IV, FOUNDER OF THE NEW RE-
LIGION ATONISM, APPEARING
IN HIS FAVORITE HEADGEAR
AND BEARING A TRAY OF
OFFERINGS. SOME EFFORT
HAS BEEN MADE TO IDENTIFY
THE NEW RELIGION AS A
FORM OF MONOTHEISM IN THE
FIFTEENTH CENTURY B.C.

STATUE OF AMENHOTEP IV, HERETICAL PHARAOH OF EGYPT, WHO OUT-
LAWED THE AMON-RA RELIGION OF HIS FATHERS, AND INTRODUCED THE
NEW CULT OF ATONISM OR WORSHIP OF THE SUN'S DISK. IN KEEPING
WITH THIS RELIGIOUS REVOLUTION, HE CHANGED HIS OWN NAME TO
AKHNATON AND REMOVED THE CAPITAL FROM THEBES TO TELL
EL-AMARNA.

Nebuchadnezzar's invasion of Canaan. The ruins of Kirjath-Sepher are located southwest of Hebron overlooking the Shephelah area into the Plains of Philistia. Its nearness to the great commercial routes cutting through Canaan north and south rendered the city very important in trade relations, while the strong fortifications now uncovered indicate the importance of Kirjath-Sepher from a military standpoint. The name of the city (signifying "book town" or "town of Scribes") encouraged excavators to expect here the recovery of records bearing on ancient Israel, but nothing of unusual importance has yet come to the surface.[9]

A third phase of the Hebrew conquest is shown in the struggles under Deborah and Barak. The period of the conquest witnessed no event more important for the establishment of the tribes in the midst of hostile neighbors than the epochal struggle of Deborah and Barak with the Canaanite forces under Sisera. The scene of the struggle was somewhere in the southwestern section of the Plain of Esdraelon, between the foothills of Mount Carmel and Mount Tabor. The distance between these two points is only fourteen miles. The biblical narratives probably indicate the exact place in their reference to the River Kishon, whose principal source is in the immediate vicinity of ancient Megiddo. While the forces of Israel were likely massed on the slopes of Tabor, it would have been impossible for the battle here described to have occurred at that place. Obviously the engagement was in the open field, with Deborah and Barak moving against the enemy from the northeast and pushing them backward toward Megiddo and the River Kishon lowlands. The battle occurred, in all probability, during the winter or early spring, when the rainy season continues with disastrous results to caravans within waterlogged areas. The Plain of Esdraelon is particularly treacherous within this period.

273

Maintaining only a slight elevation above the Mediterranean, with practically no outlet except the Kishon Basin, the great territory is drained very slowly. One can well understand the predicament of the Canaanites when pressed into this water-soaked area. Their heavy chariots of iron sank into the soft earth, horses struggled for foothold, but in vain. Deborah and Barak in their song of triumph described the helplessness of their foes, when even the stars in their courses fought against Sisera. Though poetically expressed, that was exactly the situation in Esdraelon; the discomfiture of the Canaanites was an event in which heaven and earth combined for complete destruction. The scene of this decisive engagement may be located easily on the map.

A study of the fourth and fifth chapters of Judges will set in sharp relief the splendid victory of Israel and its significance for the struggling tribes, particularly Zebulun, Issachar, Naphtali, and Manasseh, whose territory was constantly menaced by these strongly entrenched people. Indeed, it should be remembered that the tribal allotments for these groups in Israel, while the most attractive in Canaan, were likewise the most exposed to hostile forces who successfully prevented a permanent foothold on the part of Israel until the days of David and Solomon. Among these Canaanite strongholds the most powerful were Hazor, Megiddo, and Taanach, but other towns of significance engaged in the unequal combat against the ill-disciplined forces of Israel. Hazor was located four miles southwest of the Waters of Merom, Megiddo, and Taanach on the southern borders of the plain, while Harosheth stood at the entrance to Esdraelon overlooking the Kishon depression. There is some question regarding the location of Harosheth, but Megiddo and Taanach are well known through excavations, their recovered evidences pointing to conspicuous and overmastering centers from

274

earliest days. Our record is careful to state that the outcome of Deborah's victory gave to Israel a comparative rest for forty years, but the Canaanites were not subdued in those impregnable cities. They will continue to harass Israel until the era of Solomon, when the Israelite ruler himself will convert some of these cities into fortified outposts of his own kingdom. To Deborah, however, must be attributed a powerful blow at the Canaanite domination in Esdraelon and, ultimately, their disintegration in the north.

A fourth phase of the Hebrew struggles in holding Canaan during this crucial period is illustrated in the career of Gideon. Standing on the actual field of battle where Gideon attacked the overwhelming hosts of Midianites and Amalekites, one has no difficulty in visualizing even the minutest detail of the uneven struggle. Midian and Amalek pushed up from the east to encamp against Israel in the Valley of Jezreel. The invading multitudes covered the northern side of the valley along the slopes of the Hill Moreh, while the forces of Israel massed at the base of Mount Gilboa to the south. At the foot of the mountain a copious spring still gushes forth with life-giving waters. There can be no question but that by the side of this brook Gideon selected the three hundred men according to divine instruction. One can see vividly Gideon and the servant on their secret visit to the Midianite camp across the vale, can understand their joy in hearing the soldier's dream concerning the barley loaf which rolled out of Gilboa to overturn the camp of the Midianites. Under cover of night three bands of Israelites surrounded the camp of Midian prepared for a surprise attack. The weird scene of burning torches, plus the ring of shattered water jars and the exultant cry of confident soldiers, dismayed the Midianites, who attempted to

275

escape down through the Valley of Jezreel to the Jordan, the way by which they had come. Gideon and the augmented forces of Israel pursued the fleeing Midianites into Transjordania by way of Succoth, Penuel, and Jogbehah.

While the details of this event are full of interest, attention is here centered on three aspects. In the first place, the incursion of the Midianites is a recurrent phase of nomadic movements which persist in the East until now. Bedouin raids are almost inevitable, being occasioned by insufficient rainfall in arid regions, particularly along the eastern borders of Transjordania, Arabia, and the vast area immediately south of Canaan. Out of these parched wastes and barren steppes come periodic movements of desert tribes into more favored territory where nature provides water and pasturage. Midianites and Amalekites constituted only a part of this great desert population whose migrations always depended on geographical conditions. Second, the Midianite invasion struck at the richest portion of Canaan, the actual granary of the land, the possession of which was necessary not only for native security but also for livelihood. It is clear that having once obtained control of the Valley of Jezreel, the Plain of Esdraelon was open to the invaders, carrying with it easy approach to every other section of the country. Domination over this bit of territory was essential for lordship in Canaan. Gideon's repulse of the Midianites accordingly had far-reaching results regarding Israel's survival in the Land of Promise. And, finally, the victory of these northern tribes reacted favorably on the tribesmen themselves in that it foreshadowed other possible triumphs in concerted action. Unification of the scattered tribes was still a long way off, but every victory contributed something to the great ideal of Israel's leaders for a united people and country.

II. Canaan in the Tell el-Amarna Letters[10]

In the foregoing discussion of the military campaigns issuing in the conquest of Canaan, we have relied mainly on the early narratives of Joshua and Judges, to which we have added corroborative evidence from archaeology to throw light on certain pivotal centers and areas coming to the front during the process of the movement. In the present summary of Canaan in the Tell el-Amarna period which, in its latest phase, coincided with the conquest, our principal source of information is found in the Amarna Letters themselves. For, as already shown, these letters for the most part originated in Canaan; they were addressed by Canaanite subject kings to their great Egyptian overlords Amenhotep III and Amenhotep IV, especially the latter, who was then dwelling at his new capital Tell el-Amarna (Akhetaton). These letters fall within the period of 1412-1362 B.C. and are accordingly contemporary with the closing phases of Joshua's career and the early part of the era of the Elders and Judges.

The general conditions reflected in the Amarna Letters show Canaan at this particular period to be a definite part of the Egyptian Empire. Though Egyptian influence in Canaan is long anterior to the Hebrew invasion about 1400 B.C., it was during the brilliant reign of Thutmosis III, 1501-1447 B.C., that the whole territory was brought within the sphere of Egyptian imperialism, and by repeated invasion was kept subject to the Egyptian crown. This complete subjugation to Egypt is reflected in the appeals for succor addressed by the local kings of Jerusalem, Taanach, Lachish, Gezer, Hazor, etc., to Egypt. Though widely separated, all of these cities lie within the borders of Canaan north and south. It is known, of course, that these cities are the very centers affected by the Habiru-Sagaz movement. In spite of frantic appeals for help, the Canaanite cities gradually fell to the invading Habiru, and the country slips from Egyptian control. The culminating point in this process came after the Nineteenth Dynasty rulers, Rameses II and Merneptah, when independence was achieved under David and Solomon.

On the other hand, while politically dependent on Egypt during the Eighteenth and Nineteenth Dynasties, from a cultural point of view Canaan looked to Babylonia. The very fact that the Amarna Letters were written by Canaanite kings in the Babylonian cuneiform, rather than in the Egyptian hieroglyphics, or even in a Canaanite alphabetic, shows the dominance of Babylonia. It is now clear that the cuneiform system provided the common medium of communication between east and west at this very early date. But this startling revelation which has so recently come to the scholarly world, though previously unrecognized, finds intimations not only in the early records of the Hebrews but also in the then contemporary annals of Babylonia. In all probability the culture of Canaan was more dependent on Babylon than on Egypt. However, whether indebted more to Babylon or Egypt, the culture of Canaan is now shown by the excavations to have been inferior to neither. This revelation has also produced astonishment among students of Near and Middle East civilizations.

Furthermore, in addition to these general points of contact with their overpowering neighbors, culturally and politically, the Canaanites in the Amarna Letters appear in hopeless disagreement, even belligerency, among themselves. The internal conditions of Canaan reflected in the letters are completely chaotic. The immediate occasion of this state of affairs is in all likelihood found in the Habiru-Sagaz invasion which, on highest probability, is to be equated with the Hebrew conquest under Joshua. The Correspondence might be characterized not only as a collection of state documents addressed to a ruling sovereign of Egypt, but just as truly as an assortment of classics in villification, treachery, slander, suspicion, treason, insinuation, and hypocrisy. Of course, among these letters there are also expressions of perpetual loyalty and allegiance to the Pharaoh. It is likely, however, that the Pharaoh, confronted with such a chorus of charges and countercharges, protestations of allegiance and outright treachery, hardly knew his friends from his foes. Here again, it is altogether possible that this very weakness among the Canaanite rulers, their disunity and disloyalty, came to be the determining factor in their dissolution and the final success of the Hebrews. But this point is not unduly pressed, for it is equally clear that the disinterested attitude of the Pharaohs, particularly Amenhotep IV, was probably the basic cause for the collapse of his empire. Still, whatever the explanation, the Tell el-Amarna Letters describe conditions in Canaan as chaotic and desperate at the time of the Hebrew invasion.

III. The Hebrews and Canaanite Culture

In our summary of the Tell el-Amarna period in Cannan we were careful to point out that the civilization of the Canaanites was in no sense inferior to the culture of their neighbors, particularly the Egyptians and Mesopotamians, and that in some respects it might have had even higher qualities. Such a statement, however, was intended to apply to its economic status, its arts, and to other features of its external development, but not to its religious retrogression which finds no parallel among bordering people. From Kadesh-barnea the Hebrew refugees looked over into Canaan as "a land overflowing with milk and honey," but it was also a land filled with perils for their new-born faith and mission.[11] These perils are not specified in the report of the spies, but they are clearly implied in the preview of Canaan given in the following: "But in the fourth generation they shall come hither again: for the iniquity of the Amorite is not yet full."[12] It is one of the astounding facts of biblical archaeology that this very aspect of culture in Canaan appears at this period as its most sordid and debased. It is here, too, that criticism has signally missed the point in ascribing the eradication of the Canaanites to an arbitrary and bloodthirsty Deity when, as plainly implied in the Genesis passage, the retribution is based solely on moral and ethical grounds, the reaction of God to iniquity. It follows, of course, that the conflict of the Hebrews with this form of Canaanite culture was fundamentally religious; that it was actually a moral and spiritual death struggle between the Hebrews and the Canaanites, the outcome of which, though reached centuries later, demonstrated the supremacy of the Hebrew standards both for thought and conduct. For with all the vaunted culture of Canaan, with its favorable comparison with the civilizations of Egypt and Mesopotamia from which it was chiefly derived, the religion of Canaan now appears as the most sordid in any area of the Near and Middle East. Its lurid story is gradually being unfolded with the progress of excavations in Canaan.[13] "Later on, when Israel entered Canaan, they came in contact with a civilization the ingredients of which were Egyptian and Babylonian. Thutmose III had done his best to 'Egyptionize' the country.[14] He had educated the children of Syrian princes in Egypt and later returned them to govern Syrian and Palestinian city-states for him. Egyptian garrisons made the country secure. In some courts the Egyptian language was employed.[15] The gods of Egypt followed the army

280

and worship was paid to Osiris, to Ptah, and particularly to Amon. Goods of Egyptian manufacture flooded the country. It is probable that when the Hebrews invaded Palestine the political leadership of Egypt was in jeopardy, but her social prestige still challenged the Babylonian. This culture the Hebrews inherited and assimilated in taking over the country.''[16]

The chief characteristic of the religion of Canaan, like that in Mesopotamia and Egypt, was that it represented a great pantheon whose principal divinities were associated with natural phenomena, particularly those dealing with fertility in crops, in flocks, and in human kind. This conception of religion found its expression in cults of various descriptions which appealed to all that was low in human nature. The list is a formidable array of competing divinities gathered from Egypt, Babylonia, and Canaan: *Teshuv-Heppa,* storm god and female consort from North Syria; *Osiris-Isis,* fertility god and wife introduced from Egypt; *Baalath,* the lady of Gebal, who became at home in Canaan; *Shamash,* solar god of Babylon; *Haddad-Rimmon,* storm god from Syria and, probably, Asia Minor; *Tammuz-Adonis,* fertility god, and *Ishtar,* goddess of love and ''queen of heaven''; *Baal,* and *Baalim; Astarte, Anath,* etc. These were the gods and goddesses who made continual appeals to human nature at its weakest points. During the 1928 season of excavations at Kirjath-Sepher, however, we came into possession of one of the startling recoveries in archaeology, the *Serpent Stela,* which is described by Kyle as follows: ''The elements of the importance of this cult object do not lie on the surface, and its significance will not appear to those who are simply able to look at striking things and marvel. Snakes are not pretty. But to the student of ethnology, especially to the student of Palestinian culture, and above all to the student of the background of that

Canaanite life which resulted in a decree of capital punishment from Heaven itself, this object will be of the utmost importance. Some people are quite distressed at what they conceive to be a strange and unworthy representation of God in the decree of the extermination of the Canaanites. There are indeed persons who are horrified at the practice of most nations on earth, at the present time and in history, of putting to death notorious murderers, more, far more horrible indeed, than at the cruel and senseless murder that the criminal had committed. . . . So when we get a glimpse of the practices of these Canaanites, their revolting licentiousness, their horrible child sacrifice, and the debasing character of their manner of worship, here, in fact, loathsome serpent worship, the worthiness of God's dealing with such people loses its seeming objectionable features. These people from whom comes this remarkable object, whether idol or symbol, were the Canaanites living in the land at the time the Israelites came in and were designated to be the executioners of the divine sentence.''[17]

But in addition to these gross conceptions of deity, together with base cult-objects attending their worship, there was the high place. In Canaanite religion the centers of worship in the land were the High Places (bamoth). To a certain extent we can reconstruct these sanctuaries from the descriptions that have come down to us. ''A hoary but vigorous tree, hung with rags and with other votive offerings; beside it one or more pillar-stones, which served at once as images and as altars, acting as intermediaries between the material world of the worshipper and the intangible world of the being to whom he addressed his worship; a wooden post, perhaps worked rudely into a human semblance,—a well, whence water could be drawn for lustrations and for libations; a tumulus, marking the restingplace

282

of some ancient worthy, whose spirit brooded over the sanctuary and received at least a share in the ritual worship—of these elements, in various combinations, were the Canaanite and early Hebrew High Places made up."[18]

But these are not all of the abominations of the Canaanites. In a system of religions where moral and ethical conceptions had reached the vanishing point, human life was correspondingly cheap. This in turn led to the practice of human sacrifice, the subjects being for the most part infants but also including youths and adults. Though not practiced among the Hebrews as a part of their religion, there are examples of such sacrifices in the Old Testament narratives.[19] The incident of the attempted offering up by Abraham of Isaac, however, cannot be invoked in this connection except to prove that human sacrifice was *not* pleasing in the sight of God.

Finally, there is no necessity of indicating other features of the religion of Canaan which confronted the Hebrews on their arrival in the land. In the context of that which has already been given, it is apparent that the religion of the Hebrews was facing its supreme test. The Old Testament echoes with the resounding clash between Hebrew and Canaanite when the lofty and spiritual conceptions of God, the moral and ethical requirements of Israel's faith, and the demands of a contrite heart as acceptable sacrifice, were all imperiled on every hand by their opposites. It is now known that in this struggle the Hebrew finally emerged triumphant, but the conflict was none the less real and unrelenting. The Canaanite background was not therefore the environment out of which the religion of Israel *evolved,* but was rather the arena in which it fought and won its battles for spiritual religion and for the exalted conceptions of ethical monotheism.

IV. STRUGGLE WITH THE PHILISTINES

But falling across the path to the complete unification of Israel and the permanent possession of Canaan was the dark shadow of the Philistines, the hereditary enemies of the Hebrews. These people, together with the Hittites and Horites, have long been numbered among the mystery peoples of the Old Testament. But, while the history of the Hittites is slowly being reconstructed in the light of Winckler's recoveries at Boghaz-koi, and the enigmatic Horites now appear in the outstanding Hurrians of the northeast Mesopotamian area, the story of the Philistines still remains unknown.[20] Though among the most important peoples of the Old Testament, practically every fundamental question relating to their history and civilization remains unanswered.[21] We would like to know definitely the land of their origin, their primary ethnological connections, the exact time of their arrival in Canaan, the full content of their religion, and the language which they employed. These are all vital questions, but the best that we can do is to approximate the answer to each. On the other hand, though our information is not complete, we are perhaps justified in making the inferences set forth in the following paragraphs.

The great majority of critics, assuming that the Caphtor of Amos is to be equated with the island of Crete, place the *original home* of the Philistines in this sea kingdom immediately south of the Greek mainland.[22] In all probability this identification will meet fully the requirements of all future tests. At present it meets one of the requisites in Philistine movements, namely, that they were a great seafaring people, or sea-rovers, who were perhaps driven from their homeland to seek refuge elsewhere. And, strangely enough, the Knossos

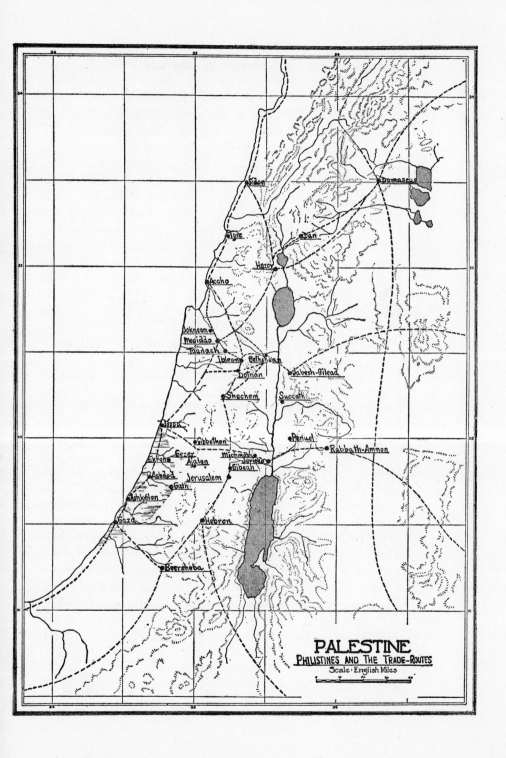

PALESTINE
PHILISTINES AND THE TRADE-ROUTES
Scale · English Miles

excavations in Crete, where Evans uncovered the marvelous Minoan civilization, would supply the background for such a forced migration at approximately the same time the Philistines are believed to have arrived in Canaan.[23] There is a difficulty in making this identification unconditional, however, for it is not known positively that the Minoans and the Philistines are the same people.[24] As will be seen later, though the Philistines may not be identical with the Minoans, it is practically certain that they came from Crete and that there was some connection between the two. Furthermore, it seems fairly certain that the Philistines were among the Peoples of the Sea (tribes of the Mediterranean area, some of them Greeks living in the Aegean Islands), "who attacked Egypt in the thirteenth and twelfth centuries B.C., having already appeared on the coasts of Syria as early as the end of the fifteenth."[25] On the basis of our present knowledge, we are not able to distinguish clearly many of these peoples or tribes as, for example, the Caphtorim, the Keftim or Keftians, the Pulesati-Purasati-Pelishti, the Zakkala, the Lycians, Mysians, Carians, Cherethites, Pelethites, etc., though we may be confident that there were intimate connections, and that actually they were all involved in the same general upheaval of Aegean peoples making their way to the littoral of the eastern Mediterranean. The great concentration effected by the Philistines resulted in the conquest of southwestern Canaan where they firmly established themselves for several centuries.

If Crete could be shown conclusively to have been the home of the Philistines, that fact would have considerable bearing on their *ethnological connections*. Crete was definitely not a part of the Semitic world; its inhabitants must be classified among the Greek or Aryan groups. General representations on the monuments show the Philistines as marked by distinctive

Greek features, including facial lines, physique, and habiliments. In the early records of the Old Testament the Philistines always appear as the great uncircumcized, the foreigners *par excellence,* totally distinct from Semitic inhabitants of Canaan. In relation to the Hebrews, the Philistines are the hereditary enemies of the people of God, from whom no concessions were asked and to whom no quarter was ever given. Though this bitter antagonism might be attributed to political and religious causes, the principal explanation probably lies in racial differences. Anti-Semitism finds in the Philistines one of its classical expressions, while anti-Aryanism on the part of the Hebrews is equally pronounced. It is usually accepted that the Cretan origin of the Philistines definitely determines their ethnological connections, thus placing them among that great mass of Aegean peoples whose antecedents are distinctly related to Hellas or Greece. In establishing themselves in Philistia, their whole life centering in the great Pentapolis—Gaza, Gath, Ashkelon, Ashdod, and Ekron—the Philistines struggled not only against the Hebrews but positively sought the preservation of their own distinctive way of life and thought.

The time of their *arrival in Canaan* can only be approximated. The majority of modern critics will not allow the great body of Philistines to arrive in Canaan before the beginning of the twelfth century B.C., the exact time being fixed by the victory of Rameses III over the Peoples of the Sea in 1194 B.C. As a result of this Egyptian triumph, the would-be invaders were thrown out of Egypt and compelled to retreat northward to Canaan. This retreat was continued until they reached the plains of southwestern Canaan where they effected their permanent settlement. There is no serious disposition to question the verdict of the monuments, and in all quarters it is freely admitted that at this

287

time, 1194 B.C., there was probably a great wave of Philistines (who were among the Peoples of the Sea) reaching Canaan. It is an open question, however, whether these were the only Philistines to reach Canaan. In all probability there were other Philistines who in earlier days established themselves in the southwestern plains around Gerar, Gaza, and Gath. It will not do to argue dogmatically that all biblical references to Philistines in the days of the patriarchs are anachronistic, and that there is no ground for allowing the presence of any Philistines in Canaan even as late as the period of the Exodus (1446 B.C.). We simply do not have in hand all the information needed with reference to these mysterious people. As already shown, there were many related tribal movements from the Aegean area headed for the Syrian coastlands as early as the fifteenth century B.C., and the Philistines may well have been among these kindred peoples. Furthermore, the recovery of the Philistine civilization progresses very slowly. Of course it is impossible now to follow up excavations under war conditions, but even prior to this period no exhaustive excavations have been in any of the strictly Philistine territory. It is true that some work was undertaken at Ashkelon, but the lack of funds necessitated its discontinuation. Petrie's excavations at Gaza (Tell Ajjul) were rather successful, but not as comprehensive as his labors at Gerar (Tell Jemmeh) nine miles south of Gaza. The treasures of Ashdod remain to be uncovered, while the hidden secrets of Ekron and Gath (whose sites are not definitely known) are safely kept until some future expedition will be fortunate enough to uncover them. Furthermore, we are not yet thoroughly informed as to the exact relations between the ceramics and various artifacts produced by the Mycenaean and Cypriote civilizations, on the one hand, and the Philistine, on the other. Consequently, we must

288

THE GREAT STELA OF HAMMURABI ON WHICH THE BABYLONIAN MONARCH
IS SHOWN RECEIVING THE LAWS FROM SHAMASH THE SUN GOD.   THE
STELA IS ONE OF THE MOST IMPORTANT DISCOVERIES IN THE HISTORY
OF ARCHAEOLOGY.   IT HAS PROFOUNDLY AFFECTED THE CRITICISM OF
THE OLD TESTAMENT.

IN THE SPRING OF 1935, TWO LARGE INSCRIBED STONES WERE WASHED
DOWN FROM MOUNT GERIZIM. THE INSCRIPTIONS SET FORTH THE SA-
MARITAN TEN COMMANDMENTS. THE LANGUAGE EMPLOYED IS THE
BEAUTIFUL SAMARITAN SCRIPT, WHICH IS CLOSELY RELATED TO THE
HEBREW. IN THE MOSLEM MOSQUE AT NABLUS THERE IS A DUPLICATE
OF THESE COMMANDMENTS BUILT INTO THE WALL.

speak with some measure of caution regarding the early presence of Philistines in Canaan. Petrie's reservation in this connection illustrates exactly the point in view: "There are references to 'the land of the Philistines,' and 'all the borders of the Philistines,' at the Exodus. But the Philistines were not present in force under Rameses II (1290), and are only shown on the monuments of Rameses III (1190 B.C.)... This limitation of the Philistines does not apply to the scanty trading centres of earlier days, as far back as the time of Abraham."[26] Again, "The evidence of abundant corn supplies, in the great granaries, and the sickles of iron and flint, give the reason for a Philistine occuying the place, as the Philistine did at Ekron in the rich grain district to the north. The export of grain to Crete would certainly be in demand, as it was rather later in Greece. Gerar was in those times the centre of trade and manufacture for N. W. Arabia, as Gaza is now."[27] Or, once more, "The appearance of a Philistine chief, son of a king, as ruling at Gerar (Gen. xxvi.8), is long before the mass immigration of the Philistines into Palestine."[28]

With regard to the *content of the religion* of the Philistines we must depend almost exclusively on the Old Testament for our information. Their principal divinity appears to have been Dagon, the name being a purely Semitic term meaning "Corn," and was associated with the art of corn-growing in the fertile plains of Philistia. In the early Akkadian language the name has a slight variation, Dagan, which signifies "lord of the fish" or simply fish-god. It will be recalled that the image in the temple at Ashdod was half man and half fish.[29] From extra-biblical sources we learn that Marna, the fish goddess, was regarded as the consort of Dagon. This worship of divinities in pairs was characteristic of early peoples. Also prominently con-

289

nected with the Philistine pantheon was Ashtoreth, a Semitic goddess of probable Mesopotamian origin where she was better known as Istar (Ishtar) the "light maker." In that capacity she was identified with the moon goddess and later with the planet Venus. Her appearance in the later Greek world was in some degree connected with Aphrodite. At any rate, in Canaan she was regarded as the goddess of war and love, the consort of Baal. Ashtoreth was powerful in Bethshean where the Philistines placed Saul's "armour in the house of the Ashtaroth."[30] "At Ashkelon, where Herodotus (i.105) places her most ancient temple, she was worshipped under the name of Atar-Gatis, as a woman with the tail of a fish, and fish were accordingly sacred to her. Elsewhere the dove was her sacred symbol. The immoral rites with which the worship of Istar in Babylonia was accompanied were transferred to Canaan (Dt. 23:18) and formed part of the idolatrous practices which the Israelites were called upon to extirpate."[31]

In addition to these we have Baal-zebub (the lord of flies) who was principally associated with the Philistine city of Ekron.[32] It is also probable that Baal-zebub was connected with the sun as a healer of disease. It seems clear that this is the same divinity as Beelzebub (chief of devils) mentioned in the New Testament.[33] The worship of Baal-zebub, or resorting to his oracles at Ekron, was apparently extensive. Again, the Old Testament reveals to us that the Philistines worshiped in temples; e.g., "the house of Dagon" at Ashdod where the ark of the covenant was placed, and at Gaza where Samson destroyed the Philistine temple in the last display of his unusual strength. Also interesting is the fact that proclamation concerning the death of Saul on Mt. Gilboa was made to the Philistines in the house of their idols.[34] These houses or temples long antedate the great Temple of Solomon in Jerusalem and are

290

actually among the first temples to appear in Canaan.[35]
Furthermore, the Philistines had priests and diviners
who claimed to be able to discover the wishes of their
gods. They specified the required offering to be presented to the gods in supplications.[36] The lords of the
Philistines are described as preparing a great sacrifice
(probably Samson himself) to Dagon at the time of
Samson's death.[37]

Now, since all of these religious conceptions have
their root in distinctive Semitic practices, it is entirely
probable that the Philistines derived their religion
mainly from the native Canaanite population, adopting
it as their own. It is significant that no outstanding
Greek ideas appear in this pantheon of Philistine divinities whatever may have been their religious conceptions
when they first arrived in Canaan.

And, finally, the language which the Philistines
originally employed has practically disappeared. There
are only a few words in the Old Testament which may
be definitely ascribed to them as, for example, Ziklag,
Phichol, Sisera, Achish, Maoch, Ittai, and Seren. Evidently they spoke a different language from that of
the Canaanites when they arrived from the Aegean
Islands, but, as indicated in the few surviving words,
it has been lost. Our biblical references to relations
between the Philistines and the Israelites do not suggest
any barriers of language in public or private dealings.
As in the case of their religion which they seem to have
taken over bodily from the Canaanites, they probably
adopted the language of the inhabitants at an early date
and persisted in its use. It is true that Nehemiah in
the days of his reformation attempts found considerable
intermarriage between Jews and women of Ashdod,
Ammon, and Moab, and that in the case of Ashdod the
children spoke a mixture of the Hebrew or Aramaic and
the language of Ashdod. We do not know whether this

Ashdod dialect was a survival of the Philistine or just a local or vernacular speech. On the other hand, we have in our possession the priceless Phaestos Disk, the terra cotta plaque found in the Cretan palace of Phaestos, and which remains to be deciphered. "On each face is a spiral band of four coils, indicated by a roughly drawn meandering line; and an inscription, in some form of picture-writing, has been impressed on this band, one by one, from dies, probably resembling those used by bookbinders. I suppose it is the oldest example of printing with movable types in the world ... There are forty-five different characters employed. It is likely, therefore, from the largeness of this number that we have to deal with a *syllabary* rather than a alphabet."[38] Assuming that the Philistines came from Crete, and that the principal figures appearing on this plaque correspond perfectly with the sea-peoples sculptured by Rameses III on the temple walls of Karnak, the Phaestos language is in all probability the language of the Philistines. At present, however, we know nothing of the content of this baffling record.

Now these are the interesting people to whom the early records of the Old Testament continually refer. Having reached the Plain of Philistia in their invasion movements, and having overcome the native Semitic population of the ancient cities of Gath, Ashkelon, Gaza, Gerar, etc., they finally succeeded in establishing themselves permanently, and thus attained dominance over all this region. The area was strategic in old world relations, is now the great connecting highway between the Nile Kingdom and the Tigris-Euphrates running through the heart of the country. Here they developed their own form of political organization, the great Pentapolis of Gaza, Gath, Ashkelon, Ekron, and Ashdod, over which were placed as sole rulers "the lords of the Philistines." Fundamentally, the Pentapolis was a military confederation, as well as cultural, and through its effective use against the disorganized tribes of Israel, the Philistines gradually entrenched themselves in every part of Canaan, as shown in the accompanying map. The result was that the Philistines maintained a stranglehold on the Israelites for many years even through the days of Samuel and Saul. David, the great leader of Israel, succeeded in throwing off this yoke. In subsequent periods they are occasionally seen but never in the role of masters. In the latter phases of Israel's history the Philistines have become a forgotten people.

"The rude tribes of Israel were forced to wage a long and stubborn fight with the Philistines for the possession of the Promised Land. For long it seemed doubtful whether Canaan would be retained by the Semitic tribes or lost to them: and it is no mere accident that the best known name of the country is derived from that of the sea-rovers. In the struggles the Hebrews learned the lessons of culture which they needed for their own advancement: and what was more important, they learned their own essential unity. The pressure of external opposition welded, as nothing else could have done, their loosely-knitted clans into a nation. This was the historic function of the Philistines; they accomplished their task, and then vanished with startling suddenness from the stage. But the chosen people were led on from strength to strength, till they too fulfilled their mission of teaching mankind to look forward to a time when the knowledge of the Lord should cover the earth as the waters cover the sea."[39]

CHAPTER FIFTEEN

THE HEBREW KINGDOMS

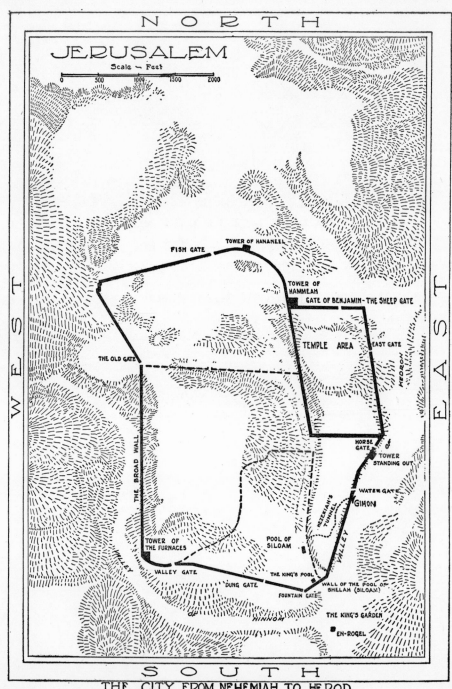

NORTH

WEST

EAST

SOUTH

JERUSALEM

Scale — Feet

0   500   1000   1500   2000

FISH GATE

TOWER OF HANANEEL

TOWER OF HAMMEAH

GATE OF BENJAMIN – THE SHEEP GATE

TEMPLE AREA

EAST GATE

THE OLD GATE

KEDRON

HORSE GATE

TOWER STANDING OUT

WATER GATE

GIHON

THE BROAD WALL

HEZEKIAH'S TUNNEL

VALLEY

TOWER OF THE FURNACES

POOL OF SILOAM

THE KING'S POOL

VALLEY

VALLEY GATE

DUNG GATE

FOUNTAIN GATE

WALL OF THE POOL OF SHELAH (SILOAM)

THE KING'S GARDEN

EN-ROGEL

of

HINNOM

THE CITY FROM NEHEMIAH TO HEROD
444-37 B.C.

THE HEBREW KINGDOMS

FROM the standpoint of archaeology the historical developments associated with the Hebrew Kingdoms have been set forth rather clearly so that we are now able to reconstruct the then contemporary life and thought with a high degree of certainty. Our information is more complete for the waning phases of Hebrew developments, particularly the rapid decline of the Northern and Southern Kingdoms, for it is in this period that the contemporary historical documents of the Assyrians and Babylonians commence to bristle with contacts with the struggling Hebrew governments, and to chronicle their steady decline among the powers of the ancient world. There was a period, however, when the Hebrew Kingdom was regarded as a respectable entity among the great world powers, when its domain stretched from the river of Egypt to the Euphrates, and from the Great Sea to the burning sands of Arabia. Those were the halcyon days of David and Solomon when foreign potentates looked with respect toward Jerusalem. But, by a strange coincidence, from the surviving monuments of this period we get not the least intimation of either David or Solomon, and from this silence one might suppose that the Hebrew sovereigns never lived. On the other hand, such an inference would be wholly unjustified. We may be sure that the historical records of the Hebrews which deal with the outstanding achievements of David and Solomon were

297

not manufactured, and that they may be accepted as authentic records of actual reigns. It must be remembered that the period itself (at least for contemporary peoples) was an era of general decline. Egypt was completely exhausted, the once proud Empire was merely a shell of its former glory; the early Babylonians had long since passed, and the ferocious Assyrians were not yet numbered among the really great. Consequently, developments among the Hebrews during the United Kingdom were unimpeded by any world powers, while the smaller tribal units of neighboring Edomites, Ammonites, and others were quickly brought under the Hebrew yoke. Even the adjacent kingdom of Aramaeans at Damascus and the Phoenicians at Tyre and Sidon were not slow to recognize the Hebrew sovereigns and to ally themselves with David and Solomon. Actually, then, all of these governments, the weak and the strong were relatively free from encroaching powers either from the southwest or from the northeast, and were allowed to pursue their own development. But scant records survive for this period of biblical interest. Save for the narratives of the Old Testament the entire period, so far as it relates to the Hebrew people, would be almost void. At this juncture of world affairs the Hebrews had reached one of their "blind spots" in which they were either unknown or overlooked, usually the latter.

In the later phases of Hebrew history, when the political affairs of the Northern and Southern Kingdoms became involved in the international cross-currents, the situation was radically changed. While it is true that the little country never attained to any dominating position as a world power, it was strategically located and remained of sufficient importance not to be ignored. Furthermore, several of the Hebrew rulers, perhaps thinking that they were farsighted in effecting

298

such alliances, became involved in foreign entanglements which were disastrous. One gets a glimpse of these foreign contacts as early as Solomon, who accepted from the Pharaoh of Egypt (certainly Shishak or Sheshonk) the city of Gezer in Palestine as a part of the marriage dowry of his Egyptian wife.[1] This Shishak was the founder of the Egyptian Twenty-second Dynasty and ruled through the period from 945-924 B.C. It was Shishak, also, who extended favors to Jeroboam, one of Solomon's lieutenants, at the time of his banishment to Egypt, and probably at the very season of his well-laid plans of insurrection against Solomon.[2] Apparently these actions were innocent enough, but the last of Shishak's movements toward Canaan was fraught with greater significance when, in the fifth year of Rehoboam, he invaded both Israel and Judah, assaulted Jerusalem, and plundered the Temple.[3] On the walls of the Temple of Karnak he ordered inscribed the names of 156 Palestinian towns which rendered tribute unto him.[4] The approximate date of this invasion may be regarded as 926 B.C., which is well within the limits of Shishak's reign. Confirmation of the Egyptian encroachment was found in recent excavations at Megiddo when the Stela of Shishak came to the surface. "In this case, the hieroglyphics named Sheshonk as the monarch in whose honor it was erected and for the first time provided contemporary evidence that the attack in the reign of Rehoboam by Shishak, as the Bible calls him, was not a mere raid for booty, but resulted at least in the temporary establishment of Egyptian garrisons on Palestinian soil."[5] Thus the hand of Egypt makes its reappearance in the affairs of Canaan; the shadow of the house of bondage still lingers over the destiny of Israel. But the end of its prestige is approaching. "This is the last Egyptian inscription of any importance to biblical history. The remaining records of the Pharaohs, right up to the Greek period, deal only with religious ceremonies and the interment of Apis bulls."[6]

The Ninth Century

At this point, with almost startling suddenness, the curtain falls on Hebrew relations with the outside world, and for more than a hundred years the narratives of the Old Testament are our only source of information on the history and developments of this period. At first thought this might be regarded as a catastrophe carrying with it no possibility of ever recapturing the content of that long century of Hebrew life and thought. Such a feeling of pessimism would soon be dissipated, however, not only because of a growing conviction of the credibility of the Hebrew chronicles, but an increasing recognition of the ability of archaeology to reconstruct and to recapture any given period or situation for which material evidences are provided. And, perhaps, in no other period is the function of archaeology more effectively illustrated. In spite of the absence of contemporary records of neighboring peoples, we know how the Hebrews lived; we know the subtleness of their temptation to religious decline and their actual apostasy under the impact of sordid and sensual Canaanite cults; we are acquainted with the general outlines of their cultural backgrounds, particularly the disintegrating force of prosperous times and the sordid influences of foreign importations both material and spiritual. With all of this as a backdrop, we also know the almost superhuman efforts of crusading and zealous prophets who move across the Hebrew stage of action in continual appeals for fidelity to Jehovah and for a true compliance with the unexampled purity of his religion.

300

About the middle of the ninth century B.C., the records of contemporary peoples commence to make mention of the Hebrews, to tell of conflicts in which the Northern Kingdom was involved, and to recite great victories over that struggling government. At this particular time the Southern Kingdom was rather in the background of current movements. Among these records there are three which may be mentioned here: *The Moabite Stone,* the *Monolith of Shalmaneser III,* and the *Black Obelisk of Shalmaneser III.* All of these are contemporary state documents of highest significance. The first, the *Moabite Stone,*[7] recounts a stirring period in the Northern Kingdom when the military might of Omri of Samaria triumphed over the lesser kingdom of the Moabites east of the Jordan. According to Mesha's inscription, the Moabites endured this subjugation for forty years but at the expiration of that period rebelled against the house of Omri, king of Israel, and succeeded in throwing off the Hebrew yoke. Though there is some difficulty with the exact chronology of this inscription which we cannot resolve in the light of our present knowledge, the account in general is clearly parallel with the narrative in 2 Kings 3:4-27, and may be regarded as complementary and supplementary. It should also be remembered in this connection that, while the Moabite Stone and the passage in 2 Kings may seem irreconcilable as to the date of this particular struggle, the difficulty may be more apparent than real. "But even here, if we knew everything, we might be able to see that the two histories are not so irreconcilable after all. For all we know, there may have been two rebellions; there may even have been two Meshas."[8] In any event, the period of time—i.e., 852 B.C.—is substantially correct and fits into the chronological framework of the Northern Kingdom from 884 to 841 B.C., when Omri, Ahab, Ahaziah, and Jehoram reigned, and of the Southern

301

Kingdom, when Jehoshaphat, 870-845 B.C., is said to have been allied with Israel in a major attack on Moab.[9]

The second of these contemporary records, the *Monolith of Shalmaneser III,* is by far the most important. Its historical significance has already been discussed in dealing with the problem of Old Testament chronology.[10] In this inscription Ahab and the Northern Kingdom are seen in the midst of international affairs when a powerful coalition of western states—including Syria and Israel—opposed the great Assyrian, Shalmaneser III, at the Battle of Karkar in 854-3 B.C. As is known, the Monolith proceeds to describe the utter defeat of the confederates and the consequent tribute which they bring to the mighty monarch. Our interest here is not in the veracity of Shalmaneser's claims but, rather, that in an engagement of old world powers we find Israel prominently involved. As a matter of fact, on the basis of his military forces, it is probable that Ahab was the most important of all the confederates.

In the third record, the *Black Obelisk of Shalmaneser III,* Jehu of Israel (erroneously referred to by Shalmaneser as the "son of Omri") is portrayed among several rulers of the Westlands bringing tribute to Shalmaneser, and is further featured in the second series of four reliefs as doing humble obeisance to the mighty sovereign. This event in the life of Jehu and Israel is placed by Shalmaneser in the eighteenth year of his reign—i.e., 841-0 B.C.—and probably marks the first year of Jehu's accession to the throne of the Northern Kingdom.

Strangely enough, and entirely unexpectedly, all of these monuments refer to the Northern Kingdom during the period of the house of Omri. It appears, therefore, that these particular monarchs were more aggressive than the contemporary rulers of the Southern Kingdom, and that they were consequently taken into consideration by the expanding powers of the ancient world. Of course, this special attention to Israel might also rest upon geographical considerations which found the Northern Kingdom more open to incursion and more easily involved in cross-currents of contending powers. But that does not modify the essential fact that Israel, and not Judah, was plainly in the view of old world empires when seeking conquests. Even their immediate neighbors the Syrians, under Benhadad I, II, III, and Hazael, overlooked no opportunity to impose their will upon the Northern Kingdom.[11] In this atmosphere of political strife must be set the battles of Aphek[12] and Ramoth-gilead,[13] when Syrians and Hebrews engaged in mutual self-destruction in spite of the impending catastrophe which would come upon them from the north. Likewise, into this atmosphere of religious deterioration one must envision the phenomenal careers of Micaiah,[14] Elijah,[15] and Elisha,[16] who understood not only the base betrayal of the worship of Jehovah and the entrenchment of Baalism by the house of Omri, but who also had deep intuitions of the real design and threat of Syria. The Old Testament narratives of these epochal phases in Israel's history are lighted up here and there by the corroborative evidences of contemporary monuments.

THE EIGHTH CENTURY

The dawn of the eighth century B.C. ushered in a period of religious and political decline which was ominous both for the Northern and Southern Kingdoms, both of which were to end ultimately in complete destruction. But their catastrophe did not come without warning. The earlier prophets, among whom was Amos, probably also Joel and Jonah, had already begun to see in the Assyrian power a real menace to all of the Westland, and to interpret the entire movement in the

light of their faith.[17] In the latter part of the century—
i.e., from 750 to 700 B.C.—the situation as regards Judah
and Samaria had greatly altered. In this latter period
we are probably justified in putting the closing phases
of the ministry of Amos and Hosea, who, for an unknown period, were certainly contemporaries. Here,
also, we witness the inauguration of the ministries of
Micah and Isaiah, whose careers ran parallel during
the reigns of Uzziah, Jotham, Ahaz, and Hezekiah in
the Southern Kingdom. Without exception, all of these
prophets were internationally conscious; they envisage
with profound clearness not only the threats of imperial
powers but also the judgment and purpose of God in the
experiences of his people. Particularly clear is Isaiah
in that series of prophetic utterances included in chapters 7:1 to 9:7. "The episode and declarations made
here present Isaiah's person and purpose most clearly
before us. In the midst of the frantic endeavors of the
nations of western Asia to preserve their existence in
the face of the Assyrian, and over against their petty
feuds with one another, Isaiah calls for a different
policy. Judah need not fear, either from Israel or from
Damascus. Assyria will attend to them before long.
Nor, on the other hand, need they whose God is Jehovah
seek for protection with the Assyrian. In Isaiah's
prophetic vision, to become involved with the great
nation of the Tigris is not only to evidence want of faith
in Jehovah, but also to incur all the misfortunes and
disasters that accompany the supremacy of Assyria.
If Judah will be content in reliance upon its God to keep
clear of all foreign complications and to live in quiet-
ness, prosperity and peace will be its position. This
was the prophet's program. But the king had already
committed himself to the opposite policy. The Assyrian,
therefore, as Isaiah sees, will certainly come and desolate the country, bringing privation, darkness, and

THE WALLS OF JERICHO FELL
OUTWARD UNDER THEIR OWN
WEIGHT. STILL IN PLACE
MAY BE SEEN A LOWER SEC-
TION AS IT APPEARED IN THE
EXCAVATION OF THE DOOMED
STRONGHOLD. OBSERVE THE
L A R G E BRICKS AND THE
MORTAR BINDING STILL
VISIBLE.

THE ROMANTIC ACCOUNT OF
THE FALL OF THE WALLS OF
JERICHO HAS ALWAYS GRIP-
PED THE ATTENTION OF BIBLE
STUDENTS. T H E EXCAVA-
TIONS AT JERICHO BY SELLIN
AND GARSTANG HAVE SUC-
CEEDED IN RESTORING THE
GENERAL OUTLINE OF ITS
UNIQUE EXPERIENCE AND ITS
HISTORY. IN THIS VIEW,
CONSIDERABLY BELOW THE
PRESENT SURFACE, IS SHOWN
A PART OF THE ANCIENT
WALL WITH THE SLOPING
REVETMENT OF HYKSOS DE-
SIGN.

THE APPROACH TO THE HIGH-PLACE IN CANAANITE WORSHIP WAS ALWAYS SIGNALIZED BY THE STANDING STONES, OR MACCEBOTH, OCCASIONALLY TRANSLATED IN ENGLISH VERSIONS AS OBELISKS. BEFORE THE GREAT HIGHPLACE AT PETRA MAY BE SEEN TWO OF THESE SIGNIFICANT STONES. ONE OF THEM IS SHOWN IN THIS VIEW.

THE CENTRAL POINT IN THE RELIGIOUS LIFE OF OLD WORLD PEOPLES WAS THE HIGHPLACE. THIS VIEW OF THE OUTDOOR SANCTUARY AT PETRA SHOWS ONE OF THE MOST ELABORATE YET DISCOVERED. THE ALTAR OF THE HIGHPLACE MAY BE SEEN IN THE FOREGROUND.

destruction in his train.'"[18] Indeed, the dreaded Assyrian had already begun to strike and always with characteristic vigor and effectiveness.

According to the Assyrian annals, in the year 743 B.C. the great Tiglath-pileser III (Pul) inaugurated a series of invasions into the Mediterranean borderlands which finally brought practically all of that territory under the Assyrian heel.[19] There is a possibility that during the early stages of this western advance Azariah (Uzziah) king of Judah was adversely affected because of an alliance which he had with the king of Hamath. Luckenbill, Hall, Sayce, and others are rather confident that the Azariah here named is the king of the Southern Kingdom.[20] While the chronology of the period would allow this possibility, the identification is not certain, and, furthermore, there is no reference in the Old Testament narratives to the alleged alliance. On the other hand, both Hebrew and Assyrian records agree regarding an early advance on Palestine by Tiglath-pileser when Menahem, king of Israel, was compelled to render tribute unto Pul in the astounding sum of 1000 talents of silver.[21] According to the narrative in 2 Kings, Menahem was inaugurated as king of the Northern Kingdom in the thirty-ninth year of Azariah (Uzziah) of Judah. His submission to Tiglath-pileser in 738 B.C. was therefore toward the close of his reign and might represent an effort on the part of Menahem to secure his throne against contenders.[22] The Assyrian confirmation of this event is found in Tiglath-pileser's chronicles and is placed definitely in 738 B.C.[23] The reference in the same account to Azariah of Yaudi, if Azariah of Judah is meant, must be fixed at 738 B.C. also. As already stated, this identification is not pressed in this connection, still there is no chronological difficulty in the general setting of the kings of Judah and Samaria in their relation to the Assyrian monarch.

But the annals of Tiglath-pileser do not end here. He was persistent and thoroughgoing in his design to subjugate the entire Westland. Once again his mighty hosts span the Euphrates in a descent on Syria and Palestine with the result that Damascus was destroyed, the kingdom of the Arameans permanently reduced, Pekah of Israel deposed, and Hoshea placed upon the throne. These events are fully corroborated both by the Assyrian and Hebrew records.[24] The date, determined by the Assyrian documents, is 734-3 B.C. In close conjunction with these events, two other developments of outstanding importance took place, namely, the inauguration of the distinctive policies of Tiglath-pileser in deporting native peoples to different areas of his Empire in an effort to weaken local resistance, and the importation of his own loyal followers into foreign territory with similar purpose. These policies are reflected in the Old Testament narratives, particularly in 2 Kings 16:29, 17:6, 24, and 26. The full operation of such policies is reflected in the Khorsabad Inscription of Sargon II which recounts that 27,290 inhabitants of Samaria were deported and peoples of other conquered territories brought in.[25] The *second* of these developments is found in the appeal of Ahaz of Judah to Tiglath-pileser for aid against Rezin of Syria and Pekah of Israel. The Scripture narratives bearing on this unusual proceeding and its dire consequences to Ahaz and Judah are set forth in two passages.[26] "We now reach the days so vividly portrayed in the Scriptures when those two *tails of smoking firebrands* Rezin of Damascus and Pekah of Israel tried to compel Ahaz of Judah to combine with them against Assyria, and Isaiah bade him fear them not (Is. 7:4). Ahaz did indeed resist the Syro-Ephraimite overtures, but foolishly bribed Tiglath-Pileser to do just what he had intended to do in any case II K. 16:7; and swiftly the Assyrian struck.

Of the gratuitous submission of Ahaz to Nineveh we have no record in the inscriptions save the bare mention of Jeho-Ahaz, king of Judah, amongst her tributaries. But the form of the name is interesting: why did the biblical writers omit the Jeho- (Jehovah) from his name? 'Possibly his reputation for unprecedented wickedness led the Jewish scribes to eliminate the divine element from his name,' is Robinson's suggestion."[27] Interesting, also, is the statement in 2 Chronicles that, in spite of Ahaz's tribute to Assyria, Tiglath-pileser strengthened him not but actually distressed him.[28]

With the completion of this western campaign in 733 B.C., Tiglath-pileser returned to his capital on the Tigris. As a result of his military exploits he could now describe himself as "the great King, the mighty King, King of the whole (world), King of Assyria, King of Babylon, King of Sumer and Accad, King of the four regions, the mighty one, the warrior."[29] But this was probably his final campaign. His death in 727 B.C. was the signal for a general uprising of suppressed peoples throughout the Empire, among whom were the Hebrews of the Northern Kingdom. "And the king of Assyria (now Shalmaneser V, 727-722 B.C.) found conspiracy in Hoshea: for he had sent messengers to So King of Egypt, and brought no present to the king of Assyria, as he had done year by year; therefore the king of Assyria shut him up, and bound him in prison."[30] From the Assyrian monuments we have no direct confirmation of Hoshea's humiliating experience at the hands of Shalmaneser, nor any inscriptional evidence concerning the beginning of the three-year siege of Samaria. The passage in 2 Kings 17:3-5 mentions Shalmaneser as the king against whom Hoshea rebelled, and clearly it is also Shalmaneser who began the bitter siege referred to in verse 5.[31] It was not Shalmaneser who conquered Samaria, however, nor does the narrative in 2 Kings

17:6 demand that identification. It is interesting to note that in both the Assyrian Canon and the Assyrian Chronicle the reign of Shalmaneser V terminated in 723-2 B.C., which allows also for the accession of Sargon II, 722-705 B.C., who claims to have conquered Samaria in the first year of his reign.[32] This conquest marks the termination of the Northern Kingdom, whose checkered history extended through a period of 209 years—i.e., from 931 B.C. to 722 B.C.

The Fall of Samaria

Strangely enough, however, it was not Sargon but the Hebrew historian who wrote Samaria's epitaph: "They rejected his statutes, and his covenant that he made with their fathers, and his testimonies which he testified unto them; and they followed vanity, and became vain, and went after the nations that were round about them, concerning whom Jehovah had charged them, that they should not do like them. And they left all the commandments of Jehovah their God, and made them molten images, even two calves, and made an Asherah, and worshipped all the host of heaven, and served Baal. And they caused their sons and daughters to pass through the fire, and used divination and enchantments, and sold themselves to do that which was evil in the sight of Jehovah, to provoke him to anger. Therefore Jehovah was very angry with Israel, and removed them out of his sight ... "In the ninth year of Hoshea the king of Assyria took Samaria and carried Israel away unto Assyria."[33] Thus the curtain falls on the capital of the Northern Kingdom. Its ancient site, towering above the adjacent plains, is marked by the present squalid village of Sebustiyeh, but back of this unimportant settlement lies the history of an illustrious city which dominated the political and religious life of Northern

Palestine for almost two centuries. Through the early excavations of Schumacher, Lyon and Reisner, together with the more recent work of the Joint Samaria Expedition of 1931-1935, we are now able to obtain a complete picture of Samaria and to reproduce its general atmosphere from the period of its founding by Omri, about 880 B.C., to its destruction in 722 B.C.[34] Its subsequent history in the era of Graeco-Roman Palestine, when it became one of the outstanding cities of Herodian culture, is not here taken into consideration.

Samaria was situated about eight miles northwest of the present city of Nablus (Shechem) on the great highway leading into the Plain of Esdraelon. Its towering eminence, 360 feet above the surrounding territory, made it both strategic and conspicuous. The practical reason underlying the selection of the site, at the expense of the former capitals Shechem and Tirzah, was obviously connected with its unusual elevation which carried with it the possibility of easy defenses. The far-seeing eye of Omri envisioned in this natural position a fortified area which would prove almost impregnable. His successors shared the same view, with the result that through the years Samaria increased in strength, particularly with regard to its encircling walls which now appear as among the most massive and effective of any Palestinian city. It was, of course, the strength of these mural fortifications that defied the great Assyrian Shalmaneser for three years, its final conquest being probably not by frontal assault but by the exhaustion of the population.

The acreage covered by Samaria during the reigns of Omri and Ahab is not exactly known. The Israelite city was certainly much smaller than the Roman settlement whose walls were approximately three miles in circumference. The center of the city, the Acropolis, was selected by Omri as the site for his palace and here he constructed a dwelling whose present foundations show it to have been of considerable proportion. On this same foundation Ahab constructed buildings of more pretentious design and proceeded to embellish them in keeping with the general prosperity of his reign and the conspicuous position which he occupied in relation to contemporary kingdoms. "During the reigns of Omri and of his son Ahab, Israel emerged as a state that in international affairs and in material prosperity could be compared with that of Solomon. A balance of power with Damascus was achieved and Israelite merchants in Ahab's time gained the same privileges in Damascus as had been granted by Omri to Syrians in Samaria."[35] Politically and culturally it was a period of great expansion, and it now appears that Samaria, in relation to the world powers of that day, was more conspicuous than Jerusalem. Nor was this prominence diminished during the reign of Jeroboam II, a century later, when the material prosperity of the Northern Kingdom reached its zenith. But there was another side of the picture which was more disturbing. "At Samaria, a sophisticated population enjoyed the pleasant luxuries of an advanced material culture. The cult of the Phoenician Baal, tolerated as an alternative to that of Jehovah, gave a cosmopolitan cachet to the court, which the whole country was soon imitating. Summer and winter houses built in the finest masonry sheltered an urbane society whose tastes (condemned by the prophets) for 'jewels and earrings,' ivory inlays and furniture, 'myrrh and aloes' and needlework, viols and flagons of wine, was no doubt encouraged by the presence and example of Jezebel and her Tyrian entourage."[36] Add to this the almost inevitable burdens of taxation to the underprivileged and small landowners, looseness in moral and ethical standards, overindulgence in luxuries, oppression of the poor, inequalities in the courts, and similar shortcomings of a society more bent on exterior grandeur than spiritual greatness!

Such was the character of Samaria, Ephraim's "crown of pride." From the standpoint of archaeology we can still traverse its streets ringing with the cries of merchantmen and their wares, hear the resounding echoes of men, horses, and chariots in material splendor, enter into the residences of a luxury-loving people, and into the palatial halls of the royal mansion where gold and ivory were used in profusion.[37] But that is not all. From the standpoint of the prophets of the Northern Kingdom who moved through this lurid atmosphere with strong appeals and heart-searching earnestness, we are also able to look again on a Samaria that inevitably fell under the weight of its own iniquity and apostasy. Amos and Hosea, prophets of impending judgments, were likewise spokesmen for Jehovah's love for his people and for his willingness to forgive and to restore. Their voices, by no means silenced either in content or timeliness by the lapse of centuries, may still be heard in the counsels of men and of nations. But Samaria was doomed. Obviously, where there was no immediate reaction to the incisive judgments of Amos, the prophet of righteousness, the heart was made of steel; where there was no eager response to the gentle pleading of Hosea, the prophet of love, there could be no genuine hope. Samaria was bent on self-destruction, nor was there the least intention of desisting from its corruption and consequent doom. The advent of Shalmaneser and his prolonged siege of the great city caused no consternation in prophetic circles; it was clearly the signal for the beginning of the judgment of God. The fall of Samaria in 722 B.C., together with the deportation of 27,290 of its inhabitants to various parts of the Assyrian Empire, was likewise looked upon with confidence and interpreted as just retribution for the permanent re-

311

jection of Jehovah. And, yet, in the midst of this national catastrophe, there was still the lingering memory of this "head of Ephraim" which might have been crowned with glory and honor, but whose sordid and base ideals caused it to miss the stars.

But the destruction of Samaria was only a preliminary to greater events which were to follow. "Sargon thus striking north and south consolidated his victories in Syria, colonized the depopulated areas with aliens, and added a new province to the Assyrian empire. Only one small portion of the land of Palestine remained unsubdued: the sole obstacle between Assyria and the much-desired conquest of Egypt was the tiny yet formidable highland state of Judah. But by one of history's strangest ironies, it was not Jerusalem which crumbled first, but Nineveh."[38] In the plan of Sargon, however, the full subjugation of the southwestern kingdoms was the matter of major importance. The two campaigns by which he sought this end are mentioned in his own records and are assigned to the years 720 B.C. and 711 B.C.[39] In the biblical records there is no reference to the first of these campaigns in 720 B.C., but the subsequent invasion of the Westlands in 711 B.C. is certainly reflected in Isaiah 20:1. Sargon's full accounts of this campaign may be found in the *Khorsabad Inscriptions* and in the *Cylinder* of Sargon discovered at Nineveh.[40] It will be observed that, while the adjacent territories were overrun by Sargon, the kingdom of Hezekiah was unmolested, probably because of its refusal to be drawn into a revolt against Sargon. This same event is more likely referred to in the passage describing the subtle attempt of Merodach-baladan of Babylon to turn Hezekiah against the king of Assyria.[41]

Though Hezekiah managed to escape these alien plots and overtures to futile attacks on Assyria, his supreme test was still to come. The death of Sargon in

312

705 B.C. provided an opportunity for widespread revolt which usually followed in the wake of a great sovereign's passing. Hence, with the accession of Sennacherib 705-681 B.C., incipient revolt flared up in all parts of the Empire. It is apparent at this critical juncture that Hezekiah, hitherto successful in warding off attempts to involve him in open rebellion against Assyria, was drawn into the vortex. The retaliation of the Assyrian Sennacherib was swift and powerful. On the Taylor Prism, dated in the third year of his reign—i.e., 702-1 B.C., Sennacherib sets forth the details of his campaign: an attack on Syria and Phoenicia which resulted in the conquest of these areas; a descent into southern Palestine engulfed not only the ancient Philistine strongholds of Ashkelon and Ekron, but also forty-six cities of Judah; a successful attack at Eltekeh on Tirhakah, the Egyptian commander, whose forces were coming to the aid of the revolting states; a long and bitter siege of Lachish during the progress of which Hezekiah dispatched an embassy which admitted the sedition of the king of Judah and, as a guarantee of good faith in the future, offered to Sennacherib 300 talents of silver and 30 talents of gold.[42] In addition to these details, other items of interest are mentioned in the complete annals.[43] From the biblical narratives we derive no direct information on the first phase of Sennacherib's campaign, but concerning the episode of his struggle at Lachish, and later threat against Jerusalem, the accounts are full.[44] It now appears that Sennacherib, probably surprised at the ready submission of Hezekiah's apology and tribute, his cupidity also being aroused by the splendid sum of money laid at his feet, determined to deal more decisively with rebellious Judah. At this point he ordered his forces to Jerusalem to demand the unconditional surrender of Hezekiah and the capital city.[45] Encouraged by the prophet Isaiah, Hezekiah

313

disregarded this ultimatum and set himself for the defense of Jerusalem. The sequel to this stirring event finds expression in the deliverance of the city, in the defeat at Eltekeh of the Egyptian forces coming to the aid of Palestinian allied states, and of Sennacherib's own defeat when his army was destroyed, probably by bubonic plague. The final scene is portrayed in the disgraceful return to Nineveh where, in 681 B.C., he was assassinated by his own sons. This latter event is corroborated by the recently discovered ''Prism S'' which recounts the circumstances of Sennacherib's death and the accession of his son Esarhaddon.[46] Though Sennacherib failed in his attempt to capture Jerusalem at this time, the threat of its final destruction lingered on through a full century.

THE SEVENTH CENTURY

The accession of Esarhaddon (681-668 B.C.) in no sense marked a decline in the prestige of the Assyrian Empire, but, on the contrary, under his sovereignty the whole imperial system was held intact and the hated power of the Assyrian over subject peoples further extended. ''It is clear from the inscriptions that Esarhaddon was the *cruel lord and fierce king* (Is. 19:4) who achieved the highest ambition of all Assyrians—the conquest of Egypt. His long struggle with the Pharaoh Tirhakah is fully described in the records.''[47] This is the same Tirhakah (then in the role of an Egyptian commander or co-regent) who was defeated at Eltekeh by Sennacherib in 701 B.C.[48] When met by Esarhaddon on his Egyptian invasion, Tirhakah occupied the throne as the third pharaoh of the Twenty-fifth Dynasty. The powerful Assyrian brushed him aside to penetrate the heart of Egypt in 674 B.C., repeated his invasion in 673 B.C. without success. In 670 B.C. Esarhaddon triumphed

314

over the forces of Tirhakah at the ancient stronghold of Memphis (Noph) which fell hardly without a struggle. On the death of Esarhaddon, his son Ashurbanipal (668-627 B.C.) succeeded to his father's throne and unfinished tasks, among which was a final thrust at Egypt that resulted in the conquest of Thebes (No-Amon) and the final disposition of Tirhakah. Now during all this period Jerusalem, while on the general approaches to Egypt, was not entered by the Assyrian hordes, nor was there any occasion to do so. Following the example of Hezekiah, his successors faithfully rendered unto the Assyrian kings the tribute of Judah as a dependent state. One possible exception to this general procedure might be preserved in 2 Chronicles which describes how, during the days of Manasseh, "The Lord brought upon them the captains of the host of the king of Assyria, who took Manasseh in chains, and bound him with fetters, and carried him to Babylon."[49] There is no confirmation of this passage in the Assyrian records, though there is a similar event chronicled wherein subject kings were commanded to report to Esarhaddon at Nineveh and to receive their orders. Among these vassal rulers was Manasseh, king of Judah.[50] No such humiliating events are chronicled concerning Amon and Josiah, who were the successors of Manasseh, and who were also the last of the kings of Judah having any relations with Assyria. It may be assumed that they sent their tribute to Ashurbanipal (668-627 B.C.) regularly. It is interesting to observe in this connection that, in spite of the long oppression under Assyria, the author of the Ezra narrative can still refer to Ashurbanipal as "the great and noble Osnappar."[51] But, whatever the merit of Ashurbanipal, the career of Nineveh, the spoiler of the nations, was about to be closed. Fourteen years after the close of Ashurbanipal's reign, Nineveh was in ashes. On the basis of the Baby-

315

lonian Chronicle, the destruction of the Tigris metropolis occurred in 612 B.C.,[52] and came as a result of a powerful coalition of Medes and Babylonians bent on retribution. "Nineveh's destruction was complete and final. One blow, and the mistress of the world crumbles into dust! It is the most dramatic example in ancient history of the operation of the divine law against unleashed wickedness."[53] In the thought of Nahum, and incidentally in the estimate of Jeremiah and Zephaniah, the fall of Nineveh was clearly an act of God in retributive justice against the most wicked of cities. "For nearly two hundred years Nineveh had been the metropolis of Western Asia. She lay in the fertile valley of the Tigris, and roads from the East and West, arteries along which moved the commerce of the ancient world, converged at her gates. Her walls were seven and a half miles in circumference, and inclosed the largest fortified area east of Egypt. The treasures of art were lavished upon her. Her libraries were among the wonders of the ancient world. The size, the wealth, the glory, the power of Nineveh were everywhere proverbial. But these evinced more of hate than admiration from the peoples. Assyria had become great and powerful by ravishing other nations. Her armies had trampled their fields, murdered their people, and plundered their treasures. There was occasion for relief and rejoicing when it was known that her fall was imminent."[54] Indeed, the whole world joined in the exultant cry of the prophet of Israel, "Nineveh a desolation, and dry like a wilderness . . . This is the rejoicing city that dwelt carelessly, that said in her heart, I am, and there is none beside me: how is she become a desolation, a place for beasts to lie down in! every one that passeth by her shall hiss, and wag his hand."[55]

Nineveh indeed was fallen, struck down by a powerful blow of emerging Median and Babylonian forces, but in her death pangs she once again had the satisfaction of seeing the world fall to pieces. By one of the strangest coincidences of history, two world-powers, Assyria and Egypt, and the struggling kingdom of Judah, collapse almost at the same time. The general outlines of the period are clear enough, but some details, particularly with reference to Josiah of Judah, are needed to complete the picture. We should like to know more of the career of this attractive son of Amon, particularly should we like to know more of the phenomenal discovery of the book of the law of Moses, which provided the background of a national revival during his reign. This great discovery is dated in the eighteenth year of Josiah's reign—i.e., 621 B.C.[56] Furthermore, we would like to have more information regarding Josiah's reasons for attempting to stop Pharaoh-Necho, the more powerful monarch, in the great Plain of Esdraelon. "At this point we again make contact with biblical history. Apparently it was not *against* the king of Assyria, but in support of him, that Pharaoh-Necho of Egypt marched his army up the Palestinian coast road towards Carchemish in 608 B.C. (II K. 23:29). Egypt, however, proved dilatory as usual. Necho lingered for sometime first at Megiddo, where he slew Josiah, king of Judah; and then at Riblah over the deposition of Jehoahaz (II K. 23:31ff). He arrived in consequence at Carchemish far too late to save the Assyrian remnant from the onslaught of the Babylonian general Nebuchadnezzar, and was himself utterly routed (605 B.C.), only the sudden recall of his adversary to receive the crown of Babylon saving the Pharaoh from complete annihilation."[57] But the remaining activities both of Egypt and Judah constitute mere shadow-boxing; the world was on the verge of being introduced to a new master, Nebuchadnezzar of Babylon.

Close on the heels of the tottering Empire of the Assyrians and from the ruins of a former glory, the New Babylonian Empire emerged in another of the fruitless attempts at world domination. Its second and most powerful monarch, Nebuchadnezzar 605-562 B.C., bulks large in the annals of ancient history. His chief claim to fame is inseparably connected with the fortunes of two great cities: Babylon, the glorious, which he rebuilt on the banks of the beautiful Euphrates, and Jerusalem, no less glorious, which he destroyed in the highlands of Judah. It is around these two outstanding centers of Babylonian and Hebrew life and thought that the historical and prophetical narratives of the Old Testament revolve for approximately one century and a half. Unfortunately, however, apart from the narratives of the Hebrew historians, we derive little information from contemporary Babylonian and Egyptian sources concerning this period. We know something of the well-laid plans of Nebuchadnezzar for extensive conquests, and from his own records we are informed of their execution when he returned from the Westlands laden with "gold, silver, precious stones, copper, palm-wood and cedar wood, everything that was costly, and in magnificent abundance."[58] Three of these campaigns are probably referred to in the Hebrew documents of this period.[59]

The *first invasion* of the Westlands was associated with Nebuchadnezzar's determination to deal with Pharaoh-Necho of Egypt, who was going to Carchemish to assist the Assyrian monarch in 605 B.C. The engagement at Carchemish resulted in Necho's complete defeat and in the withdrawal of his surviving forces to Egypt. It now appears that the victorious Babylonians followed in hot pursuit. "Jeremiah, who perhaps caught sight

318

of the rapidly moving armies from the Judaean hills, has given a vivid description of the flight in Jeremiah 46. Jeremiah considered this event so important that he began to commit his prophecies to writing (Jeremiah 36)."[60] The outcome of this struggle gave Nebuchadnezzar clearcut title to all of northern Mesopotamia, western Syria, and southwestern Palestine to the borders of Egypt. It is probable that this Babylonian movement in the southern highlands of Judah synchronizes with the third year of Jehoiakim—i.e., 605 B.C., when Jerusalem was attacked and choice young men, among whom was Daniel, were taken as hostages to Babylon.[61] This event also coincides with the first year of Nebuchadnezzar. The *second invasion* of the West as described in the Hebrew narratives falls at the end of Jehoiakim's reign in 598 B.C., which date also marks the accession of Jehoiachin, who reigned for only three months. At this time Jerusalem was besieged not only by the servants of Nebuchadnezzar, but the great king himself finally appeared on the scene. The records describe Jehoiachin's surrender and deportation to Babylon, the plundering of the Temple, and the enslavement of thousands of Jerusalem inhabitants, ranging from princes to craftsmen and smiths, leaving none "save the poorest sort of people of the land."[62] Finally, the *third phase* of Nebuchadnezzar's campaigns against the West, particularly against the mountain fortress of Judah, is definitely assigned to the ninth year of Zedekiah's reign, i.e., 589 B.C. The Hebrew accounts go on to state that this last siege of Jerusalem extended through a period of two years or more, and that the culmination came in the eleventh year of Zedekiah, i.e., 587-6 B.C., when "famine prevailed in the city, and there was no bread for the people of the land. And the city was broken up, and all the men of war fled by night by the way of the gate between two walls, which is by the

319

king's garden: (now the Chaldees were against the city round about:) and the king went the way toward the plain. And the army of the Chaldees pursued after the king, and overtook him in the plains of Jericho: and all his army were scattered from him. So they took the king and brought him up to the king of Babylon to Riblah; and they gave judgment upon him. And they slew the sons of Zedekiah before his eyes, and put out the eyes of Zedekiah, and bound him with fetters of brass, and carried him to Babylon.''[63] But that was not all. One month later, Nebuchadnezzar now on his way to Babylon, ''Nebuzaradan, captain of the guard, a servant of the king of Babylon, [came] unto Jerusalem: and he burnt the house of the Lord, and the king's house, and all the houses of Jerusalem, and every great man's house burnt he with fire. And all the army of the Chaldees, that were with the captain of the guard, brake down the walls of Jerusalem round about.''[64] The date of this unspeakable catastrophe is further fixed by the biblical records as in the nineteenth year of Nebuchadnezzar—i.e., 587-6 B.C. The shattering blow, long deferred in the providence of God, had finally been struck. The site of the city became a complete desolation; the glory of Mt. Zion was reduced to a mound of smouldering ashes. But its historic mission was not yet fulfilled; through the dark cloud of its abject humiliation there shone the unflickering light of divine purpose: ''They shall be carried to Babylon, and there shall they be until the day that I visit them, saith the Lord; then will I bring them up, and restore them to this place.''[65]

THE FALL OF JERUSALEM

Once again through the magic touch of archaeology and historical orientation we dig into the shattered

320

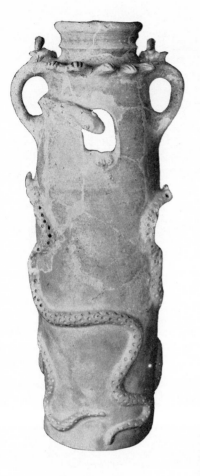

CULT OBJECTS OF VARIOUS KINDS HAVE COME TO THE SURFACE IN PALESTINE EXCAVATIONS. MOST GRUESOME ARE THE ACCOMPANIMENTS OF SERPENT WORSHIP. SERPENT WORSHIP SEEMS TO HAVE BEEN PARTICULARLY CONNECTED WITH THE CANAANITE ASHTORETH.

IN THE 1930 EXCAVATIONS AT TELL BEIT MIRSIM, ONE OF THE STARTLING DISCOVERIES WAS THE SERPENT STELA PICTURED HERE. IT WAS A CULT OBJECT ASSOCIATED WITH THE DEGRADING WORSHIP OF THE CANAANITE ASHTORETH. OTHER MONUMENTS OF THE SAME SIGNIFICANCE HAVE COME TO THE SURFACE AT BETHSHEAN AND AT SHECHEM.

IN THE EASTERN WALL OF THE OLD CITY OF THE JEBUSITES, DAVID
BUILT THE TOWER, WHICH IS NOW PRESERVED AS A NATIONAL MONUMENT.
AFTER THE CAPTURE OF THIS STRONGHOLD DAVID CONVERTED THE
CITY INTO HIS CAPITAL.

THE PRESENT WALLS OF JERUSALEM ENCLOSE PRACTICALLY ALL OF THE
ANCIENT CITY WITH THE EXCEPTION OF PORTIONS OF MOUNT ZION ON
THE SOUTHWEST AND OPHEL ON THE SOUTHEAST. THIS SECTION OF THE
WALLS STANDS ON THE NORTH SIDE LOOKING EAST TO THE VALLEY OF
THE KEDRON AND THE MOUNT OF OLIVES.

ruins of Jerusalem, city of the Great King, to reconstruct its Temple, its palatial residences, its winding streets, and its encircling walls.[66] Among the oldest existing cities of the world, Jerusalem made its first appearance about 3000 B.C., when cave dwellers occupied its site, and subsequently, about 2000 B.C., when a more pretentious settlement emerged with all the characteristics of an urban community. This was the Salem of Melchizedek and Abram at whose sacred place the Patriarch tarried to render unto God a tenth of the battle spoils taken from the Mesopotamian raiders. Above the site of Salem, which was located on the southeastern spur of Mt. Moriah, there stood the relatively lofty hill, which witnessed the attempted sacrifice of Isaac by Abram and later became the threshing floor of Araunah the Jebusite which David purchased, and finally the sacred site of the great temples of Solomon, Zerubbabel, and Herod the Great. Through many centuries of municipal development the city gradually expanded, particularly during the days of David, Solomon, Hezekiah, and Manasseh, until it included all the area now designated by the terms Ophel, Mt. Zion, the Acra, and Mt. Moriah. In addition there was considerable suburban area which greatly increased the acreage of the capital city. At the time of its destruction by Nebuchadnezzar, Jerusalem was encompassed by a wall approximately four miles in length. The population is not exactly known though it was perhaps more than one hundred thousand.

With the passing of the centuries it has become increasingly difficult to determine accurately the historic sites of the great monuments of Jerusalem. Not until recently has it been known with confidence that the city of David occupied the few acres of the southeastern hill just above the Gihon spring, but even so we do not know the exact limits of David's capital, we have no information regarding the location of his palace, nor any knowledge concerning his sepulcher. Excavations show that the Jerusalem of Solomon was extended beyond the limits of Ophel (Davidsburg), that it included all of Ophel, Mt. Zion, and Mt. Moriah, the site of the Temple. Still greater enlargement was witnessed in subsequent centuries, until by the period of Hezekiah and Manasseh Jerusalem included the whole of the Acra area (the northwestern hill), Mt. Zion, and Ophel. The Temple area was never inhabited, though, from the era of Solomon, it was always regarded as a part of the city. The whole city, consisting of approximately four square miles, was surrounded by an immense wall penetrated here and there by gates, and on the south, east, and west flanked by very deep valleys. On the northern side there were two walls, the north wall of Solomon's city which ran from the Corner Gate to the Temple, and the wall of Hezekiah and Manasseh which followed in general the present city wall from the Jaffa Gate to Herod's Gate and thence to the Temple Wall. After the destruction of Jerusalem by Nebuchadnezzar, this latter wall, according to the data in the biblical narratives, was the rampart reconstructed by Nehemiah.[67]

On the other hand, while we do not know a great deal about the monuments of Jerusalem at the time of its destruction in 587-6 B.C., we are perfectly familiar with the deep affection bestowed upon the city by all devout Hebrews. There is no question regarding the centrality of its position in the history of Canaan from the beginning through the subsequent days of Jeremiah and of Jesus. This was the city that men called "The Perfection of Beauty," "The Joy of the Whole Earth," "The Beauty of Israel," "The Daughter of Zion," "The Footstool" of the Great King.[68] "Beautiful in elevation, the joy of the whole earth, is mount Zion, on

the sides of the north, the city of the Great King. . . .
We have thought on thy lovingkindness, O God, in the
midst of thy temple. . . . Let mount Zion be glad, let the
daughters of Judah rejoice, because of thy judgments.
Walk about Zion, and go round about her; number the
towers thereof. Mark ye well her bulwarks, consider
her palaces; that ye may tell it to the generation following.''[69]

But whatever may have been the physical grandeur
of Jerusalem (and it certainly was an imposing city
from any point of view), to the pious hearts of Israel
its culminating glory was that here, on Mt. Moriah,
God had chosen to put his name. Accordingly, Jerusalem was the center of the religious life of Israel, the
place to which the tribes came up to attend the great
pilgrim feasts and to offer their sacrifices in the Temple
of Jehovah. Within its sacred precincts ministered
priests and prophets, the spiritual monitors of a none
too zealous people. Here in this holy environment there
were enacted day by day and year by year those ritual
services which had at their heart far more than the
ministering servants ever realized, and here prophetic
voices proclaimed spiritual precepts and elevated moral
ideals that have astonished the world. The seers of
ancient Israel dared to envision Jerusalem as the center
of the world and to paint with fervent colors the endless
procession of nations coming up to Mt. Zion to learn its
laws, to share its love, and to walk in its light. Some
even dared to reverse the picture and to describe the
light as breaking forth from Jerusalem to shed its rays
in every darkened area of human life and thought.
Determined in the counsels of the Almighty this latter
was to be the culmination of Jerusalem's mission but
only to a few was the glory of that mission revealed.
Indeed the final blow at the hands of Nebuchadnezzar
was interpreted in many quarters as the end of Jerusa-

lem, the termination of any purpose that it might have had. Most of all, the haughty Babylonian who reduced "The Perfection of Beauty" to smoldering ashes of complete destruction, did not pause even to make notation of his Philistinism; to him it was probably just another of his insignificant victims laid into the dust. Perhaps it is fitting that Nebuchadnezzar ignored his savagery, for in the long run he who permitted the catastrophe of Jerusalem would also cause its resurrection to new life and to an accomplished mission. Jerusalem would live again and ultimately the light would break out of it to steal over the whole world; heralds of a new order would pass out of its portals with Good News for the nations. "Standing at any point in this hallowed area, one has no difficulty in visualizing the whole procession of Israel's yesterdays, her pageantry of darkness and light. If the brilliancy of the Temple inclosure has passed, snuffed out by destructive events such as no other area in all the world has witnessed, there is still the memory of days when prophets and priests dared to proclaim here moral and spiritual ideas which challenged the nations and enhanced the glory of Israel. Consequently, the Temple area abides together with its glorious associations. One cannot write 'Ichabod' over the face of that which is immortal, nor fail to hear that cautious admonition: 'Put off thy shoes from off thy feet, for the place whereon thou standest is holy ground.' "⁷⁰

Finally, through all of these progressively deeping shadows of national decline stretching from the division of the Kingdoms to the final destruction of Samaria and Jerusalem, there developed one of the phenomenal aspects of the Hebrew religious genius—the prophetic voice. Out of the blackness of night induced by progressive deterioration in religion, there shone in marvelous fashion the spiritual discernment that has astonished the world. It was the Dark Age of a nation's decay, but at the same time the Golden Age of revelation and deep spiritual insight. Into this lurid background of national apostasies and disappointments stepped the towering figures of the moral and spiritual teachers of Israel and of Judah. While we have no tangible evidences concerning these great personages, the conditions under which they labored are being reproduced, and in the light of the reproduction by archaeology we may obtain a clearer understanding of the underlying causes of their messages. During the ninth, eighth, and seventh centuries, when the growing power of Assyria was being witnessed and when the smaller states of the Westlands became increasingly apprehensive concerning the colossus of the North, Obadiah, Jonah, Joel, Amos, Hosea, Isaiah, Micah, Nahum, and Zephaniah stood forth with their messages both to the Northern and Southern Kingdoms. But the prophets of the Assyrian period were not solely concerned with the political threats growing out of a most vicious imperialism; among these messengers who were asserting eternal providence and justifying the ways of God to men were some of the clearest voices ever heard in human counsels: Amos, incisive preacher of righteousness and divine judgment; Hosea, prophet of unchanging love and divine willingness to forgive; Isaiah, proclaimer of transcendent holiness and redeeming grace; and Micah, earnest spokesman for justice, kindness, and for an humble walk with God. But none the less outstanding in their respective missions during the Chaldean or Babylonian period were Habakkuk, Jeremiah, Ezekiel, and Daniel who interpreted faithfully and effectively the unfailing judgments of God and the ultimate purposes of his salvation. "Along the highway of those years the truths which they proclaimed stand like 'white shafts, simple and sublime'. . . .

Between the Hebrew prophets and the best moralists of other nations a great gulf is fixed. Their teachings are a result of their knowledge of God and their communion with him. Consequently their words are surcharged with a spiritual power that is utterly foreign to the ethics of Confucius and Socrates and all pagan teachers. To attribute their ideas and their abiding power over the consciences of men to mere human genius is unthinkable. The only sufficient explanation is that through the prophets God was speaking to mankind. The present writer is doubly convinced that the Spirit of the Eternal illumined the minds of the Hebrew prophets, and that their message is the Word of God.'"[71]

CHAPTER SIXTEEN

DISPERSION AND RESTORATION

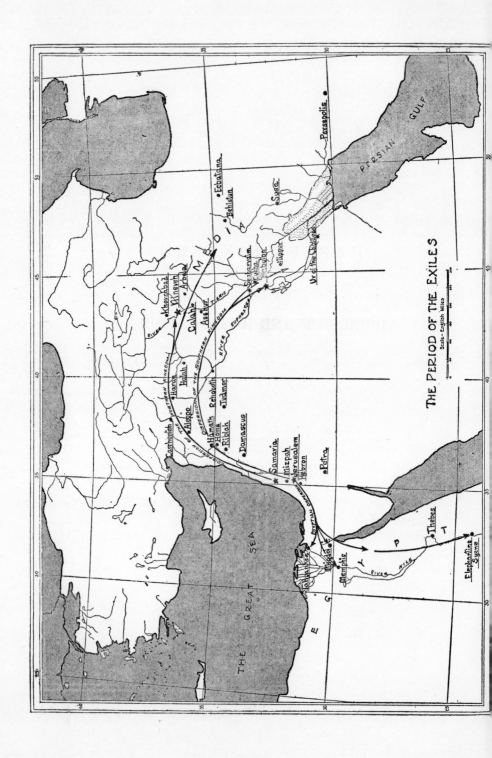

THE PERIOD OF THE EXILES

DISPERSION AND RESTORATION

THE historical and prophetical narratives of the Old Testament, extending from the ninth to the close of the fifth century B.C., constitute our principal sources of information regarding the causes that led up to the captivities of the Northern and Southern Kingdoms. They also set forth the reasons for a promised Restoration looking forward to the consummation of the purpose of God in redemptive history. In the light of these documents of contemporary importance, we may evaluate the sordid experience of Israel's apostasy and consequent dispersion, together with the similar unfaithfulness of Judah that issued in the Babylonian captivity. In these biblical records there is no disposition to minimize the horrors of the destruction of the two Kingdoms, nor is there the least intimation of exonerating either Kingdom of the seriousness of its defection. The documents stand out in broad daylight dispassionately setting forth the obvious results of disloyalty to and rejection of Jehovah. In the very nature of the case, we could hardly expect that any contemporary historian, outside of the house of Israel, should have cared for the fortunes either of the Northern or Southern Kingdom, or that he should have been interested in the fundamental causes that produced their dissolution. It followed, of course, that to the foreign observer the decline and fall of the Hebrew Kingdoms were regarded merely as inevitable results in a political and military framework of dominating world powers, and that there was no reason for expecting a political or spiritual resurrection of the fallen states. But the world now knows that such a fatalistic view of history is not always the true evaluation, and that some of its exceptions are more conspicuous than many of its inclusions. Samaria, "the pride of Ephraim," was dead, and so was Nineveh who struck her down in the day of her rejection, and in both cases the full measure of God's retributive justice was meted out. Jerusalem also was dead, and Babylon, the destroyer, was toppling on the verge of complete and permanent dissolution. But, among those who possessed an awareness of divine control in human affairs, there was not the slightest feeling that the destiny of Jerusalem ended with its destruction, or that its historic and prophetic mission could possibly have terminated with that humiliation. The records are full and complete concerning these deeper significances, both of the Exiles and the Restoration, but no one could expect that there should come to the surface any archaeological confirmation of such deep convictions on the part of men or on the abiding purposes of God. But the events themselves which culminated in the horrible judgment of Samaria and the Northern Kingdom, on the one hand, and in the subsequent catastrophe of Jerusalem and the Southern Kingdom, on the other, are accurately set forth in detail, and through the function of archaeology we may restore the general environments of these exilic experiences and the results which flowed from them.

The Dispersion of the Northern Kingdom

Apart from the Khorsabad Inscription of Sargon II, in which he chronicles the destruction of Samaria in the first year of his reign, with the deportation of

27,290 of its inhabitants, we have no extra-biblical information regarding this tragic event. But even Sargon indulges in no fanfare in thus recording the most significant conquest of his entire reign. "To him the Kingdom of Israel was but one of a hundred petty outlying states, and its royal capital but one of a thousand unimportant towns to be squeezed of all possible spoil and then crushed under foot. There is nothing whatever in all the inscriptions of the ancient East to show that any of Israel's conquerors appreciated even in the smallest degree her unique religious, literary, or cultural contribution to the world. . . . But to the Jews themselves, the Fall of Samaria was the work not of Sargon, whose name they disdained even to record, but of the Providence of Jehovah, a dreadful warning of the inevitable effect of apostasy and evil deeds. 'And it was so, because the children of Israel had sinned against the Lord their God (II K. 17:7).' "[1]

The earlier phases of the Captivity of the Northern Kingdom are clearly stated in the biblical narratives in connection with the advent of Tiglath-pileser in the Westlands about 734-3 B.C. when he disposed of Pekah (probably with the collaboration of Hoshea) and carried into captivity many of the East Jordan Israelites.[2] But the great captivity which marked the end of the Northern Kingdom came a decade later with the destruction of Samaria when "the king of Assyria took Samaria, and carried Israel away unto Assyria, and placed them in Halah, and on the Habor, the river of Gozan, and in the cities of the Medes."[3] "In the earlier deportation of the Transjordan tribes under Tiglath-pileser, the same cities are mentioned with the addition of Hara. A geographical survey of these localities shows that two general sections were affected by the Northern Captivity, first, the region centering around Haran, the early home of the Arameans; and, second, the mountains of the Medes, or the plateau country just beyond the Zagros range. In general this is the same territory as modern Kurdistan and Persia. Now in this latter section were located the unnamed cities of the Median highlands, where portions of Israel's population were to become assimilated by native peoples. In the Haran district, on the other hand, several place-names are mentioned, but there is no uniformity of opinion regarding definite locations. It is obvious that the citations call for a general territory lying east of the Euphrates river in the vicinity of Haran. Strictly regarded, this region is in the heart of Aram-Naharaim of the patriarchal period.''[4]

To the student of Old Testament history it is of extreme interest thus to find the exiles of Samaria returning to localities and scenes associated with the experiences of their forefathers. But there were many differences, and among these there was the dominance of Nineveh which, in the days of the patriarchs, was hardly more than a straggling settlement. Now it was the mistress of the eastern world. Situated on the left bank of the Tigris, the center of upper Mesopotamian highways fanning out into remotest sections north, east, south, and west, the ends of the earth literally looked to Nineveh, and for approximately three centuries she held the nations in an iron grasp. Though at present completely desolate, the once proud city presented the appearance of a magnificent metropolis. It would be difficult perhaps to exaggerate the aspects of its outward glory, its towering walls pierced by bronze gates, its colossal palaces wherein was gathered the spoil of the nations, its temples rising on elevated terraces to great heights, and its broad avenues along which citizens and military moved in unending procession. Expanding far beyond its original circuit of seven miles, Nineveh claimed considerable suburban territory including the adjacent cities of Rehoboth-Ir, Resen, Calah, Arbela, and Asshur. Its powerful monarchs, Sargon, Ashurnatsirpal, and others abandoned the crowded area of Nineveh proper and built their palatial residences in neighboring districts. The great city thus touched Assyrian life at many vital points and was at all times dominant.

It is not claimed in this connection that the helpless captives of the Northern Kingdom were brought into these particular environs of Nineveh, but the assumption is reasonable seeing that the Assyrian policy of deportation was thorough and that diffusion of captured peoples into widely separated areas was customary. At any rate, this is the region into which the exiles of the Northern Kingdom were led and where they remained. Their complete disappearance is one of the mysteries of history—the Ten Lost Tribes—and around this theme many and varied theories of explanation have revolved. But it is not likely that we shall recover any tangible evidence by which we can trace the successive steps of the Captivity of Israel or rediscover the exiles in any modern survivors. The simple fact remains that Israel never returned to Palestine to resume the exalted task and mission which had been forfeited through unexampled disloyalty and unbelief.

The Dispersion of the Southern Kingdom

Nebuchadnezzar, the great conqueror of Jerusalem, struck repeatedly at the citadel of Hebrew life in Judah and each time with increasing power and vindictiveness. From the biblical narratives these successive blows came in 605 B.C., 598 B.C., and 586 B.C. In the Babylonian records we find not the least intimation that Jerusalem ever existed, nor any notation that thousands of Judah's population were deported to Southern Mesopotamia where the major portion were to remain for more than a century. The captivity of Jerusalem and Judah was a mere incident in the daily affairs of the great city by the Euphrates; its citizens were accustomed to seeing motley throngs of prisoners of war trudging along its thoroughfares. But to the Hebrew captives this was no mere incident; it was a national calamity. In one sense their enforced trek to the East was a home-coming, but characterized by all the humiliation of a prodigal's return. Within the ranks of the more pious and spiritually sensitive exiles there were probably those who could discern in the trackless deserts the footprints of Father Abraham in his venture of faith, nor would they fail to observe that his steps pointed westward to a *Promised Land*. The children of the Great Believer are now entering upon the bitter period of suffering which was the inevitable result of unbelief. The almost endless columns of dejected captives moved slowly across the desert wastes destined for Babylon and the vicinity of Ur of the Chaldees, the city of sacred memories.

Through the recoveries of recent years we are now able to delineate the general backgrounds of the Exile of Judah. In addition to the contributions of archae-ology, we are fortunately in possession of prophetical and poetical passages in the Old Testament which set forth numerous facts regarding the location and cir-cumstances of the captives in Babylonia.[5] "The Psalmist complains that 'By the rivers of Babylon, there we sat down, yea, we wept, when we remembered Zion.'[6] This reference indicates that the center of the dispersion is probably to be sought in or near Babylon, the capital city. Another geographical note is given in the introductory statement of Ezekiel: 'I was among the captives by the river of Chebar.'[7] Several notations in Daniel claim the land of Shinar as the home of the early captivity under Nebuchadnezzar, and the city of Baby-lon as the scene of Daniel's remarkable career.[8] From

these and other Biblical references, it is clear that the
exiles were located in the heart of Babylonia, probably
in the metropolitan area of Babylon. In this event they
were hardly more than 100 miles from Ur, the native
city of Abraham. While it is likely that the majority
of the 10,000 captives were settled in Babylon, the reference to the river Chebar shows that a larger area was
affected. There is reason to believe that the Chebar
was one of the principal canals designed by early Babylonians for irrigation purposes, but subsequently converted into navigable streams. The Chebar, formerly
confused with the Habur in northern Mesopotamia,
flowed in a southeasterly direction from Babylon close by
the city of Nippur. It was part of a great inland water-
way project which was originally about 150 miles long,
receiving its waters from the Euphrates 40 miles above
Babylon, but returning to the main stream in the
vicinity of Ur.''[9]

Here, then, at Babylon we may picture the expatriated Hebrews settling to a new life under absolutely
new conditions. Instead of being in the mountain
fortress of Judah, the Hebrew captives were suddenly
placed in the center of old world contacts and conflicts.
Babylon was the focal point in all international relations. Roads from all parts of the Near and Middle
East, together with connecting highways into the Orient,
converged in Babylon. Its rivers were filled with
commercial boats; its magnificent system of canals
included a veritable network of waterways extending
in all directions; its harbors on the Persian Gulf
received imports from foreign countries, while the mer-
chandise of Babylonia found its way through the same
ports to distant lands. Merchants of Mesopotamia dealt
continually with merchants of the Mediterranean;
between East and West there was unending contact in
practically every sphere of human interest. It is rea-

335

sonable to suppose that the powerful influence of this great metropolis on the Euphrates should have reacted on the Hebrew exiles now scattered throughout its domain, and that this influence should have permanently affected the Jews in their outlook on life. Indeed, we now know that such a reaction did follow and that the Hebrews gradually experienced a revolutionary change in their historic mission.

In the first place, "The destruction of the Temple at Jerusalem created the greatest problem for the exiles, who were not only deprived of a central sanctuary, but completely cut off from the ritual and the sacrifice. The problem was partly solved, however, by the organization of a place of meeting which gradually developed into the most outstanding and potent expression of Jewish life whether in the dispersion or, subsequently, in Palestine, i.e. the Synagogue, the house of study and of prayer. It is fairly certain that the Synagogue was the product of the Babylonian Captivity. Around this central organization were grouped all of the social and religious activities of dispersed Judah; it was their unifying bond in a strange country. But other interests were seen coming to the fore, particularly the commercial. This development was obviously inevitable, since their new location in Babylon brought the exiles immediately into contact with business relations involving East and West. Babylon was at the cross-roads of world-trade and communication. The great International Highway crawled through the midst of the city toward the borderland of the Orient. The remarkable business genius which has so definitely characterized the Jew through the centuries, received perhaps its first great impulse in Babylon, and has remained to the present."[10] And, finally, here in this alien environment there came a definite religious experience that colored the whole of their subsequent history, namely, the

TELL EL-FUL, LOCATED THREE MILES NORTH OF JERUSALEM, MARKS
THE SITE OF GIBEAH OF SAUL. IT WAS NEVER AN IMPOSING CITY
THOUGH PROMINENT AS THE BIRTHPLACE OF SAUL, THE FIRST KING OF
ISRAEL. THE CITY STOOD ON THE MAIN HIGHWAY FROM JERUSALEM
AND MIZPAH TO THE NORTH.

THE MASSIVE BASTIONS OF THE HERODIAN GATE AT SAMARIA OCCUPY
PRACTICALLY THE SAME POSITION AS THE HISTORIC ENTRANCE INTO
THE CITY DURING THE DAYS OF OMRI AND AHAB. IT WAS IN A SETTING
OF THIS KIND THAT AHAB AND JEHOSHAPHAT ERECTED THEIR THRONES
TO HEAR THE COUNSEL OF THE PROPHETS.

DURING THE SAMARIA EXCAVATIONS OF 1932-1933 CROWFOOT MADE THE PHENOMENAL DISCOVERY OF THE IVORIES FROM AHAB'S PALACE. HITHERTO SCHOLARS HAVE REGARDED THE REFERENCES IN I KINGS 22:39 AND IN AMOS 6:4 AS PURELY FIGURATIVE. AS INDICATED IN THE PHOTOGRAPHS, THESE CARVED IVORIES HAVE BOTH THE EGYPTIAN AND MESOPOTAMIAN MOTIFS.

THE SAMARIA IVORIES REPRESENT A VARIETY OF SUBJECTS. HERE IS A BEAUTIFUL CHERUB OR ANDRO-SPHINX WITH THE BODY OF A LION STANDING IN A THICKET OF LOTUS FLOWERS.

rebirth of their conviction of Messianic Mission and their rededication to the requirements leading to its fulfillment. Both of these basic ideas find full confirmation in the narratives of Zechariah, Haggai, Malachi, Isaiah, Nehemiah, and Ezra. And, regardless of the privations and sufferings of the Babylonian Captivity, on the banks of the Euphrates the Hebrew exiles did learn to sing a new song whose echoes would some day be gathered up in the angelic chorus over Bethlehem.[11]

The Dispersion in Egypt

Unlike the dispersion of the Northern Kingdom into Assyria, and that of the Southern Kingdom into Babylonia, both of which were enforced at the point of the sword, the Hebrews who made their descent into Egypt were under no compulsion. Their choice of Egypt as an area of refuge was entirely voluntary, but it was no less effective in enlisting ultimately a considerable number of people. It is clear, of course, that this withdrawal into Egypt came on the heels of great persecutions in Palestine, and that refugees both from the Northern Kingdom and the Southern Kingdom were endeavoring to escape the hardships of Assyrian and Babylonian domination. It is entirely probable that a large contingent of people fled before the Assyrian invasion of Israel by Tiglath-pileser and Shalmaneser in the latter part of the eighth century B.C., and that subsequently large groups of inhabitants of Judah escaped to Egypt before the advancing hordes of the Babylonians at the close of the seventh century. The biblical records make it perfectly plain that many Hebrews forsook Jerusalem when Nebuchadnezzar began his assault on the city, and that they compelled Jeremiah to accompany them into Egypt. From the notations that we gather from the life and letters of

Jeremiah, we have hitherto been able to define a rather extensive dispersion in Egyptian setting centering around the outstanding communities of Noph, Migdol, Tahpanhes and, in the extreme southern area, of Pathros. For all this reconstruction of Hebrew life in Egypt the Scripture narratives give ample support. But there was another aspect of this Egyptian dispersion, the Hebrew colony at Elephantine, concerning which we had no intimation in the Scriptures, and of which we would have known nothing apart from the phenomenal discovery of the Elephantine Papyri.[12]

"Information regarding this colony is obtained from the recent recovery (1904, 1907) of a collection of papyrus documents giving full details concerning Jewish life in Elephantine, a garrison town located on an island opposite Syene (modern Assuan). Ezekiel refers to 'the Tower of Syene' in a passage of denunciation, but this probably had no connection with the Jews in Elephantine.[13] These papyri are written in the Aramaic language, thus showing the wide prevalence of the tongue which finally superseded Hebrew in the land of Palestine. Information contained in these ancient records refers to legal documents, temple accounts, and petitions, all pertaining to the activities of this Upper Nile community between the years 471-407 B.C. The item that has caused the greatest surprise, however, is the implication that the Jews had already been in Egypt for more than a century. They had a Temple at Elephantine which was in existence during the Persian period; we are told that Cambyses (525 B.C.) spared the edifice on his invasion of Egypt. This Temple was not an ordinary meeting place, a synagogue, but a real place of sacrifice; its altar and sacred vessels were similar to those prescribed for the Temple services at Jerusalem. While this reflects the attitude of the colonists toward the Jerusalem sanctuary, it likewise suggests their persistence in carrying out at least a part of the religious customs of their fathers in this far-off outpost. Here they were living their own life separate from the rest of the population, observing the Passover, and keeping in communication with the national center in Palestine. But we are shocked to find among these refugees a certain amount of religious syncretism, which shows the worship of Jehovah (Yahu) in a strange setting with pagan deities.[14] This latter state of affairs might have a partial explanation in the retort of the refugees in Upper Egypt when denounced by the Prophet Jeremiah for continuing to follow pagan beliefs and practices in Egypt.[15] In this connection, it is noteworthy that the Elephantine petition addressed to Bagohi, the Persian governor of Judea, is accompanied by an urgent appeal to the sons of Sanballat of Samaria to intercede in their behalf. Evidently the remnant at Jerusalem looked with disfavor on the syncretistic worship associated with the Temple at Elephantine or, as suggested by the appeal to Sanballat, there was some connection between the Elephantine Colony and the Samaritans. At any rate, one wonders what was the relation between the sons of Sanballat and the arch-enemy of the Return under Nehemiah."[16]

Restoration of the Remnant

The Assyrian captivity was the final curtain in the affairs of the Northern Kingdom; the strange interlude of a Hebrew dispersion seeking refuge in the former house of bondage had no subsequent effects which we can trace, but the captivity of the Southern Kingdom did not mark the termination of Judah's historic mission in the plan of redemption. The fall of Judah was complete; so was its resurrection in the purpose of

God. Out of the fires of Exile came the refined gold of tested character and undeviating commitment to the will and plan of God. But when the Restoration took place, only a small number of the dispersion were willing to face the austerities and uncertainties of a return to Palestine. "Many of them found life in Babylon, upon the whole, congenial. They had intermarried with foreigners, had built up good business, and had no liking for the hardships of a return journey on the score of a mere sentiment. They were at ease in Babylon."[17]

There were many others, however, who not only had exalted sentiment in connection with a return to Judah, but who, in some mysterious fashion, felt that neither their own mission nor that of the Chosen People could be accomplished without a return. It was a struggling minority that faced the perils of a desert trek back to the Land of Promise, but they had in their company a few upstanding men like Haggai, Zerubbabel, Zechariah, and others who gave them counsel, encouragement, and inspiration. In the midst of disheartening experiences and under apparently insuperable difficulties, they commenced the rehabilitation of Jerusalem and Judah; they even dared to undertake the rebuilding of the sacred Temple and to restore it to its priority in the religious life and thought of the nation. It is one of the remarkable achievements of history that the repatriated Jews completely succeeded in this program of reconstruction. A little more than half a century later, other thousands are seen making their way along the original trail of Abraham with their faces and hearts fixed on the west, on Judah and Jerusalem. These are the triumphant captives of the days of Ezra, who joined their brethren who in earlier days had dared to hold up the torch of a national revival and mission which, in the inscrutable purpose of God, held the one hope of the family of nations. The rebuilding of the

Temple, the reconstruction of the walls by Nehemiah, the rebuilding of homes, and the restoration of the distinctive way of life amid a genuine Hebrew environment—these marked the successive steps in the re-establishment of Judah in the plan of God. Here in the Hope of Israel there should forever be found the Hope of the world. Jeremiah had said with confidence on the eve of the Captivity, "Behold, I will bring again the captivity of Jacob's tents, and have mercy on his dwelling places; and the city shall be builded upon her own heap."[18] To this might have been added that overall picture of the redemptive purpose, "And in thee shall all the families of the earth be blessed."[19]

The Mission of Persia

The whole of the Restoration movement proceeded within the political framework and under the benevolent attitude of the Persian Empire. As in the case of the Babylonian captivity when all non-biblical contemporary records failed us, so here we are provided with no contemporary Persian documents setting forth the return of the Hebrew captives and the part that Persia played in that far-reaching event. Still we are not at a complete loss in being able to recapture the general conditions under which the Remnant returned to Jerusalem and its ultimate success.

In the immediate background of the Restoration stood the Persian Empire. Its continental organization included the territories of all preceding world powers. To this vast area it added other areas in the north Aegean sector across the Hellespont. "To the east Persia touched India almost as far as the Indus River; to the north, its possessions bordered the coasts of the Caspian and Euxine Seas; to the west, its outposts included not only the coasts of Asia Minor but reached

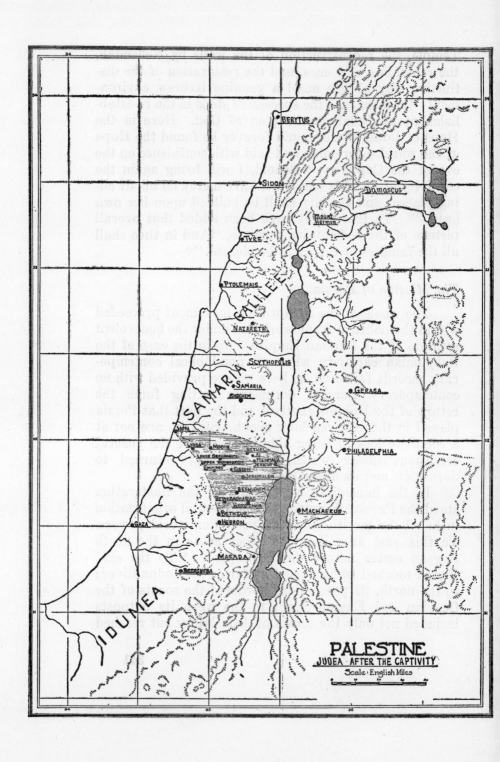

PALESTINE
JUDEA AFTER THE CAPTIVITY
Scale · English Miles

over the Aegean into Macedonia; the whole of the Mediterranean littoral, in the region of Syria, Palestine, and Egypt acknowledged the Persian rule; to the south, its boundaries reached from the Peninsula of Sinai across the Arabian desert to the Persian Gulf. The Biblical narrative suggests the extremes of this kingdom when it describes the Persian monarch, Ahasuerus, as one 'who reigned from India even unto Ethiopia, over an hundred seven and twenty provinces.'[20] These provincial units are not to be regarded as simply partitions of various states; in most cases they were large territories, embracing many nationalities.''[21] Within this framework of Persian domination and administration Palestine fell within the zone of the Fifth Persian Satrapy with its headquarters either at Damascus or Samaria. It is now known that the Jews, though occupying merely a patch of territory in the great Persian system, were made the objects of several unusually favorable state policies. In setting up the machinery for their return to Palestine, the Remnant actually received financial aid from the Persian Government. Again, there is no evidence that the Jews were the victims of repressive measures at the hands of their conquerors; they may have fared exceptionally well in comparison with their bitter experiences under Assyrians and Babylonians. ''But this is in accord with the prophetic statement regarding Cyrus, the man of mystery and mission, who was to make his appearance to accomplish two things: first, to chastise Israel's former oppressors; and, secondly, to restore the Remnant to the land of their fathers. The relations between the Jews and Persians here described were continued from the era of Cyrus (538 B.C.) to Alexander the Great (331 B.C.). They were by no means accidental. Thus for two centuries the Jews both in Palestine and Babylonia remained under the Persian yoke, receiving

343

in turn not only imperial protection, at least nominally, but encouragement in the re-establishment of the national home in Palestine.''[22]

Though their economic condition was often distressing, the Remnant persisted in their program of rehabilitation which included reconstruction of the Temple, rebuilding of the city walls, and re-establishment of the laws and customs of their fathers. Enclosed within an area of only 600 square miles, with Jerusalem as center, the struggling community survived according to the purpose of God. Here was the citadel of Jewish life and thought, the heart of Messianic hope and expectation. Babylonians, Assyrians, Medes, Scythians, Persians, Greeks, and Romans would come and go, but Judea would remain. Divinely appointed, it made a tremendous difference whether the backgrounds of Christianity were Hebrew or foreign; the preservation of this Semitic patch of territory in a constantly changing world looked forward to the day, the fullness of time when Messiah would come and be found among his own.[23]

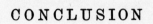

CONCLUSION

CONCLUSION

It will be readily apparent to the student of the Old Testament that, in the preceding discussions on archaeological discoveries and their bearing on the historical narratives of the Hebrew Scriptures, we have not completely solved all the biblical problems, though definite progress has been made in several areas where light was most needed. With the progress of investigation we may have confidence that further advances will be witnessed. But, as suggested, solid ground has been reached in regard to some outstanding questions which hitherto have been clamoring for explanation. Among these has been the question of the possibility and probability of early Hebrew written records contemporary with the initial and middle phases of Hebrew history—i.e., during the Patriarchal and Mosaic periods, as well as in the later era of the Monarchy where copious literary evidences are freely admitted to have existed. The net result of this inquiry, viewed in the light of ancient literary monuments among contemporary peoples and in the light of the Hebrew records themselves, leads us to believe that there was no period in Hebrew history when they could not have had current records, and that the internal evidences of these sacred documents demand an earlier date for their composition than criticism has hitherto been willing to admit. Whatever the interpolations or insertions, whatever the editorial revision or redactions, these records may be regarded as substantially the same as when first produced. The theory of oral transmission applied to such narratives of high antiquity is by no means competent to explain the estab-

347

lished accuracy of these historical records in their references to and notations of geographical, topographical, ethnological, ethnographical, and archaeological details.

Furthermore, proceeding on the justifiable assumption of early Hebrew records, we have allowed these narratives to speak from their own point of view and have insisted that their testimony be received without prejudice. This insistence has been based not only upon an exalted view of the Scriptures themselves, but also upon the archaeological discoveries of recent years which have steadily tended to elevate the sacred narratives in critical opinion. It is not mere chance that where the Bible and archaeology have met they have been found to be in substantial agreement. In those areas and incidents where they have not met we may still believe that they are not contradictory; they may be found to be complementary and supplementary. This principle has had astonishing vindication in repeated instances and may be accepted without hesitation. This is a fair and judicious attitude. One of the principal results flowing from it will be to reject decisively any misrepresentation of the respective spheres of archaeology and biblical criticism as in any sense mutually and continuously hostile. In both areas of investigation the truth is diligently sought; there is no inevitable conflict between the one and the other. To recognize this essential requirement is to make a long stride in increased knowledge of the Bible.

It will be recalled that the principle here stressed has been put into effect in all the discussions presented in this volume; the ancient records have been marshaled alongside the Hebrew narratives not as mutual antagonists but as reliable and impartial sources from which the student of the Bible could gather information in reconstructing the history and checkered experiences of the Chosen People as they led on to the fullness of time and to Christ. With that end in view, and with the abundance of biblical and non-biblical *data* placed at our disposal, there has been no great difficulty in recapturing the environment of the great Patriarch Abraham nor in rebuilding the age in which he lived, both in its Mesopotamian and Canaanite phases. When the biblical records and the ancient monuments are allowed to tell their own stories, the result has been a phenomenal agreement in circumstance and atmosphere. There have been no harsh notes in the recital of those faroff days and conditions; the facts have been consonant and convincing.

The principle has not been disappointing when applied to the outstanding experiences of the Hebrew people in the land of Egypt, nor to the culminating event of the Exodus which marked the beginning of their national life. Perhaps in no field of investigation has archaeology rendered so signal a service as here. Through the recovered evidences now at hand, discriminatively handled and interpreted, new light is being thrown on these vexing problems. It seems fairly certain that the solution of the Sojourn-Exodus problem is at hand, though one must wait for additional historical data to be absolutely positive. It is entirely possible that the recent investigations of Glueck in the Transjordan area will provide additional material on which we may found a clearer view of the whole Exodus experience. Since these investigations, mainly in the field of exploration rather than excavation, have not been fully evaluated, their implications are not invoked either in defense or refutation of an early date for the Exodus. At present this is perhaps the course of wisdom, for it is perfectly obvious that the conditions which are said to rule out of the picture any fourteenth century Exodus also necessitate a twentieth century Abraham. With a late Exodus and an early Abraham the chronological gap is further widened and additional problems are interposed. Furthermore, one would like to be more assured with reference to the biblical requirements which necessitate flourishing cities in the Sinaitic and Gulf of Akabah coastlands when the nomadic Hebrews were making their way toward the Land of Promise. In the latter phases of that movement, when they arrived in the upland areas of Moab, Ammon, and Gilead, the cities, the peoples, and the cultures which are described as contemporary are freely recognized as existent. There is no radical flaw in these narratives. We may still believe that the Thutmosis-Amenhotep Egyptian setting for the Hebrew Oppression and Exodus is the most plausible view in the light of all the collateral evidences and that no recent discovery makes necessary any radical revision of that interpretation.

In the difficult problem of Old Testament chronology substantial progress has been made in the past few years. The recovery of Assyrian and Babylonian documents of first-rate importance, together with isolated monuments bearing on the historical records of the Hebrew people, has made it possible to reconstruct a chronological framework of Old Testament history which offers help in harmonizing the Hebrew accounts with those of contemporary nations. Of extraordinary significance are the Assyrian Annals and Chronicles, the Monolith of Shalmaneser III, the Black Obelisk, the Stela of Merneptah, and the Tell el-Amarna Letters. In addition to these there are other significant monuments whose chronological data are extremely valuable. As a consequence of these discoveries the eras of Hebrew history are more clearly defined and the outstanding events of Old Testament development determined with a greater degree of accuracy.

350

And, finally, in the matter of archaeology and criticism, the areas of investigation represented by the two sciences are differentiated with the result that their combined contributions have been brought to bear on a fuller understanding of redemptive history. It is obviously a distinct loss to put archaeology and criticism into separate and hostile camps when, in their legitimate functions, they are clearly complementary and supplementary. The search for truth is a long and arduous process, and one should welcome help from every quarter. Archaeology and criticism are continually providing for us substantial corroboration of biblical statements and when constructively exercised their contributions have greatly enhanced the historical value of the Bible on every hand. As we observed in the beginning of this investigation, what is needed in the present situation involving problems of the Bible is not more conjecture, but more light, and a corresponding mental humility produced by the recognition of our limited knowledge. Thus steering clear of the so-called avenue of "blind faith" or credulity, and of a presumptuous erudition, we have sought the wide and open spaces where truth may stand and prevail. Without announcing dogmatically the solution of all our problems and the elimination of all the tangled questions confronting the earnest student of the Bible, we have sought the truth, knowing fully that it alone has any secure footing either in reason or in faith. It is earnestly hoped that in the foregoing investigations some, at least, of these purposes and goals might have been attained.

IN SOME RESPECTS JERUSALEM WAS A BEAUTIFUL CITY. THE PSALMIST
DESCRIBES IT AS WONDERFUL FOR SITUATION AND ADORNED WITH
TOWERS OF MAGNIFICENT APPEARANCE. THE SOUTHWEST SECTION HERE
IN VIEW SHOWS JERUSALEM ABOVE THE DEEP VALLEY OF HINNOM, STILL
ATTRACTIVE AND COMMANDING. THE POPULATION OF JERUSALEM TODAY.
INCLUDING THE OLD CITY WITHIN THE WALLS AND THE NEW CITY AND
SUBURBS, IS APPROXIMATELY 175,000.

MASSIVE WALLS ENCIRCLE JERUSALEM EVEN IN THE MODERN PERIOD,
BUT THEY ARE NOT AS FORMIDABLE AS THE RAMPARTS LEVELED TO
THE GROUND BY THE FORCES OF NEBUCHADNEZZAR IN 586 B.C. THIS
VIEW OF JERUSALEM FEATURES A PART OF THE WEST WALL TOGETHER
WITH THE TRADITIONAL "TOWER OF DAVID."

A BEAUTIFUL VIEW OF THE DOME OF THE ROCK, THE MOHAMMEDAN
TEMPLE AT JERUSALEM, WHICH STANDS ON MOUNT MORIAH ABOVE THE
SPOT OF THE ATTEMPTED SACRIFICE OF ISAAC BY ABRAHAM. ALWAYS
THE HOLY PLACE OF JERUSALEM, THE TEMPLES OF SOLOMON, ZERUB-
BABEL, AND OF HEROD THE GREAT OCCUPIED THE SAME SPOT. DEVOUT
MOHAMMEDANS FACE TOWARD THIS TEMPLE AS WELL AS TOWARDS MECCA
IN THEIR PRAYERS.

ON THE WEST SIDE OF THE PRESENT TEMPLE ENCLOSURE WALL IS THE
"WAILING PLACE" OF THE JEWS WHERE PRAYER IS MADE FOR THE
RESTORATION OF THE GLORY OF ZION. THIS IS ONE OF THE OLDEST
SECTIONS OF THE RAMPARTS OF JERUSALEM AND MIGHT BE OF
SOLOMONIC ORIGIN.

APPENDIXES

―――――

I.

TURNING POINTS IN ANCIENT HISTORY WITH SPECIAL REFERENCE TO THE HEBREW PEOPLE

B.C.

2080—Hyksos Invasion of Egypt
2000—Period of the Patriarch Abraham
1876—Descent of Jacob and Sons into Egypt
1876-1446—Period of the Sojourn in Egypt
1580—Hyksos Expulsion from Egypt
1526—Birth of Moses
1501-1447—Reign of Thutmosis III
1447-1420—Reign of Amenhotep II
1446—The Exodus from Egypt
1010- 970—Reign of David
1000—Capital Established at Jerusalem
970—Accession of Solomon
966—Building of the Temple
931—Division of the Kingdom
931-721—The Northern Kingdom
931-586—The Southern Kingdom
853—The Battle of Karkar
841—Tribute of Jehu to Shalmaneser III
738—Tribute of Menahem to Tiglath-pileser III
732—Accession of Hoshea of Israel
721—Destruction of Samaria by Sargon II
701—Invasion of Palestine by Sennacherib
621—Discovery of the Law of Moses in the Temple
612—Fall of Nineveh
608—Death of Josiah at Megiddo
586—Fall of Jerusalem
535—Return of Southern Kingdom Captives
520—Building of the Second Temple
458—Period of Ezra
471- 407—Period of the Elephantine Papyri
444—Nehemiah Visits Jerusalem

II.

ERAS OF CULTURAL PROGRESS IN PALESTINE

I. THE STONE AGE

Palaeolithic
Neolithic

II. THE BRONZE AGE............3000 B.C.—1300 B.C.

Early Canaanite	3000 B.C.—2000 B.C.
Middle Canaanite	2000 B.C.—1600 B.C.
Late Canaanite	1600 B.C—1300 B.C.

III. THE IRON AGE...............1300 B.C.—A.D. 636

Early Palestine	1300 B.C.— 600 B.C.
Middle Palestine	600 B.C.— 100 B.C.
Late Palestine	100 B.C.— A.D. 636

IV. THE MODERN PERIOD..................A.D. 636

Early Arab	A.D. 636—A.D. 1100
Middle Arab	A.D. 1100—A.D. 1500
Late Arab	A.D. 1500

356

III.

BIBLIOGRAPHY

Adams, J. McKee, *Biblical Backgrounds*, Second Edition, Broadman Press, Nashville, 1938.

Albright, W. F., *From the Stone Age to Christianity*, The Johns Hopkins Press, Baltimore, 1940.
Archaeology and the Religion of Israel, The Johns Hopkins Press, Baltimore, 1942.
The Archaeology of Palestine and the Bible, Fleming H. Revell Company, New York, 1932.
The Excavation of Tell Beit Mirsim, New Haven, 1932, 1933, 1938, 1943 (Annual of the American Schools of Oriental Research, Vols. XII, XIII, XVII, XXI, XXII).

Bade, W. F., *A Manual of Excavation in the Near East*, University of California Press, Berkeley, 1934.

Baikie, James, *A Century of Excavation in the Land of the Pharaohs*, Fleming H. Revell Company, New York, 1924.
The Amarna Age, Macmillan Company, New York, 1926.

Bailey, E. A., *Daily Life in Bible Times*, Charles Scribner's Sons, New York, 1943.

Barton, G. A., *Archaeology and the Bible*, Fourth Edition, American Sunday School Union, Philadelphia, 1925.

Bevan and Singer, *The Legacy of Israel*, The Clarendon Press, Oxford, 1927.

Bliss, *A Mound of Many Cities*, Palestine Exploration Fund, London, 1894.

Breasted, J. H., *Ancient Records*, University of Chicago Press, Chicago, 1907.
History of Egypt, Charles Scribner's Sons, New York, 1905.

Budge, E.A.T.W,, *Babylonian Life and History*, Religious Tract Society, 1925.
The Babylonian Story of the Deluge, British Museum, 1920.

Burney, C. F., *Israel's Settlement in Canaan*, Oxford University Press, Oxford, 1921.

Burrows, Millard, *What Mean These Stones?* American Schools of Oriental Research, New Haven, 1941.

Caiger, S. L., *Bible and Spade*, Oxford University Press, Oxford, 1936.
The Old Testament and Modern Discovery, Oxford University Press, Oxford, 1933.

Chiera, Edward, *They Wrote on Clay*, University of Chicago Press, Chicago, 1938.

Clay, A. T., *The Empire of the Amorites*, Yale University Press, New Haven, 1919.

Cook, S. A., *The "Truth" of the Bible*, The Macmillan Company, New York, 1938.
The Laws of Moses and the Code of Hammurabi, A&C Black Company, London, 1903.

Cowley, A. F., *The Hittites*, Oxford University Press, Oxford, 1926.
Aramaic Papyri of the Fifth Century, The Clarendon Press, Oxford, 1923.

Dougherty, R. P., *The Sealand of Ancient Arabia*, Yale University Press, New Haven, 1932.

Duncan, J. G., *Digging Up Biblical History*, The Macmillan Company, New York, 1931.
New Light on Hebrew Origins, The Macmillan Company, New York, 1936.
The Accuracy of the Old Testament, The Macmillan Company, New York, 1930.

Driver, S. R., *Modern Research as Illustrating the Bible*, Oxford University Press, Oxford, 1909.

Evans, Arthur, *Essays in Aegean Archaeology*, The Clarendon Press, Oxford, 1920.

Fawthrop, T. W., *The Stones Cry Out*, Marshall, Morgan and Scott, Ltd., London.

Gadd, *The Fall of Nineveh*, Oxford University Press, Oxford, 1923.

Garstang, John, *The Hittite Empire*, Richard R. Smith, New York, 1930.
The Foundations of Bible History, Richard R. Smith, New York, 1931.

Gaster, Moses, *The Samaritans*, Oxford University Press, Oxford, 1925.

Glover, T. R., *The Ancient World*, Cambridge University Press, Cambridge, 1935.

Glueck, Nelson, *The Other Side of Jordan*, American Schools of Oriental Research, New Haven, 1940.

Gordon, Cyrus H., *The Living Past*, The John Day Company, New York, 1941.

Gray, G. B., *A Critical Introduction to the Old Testament*, Edinburgh University Press, Edinburgh, 1913.

Hall, H. R., *Ancient History of the Near East*, Methnen and Company, Ltd., London, 1927.
Joint Expedition of British Museum and the University of Pennsylvania to Mesopotamia, Oxford University Press, Oxford, 1927.

Harris, C. W., *The Hebrew Heritage*, The Abingdon Press, New York, 1935.

Hilprecht, H. V., *Explorations in Bible Lands*, A. J. Holman and Company, Philadelphia, 1903.

Hogarth, D. G., *Kings of the Hittites*, Oxford University Press, Oxford, 1926.

Jack, J. W., *Date of the Exodus*, T. and T. Clarke, Edinburgh, 1925.
Samaria in Ahab's Time, Charles Scribner's Sons, New York, 1929.
The Ras Shamra Tablets, T. and T. Clarke, Edinburgh, 1935.

Jastrow, Morris, *Hebrew and Babylonian Traditions*, Charles Scribner's Sons, New York, 1914.

Johns, C. H. W., *The Laws of Babylonia and the Laws of the Hebrew People*, Oxford University Press, Oxford, 1917.

Kent, C. F., *Biblical Geography and History*, Charles Scribner's Sons, New York, 1926.

Kenyon, Frederick, *The Bible and Archaeology*, Harper and Brothers, New York, 1940.

King, L. W., *Legends of Babylon and Egypt*, Oxford University Press, Oxford, 1918.

King and Hall, *Egypt and Western Asia in the Light of Recent Discoveries*, Grolier Society, London, 1906.

Knight, G. A. F., *Nile and Jordan*, J. Clarke and Company, Ltd., Edinburgh, 1921.

Kyle, M. G., *Excavating Kirjath-Sepher's Ten Cities*, Wm. B. Eerdmans Publishing Company, Grand Rapids, 1934.
The Deciding Voice of the Monuments, Bibliotheca Sacra Press, St. Louis, 1924.

Leslie, E. A., *Old Testament Religion*, The Abingdon Press, New York, 1936.

Ludwig, Emil, *The Nile*, Garden City Publishing Company, Garden City, 1939.

Macalister, R.A.S., *The Philistines, Their History and Civilization*, Oxford University Press, Oxford, 1914.
A Century of Excavation in Palestine, Fleming H. Revell Company, New York, 1925.

Marston, Charles, *New Bible Evidence*, Fleming H. Revell Company, New York, 1934.

The Bible Comes Alive, Fleming H. Revell Company, Edinburgh, 1938.

Maspero, G., *Manual of Egyptian Archaeology*, G. P. Putman's Sons, New York, 1926.

McCown, C. C., *The Ladder of Progress in Palestine*, Harper and Brothers, New York, 1943.

McFadyen, J. E., *Use of the Old Testament in the Light of Modern Knowledge*, Pilgrim Press, Boston, 1922.

Meek, I. J., *Hebrew Origins*, Harper and Brothers, New York, 1936.

Merrill, Selah, *Ancient Jerusalem*, Fleming H. Revell Company, New York, 1908.

Naville, Edouard, *Archaeology of the Old Testament*, Samuel R. Leland, Inc., New York, 1932.

Obermann, *The Archaic Inscriptions from Lachish*, American Oriental Society, Baltimore, 1938.

Olmstead, A.T.E., *History of Palestine and Syria*, Charles Scribner's Sons, New York, 1931.

Orr, James, *The Problem of the Old Testament*, Charles Scribner's Sons, New York, 1905.

Peake, A. S., *The People and the Book*, Essays, The Clarendon Press, Oxford, 1925.

Peet, T. E., *Egypt and the Old Testament*, University Press of Liverpool, Liverpool, 1924.

Petrie, Flinders, *Palestine and Egypt*, Society for Promoting Christian Knowledge, London, 1934.

Seventy Years in Archaeology, Sampson, Low, Marston and Company, Ltd., London, 1930.

Price, Ira M., *The Monuments and the Old Testament*, Seventeenth Edition, The Judson Press, Philadelphia, 1925.

Robinson, G. L., *The Sarcophagus of an Ancient Civilization*, The Macmillan Company, New York, 1930.

Robinson, Hunkin and Burkitt, *Palestine in General History*, Oxford University Press, Oxford, 1929.

Robinson, Wheeler, *The Old Testament, Its Making and Meaning*, Hodder and Stoughton, Ltd., London, 1937.

Schofield, J. N., *The Historical Background of the Bible*, Thomas Nelson and Sons, London, 1937.

Smith, G. A., *The Historical Geography of the Holy Land,* Hodder and Stoughton, London, 1896.

Jerusalem, 2 Vols., Hodder and Stoughton, London, 1907.

Smith, J. M. P., *The Origin and History of Hebrew Law,* The University of Chicago Press, Chicago, 1931.

Speiser, E. A., *Ethnic Movements in the Near East,* The John H. Hurst Company, Baltimore, 1933.

Mesopotamian Origins, University of Pennsylvania Press, Philadelphia, 1930.

Steindorff and Seele, *When Egypt Ruled the East,* The University of Chicago Press, Chicago, 1942.

Torczyner, Harry, *The Lachish Letters,* Oxford University Press, Oxford, 1938.

Weigall, Arthur, *Tutankhamen and Other Essays,* George H. Doran Company, New York, 1924.

Welch, A. C., *Jeremiah,* Oxford University Press, Oxford, 1928.

Woolley, C. L., *Abraham,* Charles Scribner's Sons, New York, 1936.

Ur of the Chaldees, E. Benn, Ltd., London, 1929.

The Sumerians, The Clarendon Press, Oxford, 1929.

Dead Towns and Living Men, Oxford University Press, Oxford, 1920.

Digging Up the Past, Charles Scribner's Sons, New York, 1931.

Yahuda, A. S., *The Accuracy of the Bible,* Wm. Heinemann, London, 1934.

REFERENCES

CHAPTER ONE

1. Adams, *Biblical Background*, p. 18f.
2. Adams, *Biblical Background*, p. 170f.
3. Huntington, *The Transformation of Palestine*.

CHAPTER TWO

1. *The National Geographic Magazine*, August, 1928.
2. The terms "mound" and "tell" are interchangeable. Mound is probably derived from t h e Anglo-Saxon, while "Tell" is the Arabic equivalent, indicating more specifically the site of an ancient city. The Hebrew "Tel" has the same meaning.
3. See Asia Magazine, August, 1936, Article, *Marsh Arabs of Iraq*.
4. *Deuteronomy* 1:28. See also *Numbers* 13:28.
5. The science which treats of the measurement of time by divisions or periods on the basis of comparative pottery. Sir Flinders Petrie, the father of this revolutionary method, first announced the scheme in 1890 after prolonged periods of excavation in Egypt and Palestine. At present it is held that pottery chronology can be successfully applied to all phases of Old Testament history. For more detailed description and for illustrations, see Marston, The *Bible Comes Alive*, p. 18f., 134f., 246, and plates. Compare also, *How to Observe in Archaeology*, published by Trustees of the British Museum, pp. 59-94, and especially, Albright, *The Excavation of Tell Beit Mirsim I: The Pottery of the First Three Campaigns*. For further study, see, Burney, *Israel's Settlement in Canaan*, p. 3; Kyle, *Excavating Kirjath-Sepher's Ten Cities*, p. 83ff.; Macalister, *A Century of Excavation in Palestine*, p. 237.
6. See Article in *Asia Magazine*, September, 1938.
7. Duncan, *Digging Up Biblical History*, p. 130.
8. *Ibid.*, p. 107.
9. *Joshua* 6:15.
10. *Joshua* 6:36. Compare fate of Carthage at the hands of the Romans.
11. The water supply was necessarily in the city, within the walls. Excavations, particularly at Gezer and Megiddo, have revealed some perfectly marvelous engineering achievements of these early peoples in reaching water and mak-

363

ing it accessible to the population. With crudest implements of flint they cut their way through solid rock to great depth and hewed out tunnels of immense proportions. They also provided great cisterns for the conservation of rainfall.

CHAPTER THREE

1. The results of this Expedition were published between the years 1809-1822, in seven volumes, under the title, *"Description de l'Egypte."*

2. The Obelisk was set up by Egyptian priests in 185 B.C. as an expression of gratitude to Ptolemy V (Epiphanes) for remission of taxes. Its measurements are 3 feet 9 inches in length, 2 feet 4 and ½ inches in breadth, and 11 inches in thickness. It contains 14 lines of Hieroglyphics, the sacred writing of the priests; 32 lines of Demotic, the language of the people, and 54 lines of Greek *Koine* written in capital letters. See Budge, *The Rosetta Stone*, pp. 1-8.

3. For detailed discussion of the Rosetta Stone, see the following: Knight, *Nile and Jordan*, p. 446; Budge, *The Mummy*, pp. 127-152; *The Dwellers on the Nile; The Rosetta Stone;* Mahaffy, *History of Ptolemaic Dynasty.*

4. For further study, reference is made to the following: Petrie, *Tell el-Amarna;*

Maspero, *A Manual of Egyptian Archaeology;* Macalister, *A Century of Excavation in Palestine,* pp. 151-161; Barton, *Archaeology and the Bible,* pp. 36, 402-409; Price, *The Monuments and the Old Testament,* pp. 160-162; Caiger, *Bible and Spade,* pp. 96-98; Knight, *Nile and Jordan,* pp. 208-222; Handcock, *The Tell el-Amarna Letters;* Petrie, *Syria and Egypt from the Tell el-Amarna Letters;* Driver, *Modern Research,* pp. 32-37.

5. Petrie, *Seventy Years in Archaeology,* p. 160.

6. Fuller accounts of the Merneptah Stela may be found in Driver, *Modern Research as Illustrating the Bible,* pp. 38-40; Caiger, *Bible and Spade,* pp. 111-113; 191-192; Jack, *The Date of the Exodus;* Knight, *Nile and Jordan,* 243-252; Petrie, *History of Egypt.*

7. *Isaiah* 11:11. Compare Adams, *Biblical Backgrounds,* 2nd Ed., pp. 89-111; 280-283.

8. *Jeremiah* 44:1, 15, 24; *Ezekiel* 29:10.

9. Naville, *Archaeology of the Old Testament,* p. 159. See also fascinating chapter on the subject, pp. 139-174.

10. For further study, see Price, *The Monuments and the Old Testament,* pp. 385-399; Driver, *Modern Research,* pp. 27-30; Belleli, *The Elephantine Aramaic Papyri;* Cowley, *Aramaic Papyri of the Vth Century.*

11. Adams, *Biblical Backgrounds*, p. 120.

12. Knight, *Nile and Jordan*, p. 166f.

13. *The Harvard Theological Review*, April, 1932.

14. Compare Knight, *Nile and Jordan*, p. 167.

CHAPTER FOUR

1. Compare Adams, *Biblical Backgrounds*, pp. 23, 66.

2. There is a considerable body of literature on this subject. Reference is made to the following convenient works: Sayce, *Fresh Light from Ancient Monuments*; Hilprecht, *Explorations in Bible Lands*; Rawlinson, *Cuneiform Inscriptions of Western Asia*; Clay, *A Hebrew Deluge Story in Cuneiform*; Price, *The Monuments and the Old Testament*; Driver, *Modern Research as Illustrating the Bible*; Barton, *Archaeology and the Bible*; Luckenbill, *Ancient Records of Assyria*; Caiger, *Bible and Spade*.

3. Price, *The Monuments and the Old Testament*, p. 46.

4. See Langdon, *Sumerian Epic of Creation and Paradise*; Price, *The Monuments and the Old Testament*, pp. 101-108; Caiger, *Bible and Spade*, pp. 12-18; 20-27; Jeremias, *The Old Testament in the Light of the Ancient East*; King, *The Seven Tablets of Creation*; Barton, *Archaeology and the Bible*; pp. 251-280;

King, *Legends of Babylon and Egypt*; Driver, *Modern Research as Illustrating the Bible*; Rogers, *Cuneiform Parallels to the Old Testament*; Smith, *The Chaldean Account of Genesis*; Handcock, *Babylonian Flood Stories*; Hilprecht, *Explorations in Bible Lands*, pp. 190-213; Smith, *Assyrian Discoveries*; Rassam, *Asshur and the Land of Nimrod*; Ball, *Light from the East*; Hogarth, *Authority and Archaeology*; Layard, *Discoveries in Nineveh and Babylon*; King and Hall, *Egypt and Western Asia in the Light of Recent Discoveries*.

5. Hilprecht, *Explorations in Bible Lands*, p. 70f.

6. *Ibid.*, p. 187.

7. For discussion, see pp. 249-255.

8. For further study, see, Harper, *The Code of Hammurabi*; Johns, *The Laws of Babylonia and the Laws of the Hebrew People*; Smith, *The Origin and History of Hebrew Law*, pp. 181-222; Duncan, *An Introduction to Biblical Archaeology*, pp. 120-125; Cook, *The Laws of Moses and the Code of Hammurabi*; King and Hall, *Egypt and Western Asia in the Light of Recent Discoveries*; Robinson, *Bearing of Archaeology on the Old Testament*, pp. 87-89; Johns in Hastings, *Dictionary of the Bible*, V., 584-612.

9. Smith, *The Origin and History of Hebrew Law*, Appendix II, The Code of Hammurabi, translated by Luckenbill, p. 183.

10. Driver, *Modern Research as Illustrating the Bible*, p. 27.

11. See pages 249-260.

12. Illustrated article setting forth these results may be found in *Asia*, September, 1938.

13. *Asia*, September, 1938, Article, *Closing the Gap at Tepe Gawra*, p. 541.

14. Jemdet-Nasr is a small mound located eighteen miles northeast of Kish.

15. Kenyon, *The Bible and Archaeology*, p. 144.

16. Albright, *From the Stone Age to Christianity*, p. 100.

17. Woolley, *Abraham*, p. 61.

18. For full discussion of the Ur excavations and their relation to Abraham, see Woolley's splendid volume on *Abraham*.

19. Woolley, *Abraham*, p. 82.

20. Kenyon, *The Bible and Archaeology*, p. 135.

21. Woolley, *Abraham*, p. 103.

22. Kenyon, *The Bible and Archaeology*, p. 167.

23. Cf. Burrows, *What Mean These Stones?* p. 89.

24. Burrows, *What Mean These Stones?* p. 92.

25. *Genesis* 14:6; 26:20, 29; *Deuteronomy* 2:12, 22. Cf. Duncan, *New Light on Hebrew Origins*, p. 84f.; Kenyon, *The Bible and Archaeology*, p. 146.

26. Speiser, *Ethnic Movements in the Near East*, p. 31f.

27. Up to this time five volumes of Nuzi Texts, discovered by Americans, have been published.

28. Burrows, *What Mean These Stones?* p. 91f.

29. At Dog River, ten miles north of Beirut, one can see the portrait of the great military leader sculptured in the mountainside. See, Barton, *Archaeology and the Bible*, note, p. 420.

30. See Barton, *Archaeology and the Bible*, p. 418f., Price, *Monuments and the Old Testament*, p. 271f.

31. The determination of the date proceeds mainly on astronomical lines, especially on arguments advanced by F. X. Kugler, Assyriologist and Astronomer. See Barton, *Archaeology and the Bible*, p. 56f., Cambridge Ancient History, Vol. III, pp. 22, 262, 363 and Albright, *Archaeology and the Religion of Israel*, note, p. 221. See also Kugler, *Von Moses bis Paulus*, in loco. Further explanation, see this volume, Chapter X.

32. Hilprecht, *Explorations in Bible Lands*, p. 208. Compare, Kenyon, *The Bible and Archaeology*, p. 55f. See, also, King, *Bronze Plates from the Gates of Shalmaneser*, p. 17. For Balawat Translations, see Sayce, *Records of the Past*, Vol. iv, pp. 74-79.

33. Compare, Kenyon, *The Bible and Archaeology*, p. 55f., Fawthrop, *The Stones Cry Out*, p. 77f.

34. *1 Kings* 22:1-40.

35. Hilprecht, *Explorations in Bible Lands*, p. 107.

36. *Ibid.*, p. 106.
37. Driver, *Modern Research as Illustrating the Bible*, p. 17. Cf. *1 Kings* 20:15.
38. Price, *The Monuments and the Old Testament*, p. 275.
39. See Chapter X, *Old Testament Chronology*.
40. *2 Kings* 15:19-20.
41. *2 Kings* 15:23.
42. *2 Kings* 15:27.
43. *2 Kings* 15:30.
44. Angus - Green, *Cyclopedic Handbook*, p. 309.
45. See Chapter X, *Old Testament Chronology*.
46. Compare *2 Kings* 17:6; *2 Kings* 18:9-12; *Isaiah* 20:1.
47. *Helps to the Study of the Bible*, p. 41 in section *Explanation of Plates*.
48. Compare Hilprecht, *Explorations in Bible Lands*, pp. 114-138.
49. Caiger, *Bible and Spade*, p. 165f.
50. Gadd, *The Fall of Nineveh*, p. 15. In this volume one may find complete Transliteration, Translation, notes, etc., bearing on Chronicle No. 21, 901.

CHAPTER FIVE

1. Beginning with the excavations at Boghaz-koi under the German Oriental Society, many volumes have been written on Hittite movements and developments. For further study of these most interesting people, the student is referred to the following splendid works: Cowley, *The Hittites;* Hogarth, *Kings of the Hittites;* Garstang, *The Hittite Empire;* Sayce, *The Hittites;* Wright, *The Empire of the Hittites.*
2. Cowley, *The Hittites*, p. 8.
3. *Exodus* 13:5, etc.
4. See Garstang, *The Hittite Empire*, p. 317f.
5. Cowley, *The Hittites*, p. 19.
6. Smith, *Origin and History of Hebrew Law*, p. 279. Compare Barton, *Archaeology and the Bible*, pp. 369-388.

CHAPTER SIX

1. Attention is called to two illustrated articles in the National Geographic Magazine, October, 1930, and July, 1933, describing the results of excavations at Ras Shamra. Articles, *A New Alphabet of the Ancients is Unearthed,* and *Secrets from Syrian Hills.* For further study of the Ras Shamra excavations, see, Schaeffer, *The Cuneiform Texts of Ras Shamra-Ugarit;* Jack, *The Ras Shamra Tablets;* Kenyon, *The Bible and Archaeology,* pp. 153-164; and Burrows, *What Mean These Stones?* paragraph 37.
2. Jack, *The Ras Shamra Tablets,* p. 4.
3. Jack, *The Ras Shamra Tablets,* p. 4.
4. The adventures are recited in the Golenischeff Papyrus found in 1891 at El-Khibeh in Upper Egypt. See Macalister, *The Philistines,* pp. 29-37, and Barton, *Archaeology and the Bible,* pp. 410-414.

5. Caiger, *Bible and Spade*, p. 7. See, also, Olmstead, *Palestine and Syria*, for description of the Sarcophagus.
6. Kenyon, *The Bible and Archaeology*, p. 167.
7. The Tirhakah here mentioned is probably the same king referred to in the disastrous campaign of Sennacherib against Hezekiah in 701 B.C. (See 2 Kings 19:9). If this is correct, Tirhakah was acting for his cousin, Shabatoka, the ruling Pharaoh, whose death occurred in 693 B.C. Possibility of a later campaign by Sennacherib.
8. Hall, *The Ancient History of the Near East*, p. 499.
9. In the Northern Kingdom: Menahem, Pekah, and Hoshea; in the Southern Kingdom: Uzziah and Ahaz.

CHAPTER SEVEN

1. *Joshua* 10:31; 15:39; *2 Kings* 14:19; 18:13-17; 19:8; *2 Chronicles* 10:9; *Jeremiah* 34:7; *Micah* 1:13.
2. The Cylinder of Sennacherib (The Taylor Prism), now in the British Museum. See Caiger, *Bible and Spade*, p. 158.
3. See Caiger, *Bible and Spade*, p. 160. Compare *2 Kings* 18:14-15.
4. *Jeremiah* 34:6f.
5. See Marston, *The Bible Comes Alive*, pp. 181-223; Robinson, *Bearing of Archaeology on the Old Tes-*

tament, pp. 180-184; Kenyon, *The Bible and Archaeology*, pp. 190-198.
6. Marston, *The Bible Comes Alive*, p. 182.
7. Torczyner, *The Lachish Letters*.
8. *2 Kings* 18:13 to 19:37; *2 Chronicles* 32:1-24; *Isaiah* 36:1 to 37:38.
9. *2 Chronicles* 32:30.
10. Full translation of the Siloam Inscription may be found in Barton, *Archaeology and the Bible*, p. 437; Caiger, *Bible and Spade*, p. 155; Kenyon, *The Bible and Archaeology*, p. 179.
11. Hanauer, *Walks In and Around Jerusalem*, p. 349f.
12. *2 Samuel* 5:8. Cf. Duncan, *The Accuracy of the Old Testament*, pp. 113-121.
13. Adams, *Biblical Backgrounds*, p. 251.
14. Robinson, *Bearing of Archaeology on the Old Testament*, p. 173. Cf. *1 Kings* 22:39; *Amos* 3:12, 15; 6:1-6. See Caiger, *Bible and Spade*, p. 134f.
15. Jack, *Samaria in Ahab's Time*.
16. See Albright, *Archaeology and the Religion of Israel*, p. 160.
17. *Genesis* 19:30-38.
18. *Numbers* 21:26-30.
19. *Numbers* 22:1-6.
20. *2 Kings* 3:27.
21. *Ruth* 1:4.
22. For translation of Moabite Stone, see Barton, *Archaeology and the Bible*, pp. 421-423.
23. *Joshua* 10:33; 16:10; *1 Kings* 9:16. Compare Driver, *Modern Research*

as *Illustrating the Bible,* p. 46ff.

24. Driver, *Modern Research as Illustrating the Bible,* p. 52f.
25. Jack, *Samaria in Ahab's Time,* p. 44.
26. *Ibid.,* p. 46.
27. Quoted from Marston, *The Bible Comes Alive,* p. 277.

CHAPTER EIGHT

1. The block characters of the present Hebrew text are of rather recent origin, being a modification of the Aramaic and dating not earlier than 500-400 B.C. The Hebrew alphabetic script here in view is represented by the Phoenician and Gezer inscriptions, etc. It is now generally believed that its ancestry is to be traced to the Serabit el-Khadim alphabet c. 1800 B.C.
2. Naville, *Archaeology of the Old Testament,* pp. 202-208. Compare also Wilson, *Is the Higher Criticism Scholarly?* p. 144f.
3. *The Moabite Stone,* found at Dibon, Transjordan, and referring to the ninth century B.C.
4. Woolley, *Abraham, Recent Discoveries and Hebrew Origins,* p. 20f.
5. Duncan, *New Light on Hebrew Origins,* p. 6f.
6. Duncan, *New Light on Hebrew Origins,* p. 178-179.
7. Albright, *Archaeology of Palestine and the Bible,* p. 142f.

8. *Genesis* 13:1-18; 14:1-12.
9. Compare *Deuteronomy* 2:9-12, 37; 7:1f.
10. *Genesis* 14:6; *Numbers* 13:5; *Deuteronomy* 2:12.
11. Speiser, *Ethnic Movements in the Near East in the Second Millennium* B.C., p. 31f.
12. Compare, Garstang, *Foundations of Bible History,* pp. 7-8.
13. The introduction of the term *Hexateuch* indicates merely that the book of Joshua is to be considered in connection with the books of Moses (the Pentateuch)—i.e., Genesis, Exodus, Leviticus, Numbers, and Deuteronomy. All are subject to the same critical analysis.
14. North, *Archaeology and the Bible,* in Abingdon Commentary.
15. Caiger, *Bible and Spade,* p. 11.

CHAPTER NINE

1. Bradford, *Introduction, Bible and Spade,* p. 11.
2. Compare Jack, *The Ras Shamra Tablets, Their Bearing on the Old Testament.*
3. Driver, *Modern Research as Illustrating the Bible,* p. 89. See also Briggs, *General Introduction to the Study of Holy Scriptures,* p. 280.
4. Marston, *New Bible Evidence,* p. 15f.
5. Meek, *Hebrew Origins,* p. 8.

6. Kenyon, *The Bible and Archaeology*, p. 279.
7. Wellhausen, *Prolegomena*, p. 331.
8. Compare, Sayce, *Patriarchal Palestine*.
9. Driver, *Modern Research as Illustrating the Bible*, p. 23.
10. Orr, *The Problem of the Old Testament*, p. 408.
11. Naville, *Archaeology of the Old Testament*, p. 48.
12. For full discussion of these excavations, see, Woolley, *Abraham*, pp. 169-187; Duncan, *The Accuracy of the Old Testament*, p. 27f.; Caiger, *Bible and Spade*, pp. 20-27.
13. See, *Genesis* 21, and *Exodus* 20 and 21, etc.
14. The Spartoli Tablets are probably late Babylonian war songs of the Persian period, though they may have been copied from ancient authorities. It is on this assumption that they are used here. But the historicity of Genesis 14 is defended on other grounds. See pp. 119-120.
15. See Duncan, *The Accuracy of the Old Testament*, pp. 61-66; Caiger, *Bible and Spade*, pp. 31-36.
16. See particularly *Harvard Theological Review*, April, 1932.
17. Compare Woolley, The Sumerians, Abraham, etc. Compare also Sayce, *Patriarchal Palestine*.
18. Albright in the *American Scholar*, Spring 1938, Article, *Archaeology Confronts, Biblical Criticism*, p. 185f. Compare also Bulletin, American Schools of Oriental Research, October, 1937, Article, Albright, *The Archives of Mari*.
19. Hooke, chapter on *Archaeology and the Old Testament*, in *Record and Revelation*, p. 372.
20. Orr, *The Problem of the Old Testament*, p. 100f.
21. Kautzsch, *Literature of the Old Testament*, p. 9.
22. Cf. Duncan, *Accuracy of the Old Testament*, p. 26.
23. Kenyon, *The Bible and Archaeology*, p. 267.
24. See particularly, Knight, *Nile and Jordan*, pp. 171-190; and Duncan, *New Light on Hebrew Origins*, pp. 73-179.
25. Duncan, *New Light on Hebrew Origin*, p. 74.
26. Orr, *The Problem of the Old Testament*, pp. 247-284.
27. Aftermath Series, *The Crisis of Criticism*, p. 12.
28. Jack, *The Ras Shamra Tablets*, p. 6.
29. Compare Jack, *The Ras Shamra Tablets*, p. 28f.
30. Jack, *The Ras Shamra Tablets*, p. 31f.
31. Duncan, *New Light on Hebrew Origins*, p. 179.
32. Orr, *The Problem of the Old Testament*, p. 249.
33. Wellhausen, *History of Israel*, p. 9.
34. See 2 Kings 22:23.
35. Orr, *The Problem of the Old Testament*, p. 255f.
36. *Ibid.*, p. 256.
37. Albright, *The Archaeology of Palestine and the Bible*, p. 154f.
38. Orr, *The Problem of the*

370

Old Testament, p. 251.
39. *Ibid.,* p. 271.
40. Compare Smith, H. P., *Old Testament History,* p. 332.
41. Garstang, *The Foundations of Bible History,* p. 7.
42. Garstang, *Ibid.,* p. 8.
43. Duncan, *The Accuracy of the Old Testament,* p. 26.
44. Gray, *Critical Introduction to the Old Testament,* p. 58.
45. Burney, *Israel's Settlement in Canaan,* p. 11.
46. Jack, *Samaria in Ahab's Time.*
47. London Times, October 5, 1935. Compare, especially, Marston, *The Bible Comes Alive,* p. 248.
48. Marston, *The Bible Comes Alive,* p. 248f.

CHAPTER TEN

1. Cf. *Exodus,* 12:2.
2. See pp. 74-77 for a summary of the discovery, together with the Black Obelisk and the Bronze Gates of Balawat, all of which pertain to the reign of Shalmaneser III, 859-824 B.C.
3. Luckenbill, *Ancient Records of Assyria,* Vol. i, 611. Compare Sayce, *Records of the Past,* Vol. iv. 70. See, also, Pinches, *The Old Testament in the Light of the Records of Assyria and Babylonia.*
4. An Eponym refers to one who is so prominently connected with a thing as to become a figurative expression for it.
5. Sayce, *Records of the Past,* Vol. ii, p. 3. See, also,

Smith, *Assyrian Eponym Canon.*
6. Burrows, *What Mean These Stones?* p. 81.
7. See Sayce, *Records of the Past,* Vol. ii., pp. 120-127; Rogers, *Cuneiform parallels to the Old Testament,* pp. 219-238.
8. For complete translation, see Barton, *Archaeology and the Bible,* p. 419; Rawlinson, *Cuneiform Inscriptions of Western Asia,* III, 7, 8.
9. Layard, *Inscriptions in the Cuneiform Character from the Assyrian Monuments,* p. 15.
10. *1 Kings* 20:26-43.
11. *1 Kings* 22:1-40.
12. Cf. Peet, *Egypt and the Old Testament,* p. 111f.
13. *Exodus* 12:1f.
14. Problems connected with this entire period are fully discussed in Chapter XII.
15. *Deuteronomy* 34:7.
16. *Exodus* 12:40.
17. *Genesis* 1:26.
18. *Genesis* 47:9.
19. *Genesis* 47:28.
20. *Genesis* 25:26.
21. *Genesis* 12:4.
22. Discussed in Chapter XII, pp. 203-238.
23. Incidentally, this inscription also makes it clear that the Assyrian kings referred to in *2 Kings* 17:5-6 are not the same but, according to this account, Shalmaneser began the siege (*2 Kings* 18:9), while its fall three years later (*2 Kings* 18:-10-11) is claimed by Sargon II in 722-1 B.C.

24. *2 Kings* 20:12f.; *Isaiah* 39:1.
25. This is clearly the same incident as that set forth in the narrative of *2 Kings* 15:19-20.
26. Caiger, *Bible and Spade*, p. 145.
27. *2 Kings* 15:23.
28. Luckenbill, *Ancient Records of Assyria*, ii. 512, 690.
29. Summary

THE KINGDOMS
UNITED
Saul ....1010 B.C.
David ....1010-970 B.C.
Solomon .... 970-931 B.C.

SOUTHERN
Rehoboam .......................B.C. 931-914
Abijah .............................B.C. 914-911
Asa ...................................B.C. 911-870
Jehoshaphat ................B.C. 870-849
Jehoram .........................B.C. 849-841
Ahaziah ..........................B.C. 841-840
Athaliah .........................B.C. 840-834
Jehoram .........................B.C. 834-794
Amaziah ........................B.C. 794-765
Uzziah ............................B.C. 785-733
Jotham ............................B.C. 760-744
Ahaz ................................B.C. 744-728
Hezekiah .......................B.C. 728-698
Manasseh .......................B.C. 648-642
Amon ...............................B.C. 642-640
Josiah ..............................B.C. 640-608
Jehoahaz .......................B.C. 608-608
Jehoiakim .....................B.C. 608-598
Jehoiachin ....................B.C. 598-598
Zedekiah ........................B.C. 598-586

NORTHERN
Jeroboam .......................B.C. 931-910
Nadab .............................B.C. 910-909
Baasha ............................B.C. 909-886
Elah .................................B.C. 886-885
Zimri ...............................B.C. 885-885
Omri .................................B.C. 885-874
Ahab .................................B.C. 874-852

Ahaziah ...................B.C. 852-851
Jehoram ...................B.C. 851-841
Jehu ...........................B.C. 841-813
Jehoahaz ...................B.C. 813-796
Jehoash ......................B.C. 796-780
Jeroboam II............B.C. 780-747
Zechariah ................B.C. 746-746
Shallum ....................B.C. 746-746
Menahem ..................B.C. 746-735
Pekahiah ..................B.C. 735-733
Pekah .........................B.C. -732
Hoshea ......................B.C. 732-722

CHAPTER ELEVEN
1. *Genesis* 14:13-24.
2. See page 146.
3. Dates for Hammurabi are fixed by inscriptions and astronomical calculations. Abraham's migration from Haran is put at 1125 years before Solomon's Temple (967 B.C.)—i.e., 2092 B.C.
4. See Burney, *The Book of Judges*, p. lxxiv.
5. Woolley, *Abraham*, p. 45ff.
6. Section 146, *Code of Hammurabi*.
7. *Genesis* 16:6.
8. *Genesis* 21:10.
9. Woolley, *Abraham*, p. 156f.
10. *Joshua* 8:28.
11. *Genesis* 12:8.
12. *Genesis* 11:31.
13. Woolley, *Abraham*, p. 59f.
14. Special attention is called to Woolley's recent volume on *Abraham* which sets forth the full picture of Ur of the Chaldees in Abraham's day. See, also pp. 68-71.
15. *Genesis* 10:15.
16. *Genesis* 15:20.
17. *Genesis* 23:3.
18. *Genesis* 14:13f.
19. See Barton, *Archaeology and the Bible*, pp. 535-543.
20. *Genesis* 15:16.

21. Compare Petrie, *Palestine and Israel*, pp. 19-26.
22. *Genesis* 14:6; *Deuteronomy* 2:12, etc.
23. Speiser, *Ethnic Movements in the Near East in the Second Millennium* B.C.
24. *Genesis* 14:7.
25. *Genesis* 14:5; *2 Samuel* 5:18.
26. *Genesis* 15:21; *Ezekiel* 16:3.
27. *Exodus* 3:8.
28. See Petrie, *Palestine and Israel*, p. 62.
29. Orr, *Problem of the Old Testament*, p. 110.
30. Woolley, *Abraham*, p. 50. Compare, also, Gadd, *The History and Monuments of Ur*, p. 180. Albright, *The Archaeology of Palestine and the Bible*, pp. 129-151.

CHAPTER TWELVE

1. *Genesis* 15:13-14.
2. *Acts* 7:6.
3. *Exodus* 7:40-41.
4. *Galatians* 3:17.
5. *Psalm* 105:9-10.
6. Robinson, *History of Israel*, Vol. I, p. 70.
7. Peet, *Egypt and the Old Testament*, p. 106.
8. Adams, *Biblical Backgrounds*, p. 115.
9. *1 Kings* 6:1.
10. Garstang, *The Foundations of Bible History*, p. 55.
11. *Cambridge Ancient History*, p. 160.
12. Peet, *Egypt and the Old Testament*, p. 111f.
13. *Acts* 13:19-20.
14. Burney, *Judges*, p. 304.
15. Garstang, *The Foundations of Bible History*, p. 59.
16. The period of Hyksos domination constitutes more than a mere interlude in Egyptian affairs. Manetho, the Egyptian historian, states that the Hyksos Era embraced 500 years. Their Dynasties are referred to as the fifteenth and sixteenth. The seventeenth Dynasty represents a period of intense struggle between the foreign Hyksos and native Theban princes who finally triumphed. The expulsion of the Hyksos in 1580 would therefore determine the beginning of the domination at approximately 2080 B.C., thus synchronizing with the date of Abraham's descent into Egypt and including the subsequent experiences of Joseph, Jacob, and Israel in Egypt. Modern critical opinion does not reject entirely the estimate of Manetho. It is altogether possible that there were several infiltrations of these Asiatics into the Nile area. See Knight, *Nile and Jordan*, pp.98-125.
17. Josephus, *Contra Apionem*, i.14. See, also, Hall, *Ancient History of the Near East*, pp. 403ff.; Jack, *Date of the Exodus*, pp. 169-176.
18. *Exodus* 1:12.
19. *Genesis* 12; *Genesis* 46 and 47; *Genesis* 39 and 40.
20. *Contra Apionem* i.14.
21. Burrows, *What Mean These Stones?* p. 93.

22. Josephus, *Contra Apionem*, ii.2.

23. *Pharaohs of the Nineteenth Dynasty.*
Horemheb......1350-1315 B.C.
Rameses I.....1315-1314
Seti I.................1314-1292
Rameses II....1292-1225
Merneptah ..1225-1215
Amenmose......1215-1214
Rameses-
Siptah..........1214-1209
Seti II.............1209-1205
Anarchy..........1205-1200

24. Barton, *Archaeology and the Bible*, p. 37f.

25. See Knight, *Nile and Jordan*, p. 241f.

26. Robinson, *Bearing of Archaeology on the Old Testament*, p. 178.

27. Robinson, *Ibid.*, p. 178. See, also, McCown, *The Ladder of Progress in Palestine*, p. 165.

28. Caiger, *Bible and Spade*, p. 112.

29. *Ibid.* See, also, Peet, *Egypt and the Old Testament*, p. 109.

30. See Barton, *Archaeology and the Bible*, p. 339; Knight, *Nile and Jordan*, p. 244.

31. Peet, *Egypt and the Old Testament*, p. 110.

32. Peet, *Ibid.*, p. 111.

33. *Pharaohs of the Eighteenth Dynasty*—B.C.
Amosis.................. 1580-1558
Amenhotep I.... 1558-1545
Thutmosis I....... 1545-1514
Thutmosis II..... 1514-1501
(Hatshepsut)...(1514-1480)
Thutmosis III.. 1501-1447
Amenhotep II.. 1447-1420
Thutmosis IV... 1420-1412

Amenhotep III 1412-1376
Amenhotep IV. 1376-1362
Sakere................. 1362-1360
Tutankhamen.... 1360-1350
Ai II................. 1350-1346

34. See page 87.

35. See pages 45-48.

36. Meek, *Hebrew Origins*, p. 20.

37. Robinson, *Bearing of Archaeology on the Old Testament*, p. 60.

38. See Burney, *Israel's Settlement in Canaan*, p. 92.

39. Jack, *Date of the Exodus*, pp. 157-163.

40. Olmstead, *History of Palestine and Syria*, p. 197.

41. Hall, *The Ancient History of the Near East*, p. 409.

42. See Steindorff and Seele, *When Egypt Ruled the East*, pp. 201-247.

43. Knight, *Nile and Jordan*, p. 221.

44. Omitted.

45. Omitted.

46. *Ibid.*, p. 218f.

47. *Ibid.*, p. 219.

48. Knight, *Nile and Jordan*, p. 219.

49. *Ibid.*, p. 219f.

50. See Garstang, *Foundations of Bible History*, p. 140-148. For further details regarding destruction of Ai and Hazor, see pp. 149-161 and 183-198.

51. Knight, *Nile and Jordan*, p. 222.

52. Garstang, *The Foundations of Bible History*, p. 54f.

53. Kenyon, *The Bible and Archaeology*, p. 260f.

54. *Exodus* 1:8.

55. *Exodus* 2:23.

56. Knight, *Nile and Jordan*, p. 148.
57. Knight, *Nile and Jordan*, p. 153.
58. The fifty-three years are included within the period stretching from 1515-1461 B.C., according to Knight, while the additional twenty-one years are involved in the reign of his father, Thutmosis II, and probably his grandfather, Thutmosis I. His co-regency with Hatshepsut terminated with her death about 1480, but its actual beginning is not known.
59. Knight, *Nile and Jordan*, p. 153f.
60. Assuming 1446 B.C. as the Exodus date, Moses was then 80 years of age. His birth would then be reckoned as 1526 B.C., the 19th year of the reign of Thutmosis I.
61. See *Acts* 7:21-23.
62. *Exodus* 2:23.
63. *Exodus* 7:7. Cf. also, *Deuteronomy* 34:7.
64. An immense red granite slab fourteen feet in height, standing immediately in front of the Sphinx. On this stela is recorded a dream which Thutmosis is said to have had in which the Sphinx promised that one day Thutmosis would be king, "and when that day arrived, he must remove the sand from the feet of the god who had foretold to him his succession to the throne" (Knight, *Nile and Jordan*, p. 163).
65. Caiger, *Bible and Spade*, p. 74. For translation of this stela, see, Sayce, *Records of the Past*, Vol. ii.52-56.
66. *Exodus* 12:12; *1 Kings* 6:1.

CHAPTER THIRTEEN

1. Price, *The Monuments and the Old Testament*, p. 314.
2. An English Translation by A. Walther may be found in Smith, *The Origin and History of Hebrew Law*, pp. 247-274. See, also, Barton, *Archaeology and the Bible*, pp. 369-388.
3. An English Translation by Luckenbill and Geers may be found in Smith, *The Origin and History of Hebrew Law*, pp. 223-243. Compare, also, Driver and Miles, *The Assyrian Laws*. See, also, Barton, *Archaeology and the Bible*, pp. 389-399.
4. Compare, Meek, *Hebrew Origins*, pp. 46-75. Smith, *Origin and History of Hebrew Law*, pp. 15-169. See, especially, Johns, *The Laws of Babylonia and Laws of the Hebrew People*, pp. 24-48; and, Kent, *Israel's Laws and Legal Precedents*.
5. Price, *The Monuments and the Old Testament*, p. 314.
6. Special attention is called to Johns, *The Laws of Babylonia and Laws of the Hebrew People* for an exhaustive and scholarly treatment of the entire subject.

7. English Translations of the Code of Hammurabi may be found in Smith, *Origin and History of Hebrew Law*, pp. 181-222; Barton, *Archaeology and the Bible*, pp. 340-368.

8. Meek, *Hebrew Origins*, p. 56f.

9. Meek, *Hebrew Origins*, p. 60f.

10. Compare Burrows, *What Mean These Stones?* p. 245.

11. Compare Johns, *The Laws of Babylonia and Laws of the Hebrew People*, p. 48ff., and Albright, *The Archaeology of Palestine and the Bible*, pp. 151ff.

12. Meek, *Hebrew Origins*, p. 63.

13. Barton, *Archaeology and the Bible*, p. 367.

14. Compare Meek, *Hebrew Origins*, pp. 64-75. See, also, Burrows, *What Mean These Stones?* pp. 56f., 285f.

15. Driver, *Modern Research as Illustrating the Bible*, p. 27. See, also, Johns, *The Laws of Babylonia and Laws of the Hebrew People*, p. 21f.

16. See Clay, *Amurru; The Empire of the Amorites; The Origin of the Biblical Traditions.* See, also, Barton, *Archaeology and the Bible*, Appendix, pp. 535-543.

17. Smith, *Origin and History of Hebrew Law*, p. 279.

18. Johns, *The Laws of Babylonia and Laws of the Hebrew People*, p. 23.

19. Johns, *The Laws of Babylonia and Laws of the Hebrew People*, p. 21.

20. Barton, *Archaeology and the Bible*, p. 368.

21. Compare, also, Deuteronomy 5:6-21.

22. Smith, *Origin and History of Hebrew Law*, p. 8.

23. Johns, *The Laws of Babylonia and Laws of the Hebrew People*, p. 61f.

24. Sampey, *The Baptist Review and Expositor*, July, 1904, p. 242.

CHAPTER FOURTEEN

1. Compare Garstang, *The Foundations of Bible History*, p. 7f.

2. For English Translation of the Tell el-Amarna Letters, see Sayce, *Records of the Past*, Vol. V. pp. 54-101.

3. Compare Burney, *Israel's Settlement in Canaan;* also, *Judges.*

4. See Chapter Twelve, pp. 210-212 for comment on the length of the *Period of the Judges.* Compare, Garstang, *The Foundations of Bible History*, pp. 51-66.

5. Garstang, *The Foundations of Bible History*, pp. 140-148. See, also, Jack, *The Date of the Exodus*, pp. 142-168; Marston, *New Bible Evidence*, pp. 124-150.

6. *1 Kings* 16:34.

7. *Numbers* 13:22.

8. *Genesis* 13:18; 14:13; 23:-
1-20; 25:9-10; 35:27; 37:-
12-14; 1:13; *Joshua* 10:-
36; 14:6-15; *2 Samuel*
3:2-5; 4:8-12; 5:4-5; 15:-
10.
9. Kyle, *Excavating Kirjath-
Sepher's Ten Cities.*
10. See English Translations
of *Tell el-Amarna Letters*
in Sayce, *Records of the
Past,* Vol. II, pp. 57-71;
Barton, *Archaeology and
the Bible,* pp. 402-409.
11. Compare *Numbers* 13:26-
33.
12. *Genesis* 15:16.
13. For further study see,
Macalister, *A Century of
Excavation in Palestine,*
pp. 266-325; Harris, *The
Hebrew Heritage,* pp. 151-
165; Burrows, *What Mean
These Stones?* pp. 198-
249.
14. Bertholet, *History of Hebrew Civilization,* p. 81.
15. *Ibid.,* p. 49.
16. Harris, *The Hebrew Heritage,* p. 132f.
17. Kyle, *Excavating Kirjath-
Sepher's Ten Cities,* p.
130.
18. Macalister, *A Century of
Excavation in Palestine,*
p. 171f.
19. *Judges* 11:30f; *1 Kings* 16:-
34; *2 Kings* 23:10.
20. Special reference is made
to the following works
bearing on the Hittites:
Garstang, *The Hittite
Empire;* Cowley, *The
Hittites;* Hogarth, *Kings
of the Hittites.* For latest
information regarding the
Hurrians, see, Speiser,
*Ethnic Movements in the
Near East in the Second
Millennium* B.C.
21. For the most comprehensive and scholarly treat-
ment of the Philistines,
see Macalister, *The Philistines: Their History
and Civilization.*
22. *Amos* 9:7.
23. The Minoan **Civilization is**
regarded as falling into
three distinct periods:
Minoan I, II, and III. The
earliest of these is dated
about 3000 B.C., the last
phase about 1400 B.C.
when the great migration
occurred.
24. *The Cambridge Ancient
History,* pp. 283-295.
25. *Ibid.,* p. 276.
26. Petrie, *Palestine and Israel,*
p. 56f.
27. Petrie, *Seventy Years in
Archaeology,* p. 257.
28. Petrie, *Palestine and Israel,*
p. 62.
29. *1 Samuel* 5:1-4.
30. *1 Samuel* 31:10.
31. *The International Standard
Bible Encyclopaedia,* Article, *Ashtoseth,* p. 271.
32. *2 Kings,* 1:2f.
33. *Matthew* 10:25f.
34. *1 Samuel* 31:9.
35. Compare *Judges* 19:46f.;
1 Samuel 1:9.
36. *1 Samuel* 6:1f.
37. *Judges* 16:23.
38. Macalister, *The Philistines,
Their History and Civili-
zation,* p. 83. But see,
also, pp. 79-87.
39. Macalister, *The Philistines,
Their History and Civili-
zation,* p. 130.

CHAPTER FIFTEEN

1. *1 Kings* 9:16.
2. *1 Kings* 11:26.
3. *1 Kings* 14:25-28; *2 Chronicles* 12:2-9.
4. See Breasted, *History of Egypt*, pp. 527-531.
5. McCown, *The Ladder of Progress in Palestine*, p. 171.
6. Caiger, *Bible and Spade*, p. 127.
7. For translation, see Caiger, *Bible and Spade*, p. 137f.
8. Macalister, *A Century of Excavation in Palestine*, p. 267.
9. *2 Kings* 3:7.
10. See Chapter X.
11. The story of the Benhadads and Hazael is recounted in *1* and *2 Kings*.
12. *1 Kings* 20:26.
13. *1 Kings* 22:3ff.
14. *1 Kings* 22:8ff.
15. *1 Kings* 19:15.
16. *2 Kings* 6:12.
17. Cf. Goodspeed, *Israel's Messianic Hope*, p. 102.
18. Goodspeed, *Israel's Messianic Hope*, p. 103.
19. See Sayce, *Records of the Past*, The Nimrud Inscription of Tiglath-pileser III, v.,115-128.
20. Compare Caiger, *Bible and Spade*, p. 145.
21. *2 Kings* 15:19-20. The tribute amounted to approximately $1,500,000.00. See also, Price, *The Monuments and the Old Testament*, p. 291f.
22. *2 Kings* 15:19.
23. See Luckenbill, *Ancient Records of Assyria*, i.772.
24. See Luckenbill, *Ancient Records of Assyria*, i.776, 777; *2 Kings* 15:29-31.
25. See Luckenbill, *Ancient Records of Assyria*, ii.4.
26. See *2 Kings* 16:5-9; *2 Chronicles* 28:6-21.
27. Caiger, *Bible and Spade*, p. 145.
28. *2 Chronicles* 28:20.
29. Cf. The Nimrud Inscription of Tiglath-pileser III, Sayce, *Records of the Past*, v.120.
30. *2 Kings* 17:4.
31. Shalmaneser is specifically mentioned in a parallel passage in *2 Kings* 18:9.
32. See Luckenbill, *Ancient Records of Assyria*, ii.4.
33. 1. *2 Kings* 17:15-18. 2. *2 Kings* 17:6.
34. See Jack, *Samaria in Ahab's Time*.
35. Hamilton, *Guide to the Historic Site of Sebastieh,"* p. 14f.
36. *Ibid.*, p. 15.
37. Compare Duncan, *Digging up Biblical History*, pp. 249-263; Jack, *Samaria in Ahab's Time*, pp. 1-36.
38. Caiger, *Bible and Spade*, p. 150.
39. Compare, *Ibid.*, pp. 149-152.
40. Luckenbill, *Ancient Records of Assyria*, ii.30, 195.
41. *2 Kings* 20:12; *Isaiah* 39:1-8.
42. *2 Kings* 18:13-16. In the Assyrian records Hezekiah's tribute is said to have been 800 talents of silver, instead of 300 as specified in this passage. The alleged discrepancy can probably be explained on the basis of the differ-

378

ence between the light and heavy talent, the Assyrian being the former.

43. For translation, see Luckenbill, *Ancient Records of Assyria* ii.240; see, also, Caiger, *Bible and Spade,* pp. 156-162.

44. *2 Kings* 18:13 to 19:37; *Isaiah* 10:24-34; 36:1 to 37:38.

45. *2 Kings* 18:17.

46. See Luckenbill, *Ancient Records of Assyria,* ii.501-5; see, also, *2 Kings* 19:-37, and *Isaiah* 37:36f.

47. Caiger, *Bible and Spade,* p. 164.

48. *2 Kings* 19:9; *Isaiah* 37:9. Cf. Caiger, *Bible and Spade,* p. 157.

49. *2 Chronicles* 33:11. The appearance of Babylon in this passage, instead of being regarded as a scribal error, is now known to be entirely appropriate. After its conquest by the Assyrians, Babylon was regarded as a second capital of the Assyrian Empire.

50. See Luckenbill, *Ancient Records of Assyria,* ii.690.

51. *Ezra* 4:10.

52. See translation of the *Babylonian Chronicle* by C. J. Gadd.

53. Harrell, *The Prophets of Israel,* p. 111.

54. Harrell, *The Prophets of Israel,* p. 109f.

55. *Zephaniah* 2:13, 15.

56. As already indicated, the date of the *discovery* of the Mosaic Law is not here in question, but the generally accepted view that requires 621 B.C. as the date of its *composition,* which is an entirely different matter. It is hoped that both the supposed motive (a pious fraud to create revival fires) and the time (near the close of the seventh century) have been shown to be erroneous. But see discussion, Chapter IX.

57. Caiger, *Bible and Spade,* p. 170. The biblical passages may be found in *2 Kings* 28:29-37.

58. Caiger, *Bible and Spade,* p. 172.

59. *2 Kings* 24:1-16; 24:17 to 25:10; *Jeremiah* 46.

60. Barton, *Archaeology and the Bible,* p. 33.

61. *Daniel* 1:1-6; Compare *2 Kings* 23:34 to 24:7.

62. *2 Kings* 24:14. Compare the entire passage from 24:8-16.

63. *2 Kings* 25:3-7.

64. *2 Kings* 25:8-10.

65. *Jeremiah* 27:22.

66. See Adams, *Biblical Backgrounds,* pp. 367-399.

67. *Nehemiah* 2:12 to 6:19.

68. *Lamentations* 3:1-22.

69. *Psalm* 48:2, 9, 11-13.

70. Adams, *Biblical Backgrounds,* p. 379.

71. Harrell, *The Prophets of Israel,* p. 228f.

CHAPTER SIXTEEN

1. Caiger, *Bible and Spade*, p. 148f.

2. *2 Kings* 15:29-30. This campaign is definitely mentioned in the Assyrian records. See, Luckenbill, *Ancient Records of Assyria*, i.815.

3. *2 Kings* 17:6.

4. Adams, *Biblical Backgrounds*, p. 272.

5. For comprehensive survey of excavations in Assyria and Babylonia up until 1902, see Hilprecht, *Explorations in Bible Lands*, pp. 1-577. More recent investigations are set forth in Woolley's, *The Sumerians, Abraham*, etc.

6. *Psalm* 137:1.

7. *Ezekiel* 1:1.

8. *Daniel* 1:1-2, 4; 2:49; 3:1; 4:28-30, etc. Compare also, *Isaiah* 11:11.

9. Adams, *Biblical Backgrounds*, p. 276f.

10. Adams, *Biblical Backgrounds*, p. 279f.

11. *Psalm* 137:4; *Luke* 2:10f.

12. See pages 49-51.

13. *Ezekiel* 30:6.

14. Compare Driver, *Modern Research as Illustrating the Bible*, pp. 28-30; Margolis, *The Elephantine Documents*, Jewish Quarterly Review, New Series, ii. 419.

15. *Jeremiah* 44:15-19.

16. Adams, *Biblical Backgrounds*, p. 282f. Compare *Jeremiah* iv.1f.

17. Levison, *The Jew in History*, p. 38.

18. *Jeremiah* 30:18.

19. *Genesis* 12:3.

20. *Esther* 1:1.

21. *Adams, Biblical Backgrounds*, p. 286f.

22. *Ibid.*, p. 290.

23. *John* 1:11.

380

INDEX

Aaron, 152, 237.

Ab, Month of, 81.

Abdi-Khiba, 227.

Abel-Shittim, 267.

Abiv, Month of, 174.

Abraham, 9, 10, 11, 12, 13, 15, 17, 19, 69, 70, 71, 72, 74, 85, 86, 106, 113, 116, 117, 120, 123, 142, 143, 144, 146, 167, 174, 187, 188, 189, 190, 191, 192, 193, 194, 195, 196, 197, 198, 199, 200, 204, 205, 206, 207, 208, 213, 215, 242, 252, 254, 255, 271, 272, 283, 289, 334, 335, 340, 349, 350.

Abram, 6, 145, 189, 321. See Abraham.

Accadian. See Akkadian.

Achan, 269.

Achish, 291.

Achor, Valley of, 269.

Acra, 321, 322.

Acre, Plain of, 15, 25.

Ader, 120.

Adonis, 281.

Adonis Cult, 93.

Aegean Islands, 286, 291.
Peoples, 286, 287.
Sea, 343.
Sector, 341.

Africa, 17, 50, 232.

Agade, 13, 72. See Akkad.

Ahab, 75, 76, 96, 104, 105, 161, 168, 170, 176, 209, 269, 301, 302, 309, 310.

Ahasuerus, 343.

Ahaz, 78, 181, 182, 304, 306, 307.

Ahaziah, 170, 176, 301.

Ahiram. See Akhiram.

Ai, City of, 120, 159, 193, 194, 226, 269.

Ajalon, 226, 269.

Akabah, Gulf of, 154, 350.

Akerblad, 45.

Akhetaton, 277.

Akhiram, 162.
Inscriptions of, 109.
Sarcophagus of, 94, 114.

Akhnaton, 46, 47, 148, 224, 225, 226, 227.

Akkad, 13, 65, 72, 92, 307.

Akkadian Culture, 71.
Empire, 72.
Language, 73, 192, 289.
Texts, 93.

Albright, W. F., 68, 119, 157.

Aleppo, 11, 14, 87, 91, 169.

Alexander the Great, 12, 187, 343.

Alexandria, 44.

Alluvial Deposits, 17, 31.

Al-Muqayyar, 68, 69. See Muqayyar.

Alphabet, 53.
Cuneiform, 93.
Demotic, 45.
Hieroglyphic, 45.

Alphabetic Writing, 53, 93, 114.

Al-Ubeid, 196.

Amalekites, 5, 199, 275, 276.

Amanus Mountains, 85.

Amarna, Tell el, 224, 277.
Letters, Tell el, 45, 47, 48, 60, 92, 101, 114, 148, 149, 222, 223, 224, 225, 226, 227, 228, 234, 236, 238, 263, 264, 266, 267, 277, 278, 279, 350.
Period, 93, 107, 229, 277, 279.
Tablets, Tell el, 51, 72, 226, 258.

Amaziah, 177, 181.

Amen, Temple of, 233.

381

Amenhotep I, 235.

Amenhotep II, 221, 229, 236, 237, 238, 350.

Amenhotep III, 46, 48, 148, 224, 225, 229, 277.

Amenhotep IV (Akhnaton), 45, 92, 93, 148, 224, 277, 279.

American School of Oriental Research, 73.

Ammon, 291, 350.

Ammonites, The, 16, 106, 211, 298.

Amon, 280, 317.

Amon-Ra, 46, 94, 95, 224.

Amorite-Canaanite Foundation, 91, 92.

Amorites, The, 10, 14, 16, 17, 28, 29, 71, 91, 121, 123, 198, 199, 200, 215, 251.
Iniquity of, 280.
Strongholds of, 269.

Amos, 284, 303, 304, 311, 325.

Amosis, 230, 235.

Amraphel, 86, 123, 189, 190. See Hammurabi.

Amurru, 251.

Anath, 281.

Ancestral Gods, 70.

Andrae, 67.

Ankara, 19.

Anthropology, 57.

Anti-Lebanon Area, 198.
Mountains, 10, 14, 87.
See Lebanon Mountains.

Antioch, 91.

Anti-Semitism, 287.

Aphek, Battle of, 75, 303.

Aphrodite, 290.

Apis Bulls, 300.

Arabia, 195, 198, 254, 276, 289, 297.
Desert of, 18, 30, 57, 264, 343.

Arabs, The, 36, 68.

Aram (Aram Naharaim), 10, 195, 198, 332.

Aramaic Language, 50, 51, 291, 338.
Papyri, 51.

Aramean Nomads, 190.

Arameans, The, 91, 200, 298, 306, 331.

Araunah, The Jebusite, 321.

Arbela, 333.

Archaeologist, 37, 80, 129, 131.

Archaeology, 6, 9, 23, 24, 69, 131, 134, 140, 168, 351.
British School of, 159.
And the Hexateuch, 140-162.

Arioch, 189.

Armenian-Taurus. See Taurus Mountains.

Arnon River, 211.
Valley of, 154.

Aroer, 211.

Arpad, 91.

Aryan Groups, 286.

Aryanism, 287.

Ascalon. See Ashkelon.

Ashdod, 15, 178, 179, 287, 288, 289, 290, 291, 292.

Asherah, 93, 308.

Asherim, 93.

Ashkelon, 15, 223, 226, 287, 288, 290, 292, 313.

Ashtareth, 290.

Ashtaroth, 119.

Ashtaroth, City of, 119;
House of, 290.

Ashurbanipal, 80, 184, 245, 315.
Library of, 62, 63, 178.
Records of, 80.

Ashurnasirpal II, 75, 245, 333.

Asia Minor, 13, 19, 20, 41, 66, 74, 85, 91, 92, 99, 130, 197, 232, 241, 242, 243, 244, 281, 341.

Asshur, 333.

Assuan, 17, 43, 49, 50, 338.
Temple of, 43.

Assyria, 5, 61, 74, 75, 78, 87, 244, 245, 303, 304, 305, 306, 307, 308, 311, 312, 313, 314, 315, 316, 317, 325, 331, 337.

Assyrian Canon, 169, 170, 175.
  308.
  Captivity, 339.
  Chronicles, 169, 170, 175, 308,
    350.
  Code, 247, 248, 258.
  Documents, 61, 74-81, 297,
    350.
  Invasion of Palestine, 50.
  Laws, 252.
  Rulers of, 60, 74, 307.
  State Policies, 333.
Assyrians, 11-13, 29, 59, 60, 99,
    124, 167, 244, 245, 259, 298,
    318, 343, 344.
Assyriology, 61.
Astarte, 281.
Astruc, Jean, 135.
Atar-Gatis, 290.
Aton, 46.
Avaris, 229.
Azariah, 181, 182, 305. See
  Uzziah.

Baal, 93, 281, 290, 308.
  Phoenician, 310.
  Of Tyre, 95.
Baalath, 281.
Baalim, 281.
Baalism, 303.
Baal-Zebub, 290.
Babel, Tower of, 12.
Babylon, 12, 13, 57, 59, 71, 142,
    151, 184, 194, 195, 241, 242,
    281, 312, 315, 317, 318, 319,
    320, 330, 334, 335, 336, 340.
Babylonia, 5, 61, 67, 86, 132,
    194, 196, 253, 254, 259, 278,
    281, 290, 334, 335, 337.
Babylonian Account of Deluge,
    61, 63.
  Captivity, 329, 336, 337, 341.
  Chronicle, 81, 315, 316.
  Code, 247, 248.
  Cuneiform, 47, 62, 65, 222, 263,
    278.
  Documents, 350.
  Dynasty, First, 64, 251.
  Empire, New, 318.
  History, 81, 297.

Invasion of Palestine, 50.
Laws, 145, 192, 251, 252, 254,
    255.
Legends, 62.
Records, 80, 92, 187, 333.
Tablets, 187.
Tradition, 143, 144.
Babylonians, 11, 12, 19, 28, 59,
    60, 80, 81, 99, 113, 124, 144,
    167, 242, 243, 245, 254, 259,
    298, 316, 318, 335, 337, 343,
    344.
Bagdad, 13, 61, 70.
Bagohi, 339.
Balak, 211.
Balawat, Bronze Gates of, 168.
  Bronze Plates of, 75.
Bamoth, 282.
Barak, 16, 267, 273, 274.
Barton, G. A., 217.
Basalt, 44.
Bashan, Territory of, 16.
Bas-reliefs, 77.
Basra, 68.
Bdellium, 77.
Bedouin Sheikh, 195.
Beelzebub, 290.
Beeroth, 269.
Beersheba, 15, 193, 226, 270, 271.
Beginnings, Land of, 10.
Behistun Inscriptions, 60, 142.
Behistun Rock, 59, 61.
Beit-Jibrin, 101.
Belshazzar, 69.
Benhadad, 75, 76, 77, 170, 209,
    303.
Berlin, 47.
Berossus, 194, 195.
Bethel, 15, 120, 193, 194, 226,
    269, 271.
Bethlehem, 15, 271, 337.
Bethshean, 25, 36, 37, 104, 217,
    226, 290.
Beth-shemesh, 227.
Biblical Criticism, 109, 129.
  History, 80.
  Sources, 73.

383

391

392

Olmstead, A. T., 223.
Olympic Games, 167.
Omri, 104-106, 161, 301-303, 309, 310.
On, Obelisk of, 31.
Ophel, 102, 103, 321, 322.
Oppert, M. J., 61, 241.
Oppression, The, 49, 118, 221, 350.
    Pharaoh of, 217, 218, 234, 238.
Orient, The, 335, 336.
Orontes River, 10, 75, 85, 86, 91, 169.
Orr, James, 151, 156.
Osiris, 280, 281.
Osnappar, 80, 184, 315.
Othniel, 272.
Oxford, 47.

Palestine, 13, 25, 26, 28, 31, 34, 35, 41, 46, 49, 51, 66, 74, 75, 78, 79, 86, 99, 102, 119, 130, 159, 193, 200, 216, 219, 221, 222, 225, 227, 242, 280, 281, 289, 305, 306, 312, 313, 319, 333, 336-340, 343, 344.
Pantheism, 134.
Papyri, 44, 100.
Paran, Wilderness of, 154, 266.
Parrot, M. Andre, 71, 146.
Passover, The, 339.
Pathros, 50, 338.
Patriarchal Era, 5, 117, 142, 145, 146, 148, 175, 347.
Patriarchs, 10, 15, 141, 145.
Paul, 206, 210.
Peet, T. Eric, 207, 209.
Pekah, 77, 78, 182.
Pekahiah, 78, 182.
Pelethites, 286.
Pelishti, 286.
Pentateuch, 4, 114, 115, 117, 118, 124, 125, 134-137, 150, 152, 155, 158, 160, 247, 252, 260.

Pentateuchal Codes, 153.
    Laws, 246, 247, 250, 252, 253, 255, 256, 258, 260.
    Criticism, 136.
Penuel, 276.
Peoples of the Sea, 286-288.
Persepolis, 59.
Persia, 59, 66, 200, 332, 341-344.
    Empire of, 341.
    Government of, 12, 343.
Persian Gulf, 10, 11, 57, 74, 80, 196, 242, 335, 343.
    Period, 338.
    Rule, 343.
Persians, 11, 51, 99, 124, 343, 344.
Petrie, Sir Flinders, 27, 35, 48, 52, 53, 146, 162, 217, 219, 221, 288, 289.
Phaestos, 292.
    Disk, 292.
Phichol, 291.
Philistia, Plain of, 15, 199, 273, 287, 289, 292.
Philistine Civilization, 288.
    Pantheon, 290, 291.
    Pentapolis, 287, 292.
Philistines, 17, 20, 178, 199, 266, 267, 284, 286-293, 324.
Philo, 259.
Phoenician Inscription, 94.
    Laws, 251.
    Script, 107, 108.
Phoenicians, 14, 19, 53, 91, 153, 298, 313.
Phrygian Areas, 86.
Pinches, T. G., 78.
Pithom, 217.
Plagues, The Ten, 237.
Polytheism, 144.
Pompeii, 30.
Pool of Siloam, 102, 103.
Pottery Chronology, 27.
Pre-Patriarchal Accounts, 145.
Pre-Patriarchal Era, 142, 143.
Preusser, 67.
Price, Ira M., 247.

393

397